Economics Kidnapped

Economics Kidnapped

Economic Common Sense Undiscovered by Investors

Dong Fang Dao

Strategic Book Publishing and Rights Co.

Strategic Book Publishing & Rights Co., LLC
USA | Singapore
www.sbpra.net

For information about special discounts for bulk purchases, please contact Strategic Book Publishing and Rights Co. Special Sales, at bookorder@sbpra.net.

ISBN: 978-1-68235-439-1

About the Author

An Economist Offering the Objective Existence Hidden for the Stream of Consciousness to Thinkers

Dong Fang Dao is an independent economist with scientific sustainable development viewpoint in the international context. The author has researched political and economic issues worldwide with an independent mind for nearly three decades. He has insisted on studying representative works in the political and economic fields at home and abroad, and thinking and writing in a long time. He always elaborates current economic problems on his own original ideas all over the world.

In addition Dong Fang Dao is an ordinary and distinctive scholar, and poet. He authored the *Democracy in China* for a unique, profound, and systemic exposition of Chinese fundamental issues through his research on the political philosophy. He also published the *Ultra Bubble: China Real Estate Finance Decryption* to first introduce the liberal economic theory meticulously into China through his research on economics, in which some sections and chapters became the basis for influencing the economic decision-making of China government. As a poet he wrote a poetry anthology, the *Unsearchable Psychological Realm of Loves*, awaking pure universal loves.

Recently the Dong Fang Dao created another classic masterpiece, a new book *ECONOMICS KIDNAPPED* in the spirit of originality over years. The author expounds various unknown arcana in the global economic operation today with his encyclopedic economic knowledge, rigorous, thorough and logical analysis, and eloquent expressiveness in easy-to-understand and profound language to open a shortcut to wealth for different kinds of investors. Commendably the author refutes in depth systemic theoretical defects in macroeconomics that governs currently the world based on the new peak of economic world, and innovates hereby a new macroeconomic theory and model. Perhaps the series of spic-and-span theories are beneficial to current economies of countries in crisis, and these original perspectives provide another theoretical support for international economic policies.

Almost every economic blog post of Dong Fang Dao was forwarded by important media, and net friends. New ideas on money, real estate, and the political restructuring reform were first proposed by the author, and later attracted widespread attention from the society in the past few years, which have a momentous influence on the healthy development of China. As a result,well-known economists, and national leadership browse his blog posts from time to time. Furthermore **the Dong Fang Dao Blog was included in the Celebrity Blog, and Elite Blog.**

Dong Fang Dao
Email: bj889@126.com

Preface

To Readers,

This book interprets profoundly economic truths at first in the human history that are known rarely but should be understood clearly by investors in terms of four arcana of money issuance, macro and micro economic policies, real estate, and national wealth.

For example: What is the root cause of currency inflation in the final analysis? Why excessive money, which was created for stimulating the economy, would not lead to rising commodity prices? Who benefits most when the loan of power support is adopted to stimulate the economy? And why would the China's increasing money issuance actually help the United States overcome crisis?

This book starts around aforementioned core questions to set forth the rule of contemporary monetary operation deeply, and uniquely, for the first time in human history revealing theories of the mutual conversion between deposits, and loans in the money supply, the co-extension of monetary base and money supply, and the loan of power support leading to low production efficiency. Besides, this book analyzes the essential relationship between money supply and housing price. Today, only when you are aware of the truth about monetary operations can the governmental intention be perceived profoundly and the investment trend be grasped authentically to lay a solid foundation for various investments. **Hereby the first truth this book will unveil is: the arcana of monetary operation, which needs to be recognized if you want to make a profit!**

Actually it is easier to get rich within the territory of China than foreign countries! On all accounts those who decoded the governmental information can only achieve. The Western government does not set economic target so it is difficult to consider for an oversea investor while China has the five-year economic planning, annual *Central Economic Working Conference*, *Government Work Report*, and regular bulletins of various governmental information. Much important information breakdown is enough for smart investors to make a fortune. Exhaustively the second part in this book tells you: How to analyze the *China Five-Year Planning*, the information in *Central Economic Working Conference*, as well as the data in *Government Work Report* specially. **Hereby the second truth this book will unveil is: the arcana of governmental economic operation, which needs to be recognized if you want to make a profit!**

In many countries the real estate is regarded as the largest household income. To make a fortune by virtue of real estate, you must above all pursue the maximum nominal income, and learn to apply various information that affects both supply and demand to analyze price trends. Government regulation affects either supply or demand, and does not work. Whether regulation and control are effective is subject to the implementation instead of the official document! You can grasp the tendency of real estate, and earn the maximum nominal income when making the relation between supply and demand clear! At the same time if the CPI (consumer price index) also increases several-fold, such as a factor of three, your actual income is only one third after earning the nominal income! To be specific, if you bought a house in 2003, and gained CNY one million by the end of 2013 whereas your real income earned was only CNY 200,000 when the CPI in 2013 was 5 times that of 2003! **Hereby the third truth this book will unveil is: a dime a dozen when everyone makes a lot of money!**

Maybe GDP, CPI and M2 data bulletined by government sometimes contradict with each other due to an error in calculating domestic GDP. For this reason, this book calculates initially the China nominal growth rate, actual growth rate, actual GDP, nominal inflation rate, and actual inflation rate, and others in recent years with the aid of well-knit logic system, and scientific methodology to reduce unambiguously the truth of China GDP growth according to the data released by the National Bureau of Statistics, People's bank of China, and other authoritative institutions. Additionally this book refutes first and foremost the theoretical fallacy in economics that governs currently the world by innovative thought, and systematic theories. Specifically it discusses the relationships between nominal GDP and actual GDP, and actual GDP and CPI to create several new models for the GDP calculation. Perhaps the series of spic-and-span theories are beneficial to current economies of all countries in crisis, and these original perspectives also provide another theoretical support for the international liberal economy. **Hereby the fourth truth this book will unveil is: only by identifying the nominal income can you pursue the real income.**

The first draft of this book was completed in 2011, and a decade has passed since then. In the past decennia, the author has changed the manuscript several times to ensure the quality of this book. At all events, various intervention policies of global governments were pointed out by the author as for the 2008 economic crisis ten years ago, governments of various countries almost follow the same old disastrous road by the time of the economic crisis in 2020, and thus verifying the correctness of views in this book. The author reminds of readers that some examples, and data analyzed in this book are several years ago, only used as an illustration without prejudice to analysis methods, and conclusions, furthermore are shown accuracy over time, and thus are still used today and not updated.

Dong Fang Dao
In March 2021

Table of Contents

Part Two
Arcana of Economic System

Part Three
Arcana of Real Estate System

Part Four

Arcana of National Wealth System

Part One

Arcana of Monetary System

Introduction

If you want to make a profit,

First of all you need to understand thoroughly the arcana of monetary system.

If you want to make a fortune, you must figure out how government operates the monetary system at first! Exactly some core issues below have investors scratching their heads day and night:

1. What are currency, monetary base, and money supply? That is, how is money created?
2. How do commercial banks create money through making loans?
3. When the government encourages loan-taking to stimulate the economy, who will most benefit from it?
4. Why would the China's increasing money issuance actually help the United States overcome crisis?
5. Why would excessive money, which was created to stimulate the economy, skyrocket housing prices, and transfer the wealth to only a handful of people?

For the first time in human history, the author expounds the rule of contemporary monetary operation deeply and uniquely around core questions above, revealing theories of mutual conversion between deposits, and loans in the money supply, the co-extension of monetary base and money supply, and the loan of power support leading to low production efficiency. Besides, the author analyzes the essential relationship between money supply, and housing prices. In the contemporary society, only when you are aware of these monetary operational rules can you truly read the governmental intentions, and grasp the trend in investment, so as to lay a solid foundation for various investment opportunities.

Key point of this part:

If you want to make a profit, first of all, you need to understand thoroughly the arcana of monetary system!

Chapter 1

The Mystery of Monetary Disappearance

At the beginning of the book we will go straight to the core and analyze the money supply and commodity price trends from 2001 to 2019, because it is very important to predict on the money supply, and CPI in these years. To have an accurate analysis we need to comprehend first the connotation of GDP growth rate, and then the implication of commodity price stability.

An average of 7% annual GDP growth rate during the *Twelfth Five-Year Planning* can be understood as growth rates around 7%. Because the growth rate of economics is closely related to that of money stock. National Bureau of Statistics of China has never revealed the actual GDP in a timely manner. The target setting of GDP growth rate indicates (or implies) that of increase of monetary aggregates. Hereto, what is the internal logic between the growth rate of GDP, and monetary aggregates in China? It can only be answered on the basis of past rules.

I. The Government Set the Goal of GDP Growth Rate at 7% per Year during the Tenth Five-Year Plan (2001-2005). Consequent Statistics of GDP, CPI and Money Supply Growth Rates from 2001 to 2005 Were as Follows.

Table 1: Annual GDP, CPI and money supply growth rates during the *Tenth Five-Year Plan* period, unit (%)

Each year of the *Tenth Five-Year Plan*	GDP growth rate	CPI growth rate	Sum of two items	M2 growth rate	M2-sum of two items
2001	8.3	0.7	9.0	17.6	8.6
2002	9.1	-0.8	8.3	16.8	8.5
2003	10	1.2	11.2	19.6	8.4
2004	10.1	3.9	14.0	14.7	0.7
2005	10.4	1.8	12.2	17.6	5.4

II. The Annual Growth Rate Was Set at 7.5% during the Eleventh Five-Year Planning Period (2006-2010)

Table 2: Annual GDP, CPI and money supply growth rates during the *Eleventh Five-Year Planning* period, unit (%)

Each year of the *Eleventh Five-Year Planning*	GDP growth rate	CPI growth rate	Sum of two items	M2 growth rate	M2-sum of two items
2006	11.7	1.5	13.2	15.7	2.5
2007	11.9	4.8	16.7	16.7	0.0
2008	9.8	5.9	15.7	17.8	2.1
2009	9.3	-0.7	13.6	27.7	14.1
2010	11.4	3.3	14.7	19.7	5.0

Table 3: Annual GDP, CPI and money supply growth rates during the *Twelfth Five-Year Planning* period, unit (%)

Each year of the *Twelfth Five-Year Plan*	GDP growth rate	CPI growth rate	Sum of two items	M2 growth rate	M2-sum of two items
2011	9.2	5.4	14.6	13.6	-1.0
2012	7.8	2.6	10.4	13.8	3.4
2013	7.7	2.6	10.3	13.6	3.3
2014	7.4	2.0	9.4	12.2	2.8
2015	6.9	1.4	8.3	13.3	5.0

Table 4: Annual GDP, CPI and money supply growth rates during the *Thirteen Five-Year Planning* period, unit (%)

Each year of the *Thirteen Five-Year Planning*	GDP growth rate	CPI growth rate	Sum of two items	M2 growth rate	M2-sum of two items
2016	6.7	2.0	8.7	11.3	2.6
2017	6.9	1.6	8.5	8.2	-0.3
2018	6.6	2.1	8.7	8.1	-0.6
2019	6.1	2.9	9.0	8.7	-0.3

The four tables above are excerpted from the data released by the National Bureau of Statistics, and the central bank. But whenever the National Bureau of Statistics bulletins the GDP, GDP growth rate, and inflation rate, the statistics would be questioned by some experts, scholars, and net citizens in the society. Critics are resulted from two sides, one is indeed major flaws in the data, and the way how the Bureau of Statistics presented the data; and the other is that net citizens lack the basic knowledge of

5

statistics. After making full sense of these data, we can analyze the internal logical relation among M2, GDP, and CPI growth rates.

Tables 1 and 2 show that data cannot hold water in most years. In accordance with the K-Percent Rule that was proposed by the monetarist master Milton Friedman after economic laws of countries throughout the world were summarized, the real GDP growth rate plus inflation rate should approximately be equal or close to the growth rate of money supply every year.

Table 1 indicates that merely the data in 2004 during the *Tenth Five-Year Plan* were basically complied with the K-Percent Rule. 8.5% (approximately CNY 1.3 trillion) of the average annual growth rate of money supply disappeared without a trace from 2001 to 2003 as well as 5.4% (approximately CNY 1.4 trillion) in 2005.

Table 2 indicates that the growth rate sum of GDP and CPI in the year of 2007 was only equal to the increase of money supply, which was in line with the Milton Friedman law. 14% (about CNY 6.6 trillion) of the money supply growth rate in 2009 disappeared without a trace as well as 5% (about CNY 3 trillion) in 2010 at all events. According to the growth law of money supply, the amount of additional money issuance reflects either the increase in actual commodity output or the rise in prices. A situation that huge amounts of currency being vanished into thin air every year is probably caused by the new addition cash hidden in a place by some people at home or being transferred abroad.

Only in this way can this phenomenon be explained: The cash hidden or transferred abroad by some people was used to make neither purchase nor investment, and thus did not generate corresponding economic growth or rise in commodity prices. If this way is ubiquitous, the effect of rapid increase of money supply every year would be partly shown through the increase in actual output, partly the rise in prices, and the rest cash being hidden or exported. Only in that case can the question of high-speed money issuance without large inflation be explained clearly in China.

Nonetheless the data for 2011 was particularly unusual. The sum of GDP growth rate, and CPI growth rate was 14.6%, and the growth rate of money supply in the year was 13.6%, which is untenable. It turned out to be a computational mistake made by the central bank. Money supplies at the end of 2010, and 2011 were CNY 72.6 trillion and CNY 85.2 trillion, the year-on-year increase should be CNY 12.6 trillion, and monetary growth rate should be 17.3% instead of 13.6%.

GDP, and money supply growth rates in Tables 1 and 2 show that the average annual growth rate of money supply arranged should be at about 7.7% (higher than the economic growth rate) when the economic growth goal was determined at 7%, and should be at about 8.7% (higher than the economic growth rate) when the economic growth rate was determined at 7.5%. Certainly specific money supply growth rate arranged varies greatly from one year to another year in China. During the *Twelfth Five-Year Planning*, whether China can develop sustainably in a mode where the money supply growth rate was 7% higher than the economic growth rate (i.e., the growth rate of M2 was more than 14%) is worthy of discussion, and investigation. If the M2 growth rate maintains the previous 17% or so, China's money supply would reach CNY 160 trillion, CNY 349 trillion, and CNY 1,677 trillion by the end of 2015, 2020, and 2030! By then, every the Chinese will have CNY 1.23 million on average, and be a millionaire!

Contents mentioned above were written in 2011, ten years ago. The total M2 in China was CNY 219 trillion by the end of March 2020, and the money issuance amount was reduced cumulatively by about CNY 130 trillion compared with 2011. The government had lowered the growth rate of M2 from 16% to about 8% since 2013, and thus avoiding the risk of extreme currency depreciation.

Chapter 2

Loans as the Primary Reason for Banks to Create Money

Lately an economist wrote an article titled the *Excessive Money Issuance Is Misjudgment*. The majority of readers are frightened by the writer's exaggerated tone, and a few people sneer because he had such a confused appreciation towards money supply, and obviously distorted common sense. Hereby I summarize his main opinions on the money supply as follows:

1. He believes that the judgment of excessive money issuance must be understood into a false equivalence of loan amount to issuance amount;
2. He believes if deposits are not converted into loans, then they would turn to unemployment, which is loss for both capital and labor;
3. He believes that the rise in price of labor has nothing to do with increasing money issuance amounts.

Whether his opinions are right? Without doubt, they cannot withstand scrutiny, and are contrary to common sense. Suppose his opinions are put into practice, China will be immediately caught in hyperinflation, and unable to extricate itself, and the people will suffer midst dire straits.

The amount of bank loan issuance is a primary component of state expansion with respect to the money supply (the concept of money issuance amount had long been outdated, and now the concept of money supply is used). It is often said that the central bank overprints, and over-issues too much more money which lead to inflation. This standpoint is not wrong. Though, the terminology money issuance amount is not accurate. Monetary aggregate or money supply would be more appropriate. Monetary aggregate, i.e., the sum of the money supply contains below:

1. Currency in circulation. The sum of numerical values as for banknotes and coins held by the public outside the banking system is called M0, which are the objective tangible money that can be touched by hand.

For instance, a CNY 100 large nominal value banknote in your pocket is a rectangular palm-sized red paper. The front is printed with words "People's Bank of China", the head portrait of Mao Zedong, amount in figures "100" and in words "CNY One Hundred", and other patterns and numbers. The reverse side is also red, and is printed with an image of the Great Hall of the People, and amount in figures "100". If you hold this banknote in your hand, and rub hard the collar of the Mao Zedong's head portrait with your thumb, you can feel the protrusion. Likewise the tangible money with CNY 100, 50, 10, 5, 1, coins, and other denominations in the people's hands, is precisely currency or cash used for transaction and shopping at any time. The cash was designed, printed and issued solely by the national central bank whereas by anyone else would be considered as illegal, and counterfeit.

Needless to say the counterfeit money have been encountered, and accidentally used by many people in the market. Yet it is not acceptable by normal consumers, and does not constitute as the money supply because there is a risk of rejection in shopping. If the scale of counterfeit money circulation in one country market was huge, its impact on the money supply should be considered because as long as the counterfeit money circulates in the market, prices will rise. Therefore, to better research the inflation, the authority should take into the consideration of counterfeit money during investigating the influence on commodity prices.

2. Apart from Stock Cash in Commercial Banks

Presuming that a very small country issued its own money, and did not have any bank within its territory, the total money supply was the sum of cash held by the people in this country. Since there is no commercial bank, for instance, the state government only minted 100,000 coins with one yuan denomination in total, and issued all of them to the people of this country. The monetary aggregate of the country is equal to the total currency in circulation which is 100,000 yuan. Nonetheless the emergence of bank makes the situation complicate. As mentioned above the currency in circulation refers to the cash held by the public outside the banking system. Now that there is the cash outside banking system, there should be naturally the cash stored within banking system. The bank here refers to a commercial bank, both accepting deposits, and making loans. All commercial banks, such as Industrial and Commercial Bank of China, China Construction Bank, Agricultural Bank of China, Bank of China, China CITIC Bank, China Minsheng Banking Corp. Ltd., and other commercial banks in various provincial capital cities such as Bank of Beijing, all possess a certain amount of cash. The sum of cash owned by all commercial banks in one country is the bank reserve. Whereabouts the cash held by the commercial bank includes only two ways below: 1. placing in own vault or the central bank vault; 2. loaning to someone outside the banking system. Consequently all the cash in the vault of commercial banks (including ATMs) is called the bank reserve. How much money does all the commercial banks in China own? It's a puzzle. Although the total cash held by all commercial banks in China varies, we can roughly estimate. As long as the headquarters of every commercial bank has constantly on the track of cash in every branch altogether, the total cash of every commercial bank could be calculated.

The total cash inside the commercial banking system plus the total cash (currency) outside the system constitute the monetary base of one country. The so-called monetary base stands for the sum of denominations including various banknotes and coins, and the amount of tangible banknotes printed and issued, and coins minted by one country in layman's terms. In fact there is no need for commercial banks to conduct analysis because the power to print money is monopolized by the central bank, and only the central bank itself knows exactly the amount of banknotes, and coins issued. In other words the central bank just needs to sum the total amount of banknotes, and coins in different versions that were issued at different periods, the total monetary base of the country can be gotten.

3. Apart from Cash Deposited by Commercial Banks in the Central Bank

Not all cash of the commercial bank can be deposited in own vaults to operate by itself at any time. Nowadays the central bank requires all commercial banks to hand in reserves against deposit in proportion. The ratio of deposits paid by the commercial bank as reserves to total deposits is called the deposit reserve ratio. By way of illustration the central bank stipulates that the deposit reserve ratio of commercial bank is 20%, which signifies that the commercial bank must deposit 20 yuan every 100 yuan deposited by a customer to the head office or local agencies of the central bank for safekeeping. Statutory reserve is a crucial means for the central bank to control the risk of various commercial banks, and cannot be lent to any client by commercial banks. Supposing that the statutory reserve ratio is increased from 10% to 20%, the multiplier for commercial bank to create money should be a factor of 10 to 5 lower. For instance, the total deposit of a bank amounts to 10 billion yuan, the commercial banking system can create 100 billion yuan deposits at the utmost in the event of the reserve ratio at 10%, and 50 billion yuan deposits in case of the reserve ratio at 20%. Ergo the raise in statutory reserve ratio is the fastest measure to reduce the money supply.

4. All Current and Time Deposits of Individuals and Enterprises.

The sum of currency (M0) and current deposit is known as M1, and that of currency, current deposit and time deposit is known as M2. By and large money supply refers to the total amount of M2. In reality different countries have different total computational methods for monetary aggregates. The relation between each part of monetary aggregates and commodity prices is also different. Taking the cash in individual pocket as an example, the cash can be applied to buy goods and services to push up commodity prices at any time whereas sometimes tens of millions of cash are locked in safes, and do not buy anything for a decade, merely conducive to plummet the money supply and commodity prices. For that reason banks hate corrupt officials most, and cannot earn interest spreads of deposits and loans with such cash, assuming which in the hands of the public increases, the deposit and the base to create money decreases for commercial banks.

Provided a country has only one commercial bank, and the national cash sums to 10 billion yuan. Most of all 1 billion yuan cash is held by the people, 9 billion yuan is deposited in the commercial bank, and the reserve ratio is 10%, the maximum money supply will be 91 billion yuan (1 billion yuan plus 90 billion yuan). Secondly the public withdraw 1 billion yuan cash from the bank, and the reserve ratio is 10%, the money supply will be 82 billion yuan (2 billion yuan plus 80 billion yuan). Thirdly the public withdraw all the 9 billion yuan deposits from the commercial bank, and put them in own homes, and the money supply will be 10 billion yuan. As a result what the commercial bank hates most is that clients withdraw cash from its business department. Provided that clients withdraw large amounts of cash from the business department, the clerk of bank must be unhappy because their operational "capital" will be reduced drastically. The commercial bank is most worried about the central bank firstly that takes up their reserves, and clients secondly that withdraw cash. Otherwise the central bank enhances the reserve ratio to 100%, the deposit of 9 billion yuan in the commercial bank will be all handed over to the central bank treasury for freeze, and the money supply will be also 10 billion yuan as to the country above-mentioned.

The relationship between current deposit and commodity prices is complicated. In China on the assumption that current deposit is expressed as a passbook, unable to buy things, only by cashability of deposits in the passbook can you go shopping. The liquidity of current passbook is poorer than cash conducive to falling commodity prices. Assuming the current deposit is represented as a debit card, cardholder can go shopping to push up commodity prices whenever and wherever. Commercial banks are very fond of current deposits due to scarcely interest accrued, and multiple money supplies created by making loans with current deposits. Be that as it may current deposits or debit cards push up commodity prices most easily.

The relation between time deposits and commodity prices is also very complicated. All commercial banks are fond of time deposits. For example, 9 billion yuan is time deposits for one year in above country, the money supply will change somewhat, i.e., 1 billion yuan (currency) + 90 billion yuan (deposit) - 9 billion yuan (time deposit) = 82 billion yuan, because 9 billion yuan certifications of time deposits in the hand of the public cannot be used for shopping (certifications of time deposits are generally not tradable in China unlike some countries), and as a rule should be subtracted from the money supply.

Commercial banks are fond of time deposits just that they can use the deposits at ease to steadily multiply the money supply within the agreed time limit. Major functions of commercial bank are to convert time deposits into current deposits through loans, thereby amplifying the money supply. The reason why the applicant for a loan from the bank is that he is in urgent need for money to buy things, once the money is lent, it must be paid for a certain purpose. For this reason the loan is ordinarily re-deposited in the bank in the form of current deposit as working capital. Manifestly loans are the source of money created by commercial banks.

The creation of all deposits on all accounts is based on the monetary base issued by the central bank. As above example one country only has the monetary base of 10 billion yuan with total numerical values on the condition of 10% deposit reserve ratio, the bank will create up to the money supply of 100 billion yuan deposits even if its citizen deposits all the currency in the commercial bank. Only when the central bank injects new money or refunds the reserve into the commercial bank has it the "foundation" to create money so the reserve is also called "bank foundation".

[Viewpoint Collision]
Excessive Money Issuance Is Misjudgment

This writer believes that China has never implemented the behavior of inflation policy without such incentive although the currency inflation has always been a product of governmental policies. Consequently so-called judgment of excessive money issuance must be a false equivalence of loan amount to the issuance amount.

At present most people think that the China's money issuance is too excessive, and even specific overshoot in trillion is calculated. The writer considers that this is a wrong judgment that does not conform to national conditions. Currency inflation has always been a product of governmental policies. In order to shift the fiscal crisis, the government deliberately issues excess banknotes to devalue artificially the money, draining the wallet of ordinary people, and enterprises. That is to say all excess money issuance is conscious, and is out of the question in an inadvertent way. Hence the central government should have known clearly whether, and what the money is over-issued, anything but needs to be calculated by scholars or statistical departments. Our government is responsible for people, and has controlled the fiscal revenue to increase at a double-digit rate, by no means carry out the motivation of inflation policy, and never have such an action. As a result the so-called judgment of excessive money issuance must be a false equivalence of loan amount to issuance amount.

First of all incontrovertibly there is currently a huge discrepancy between deposits and loans in Chinese bank accounts. A large amount of money is idle, and actually has not entered the field of circulation though they are deposited in banks, and there is no essential difference from being buried underground. In case these currencies enter the circulation field, and the turnover speed will be accelerated, and the so-called M0, M1, and M2 will be impossibly as much as they are currently. Regardless of the amount of money caused by this situation, they are all issued economically but financially or printed by banknote printing, and minting factory out of thin air. Namely they are all supported by material objects, and economic behaviors. Only when the amount of loans is greater than that of deposits are banknotes over-issued, resulting in depreciation, and inflation.

Economic common sense indicates if deposits cannot be converted into loans, then they would turn to unemployment, which is loss for both capital and labor. For a long time large amounts of deposits have been overstocked in banks, and the mechanism of monetary conversion into capital has been severely inhibited by the examination and approval economy to result in so-called four surpluses of production capacity, products, liquidity, and manpower in China. Such a country unexpectedly exists in the currency inflation, no matter what the expected size it is a confused concept in between nowhere. For decades China export like gifts and the domestic extreme economic exploitation allow a few people to become suddenly rich in a short period, high GDP, and low proportion of people income in GDP due to an inadequate social security. The people dare not consume, and have no money to expand consumption. People with low incomes have to deposit in banks for family self-insurance. Whereupon deposits grow abnormally, and loans have been significantly lower than deposits for a long time. A large number of products cannot achieve value, and have to rely on export like gifts. A large amount of capital is unemployed while it is difficult for small and medium-size enterprises

(SMEs) which create more than 95% of jobs in China to obtain loans, and their financing costs are up to about 20%. Given that there is no so-called black money, whether and how many SMEs can survive in China? How difficult their survival is! Whereas so much money is backlogged in banks. That is to say the so-called liquidity forbids flow, how could it be surplus? Deposit reserve ratio is extremely high in long-term. Similarly the dam is continuously heightened to close tightly the water in the reservoir, and meanwhile the land dried and cracked, and crops died of drought, being nervously frightened by the flood every day. The notion of so-called excess liquidity shall be stopped!

Actually this psychological disorder is terrified by the so-called high growth more than 30 years. The absolute increase of China GDP by 10% is not as great as that the United States by 1% although countries at different developmental stages has incomparable growth rate. Average GDP growth rate about 10% is not high for developing countries at all whereas the annual growth rate of 3% is a remarkable high for developed countries. Current increases in social crime rate and immigration tendency in China all illustrate that the class division and the extreme economic exploitation are becoming more and more serious. The few suddenly wealthy people are unassertive, and insecure. Accordingly the GDP growth rate about 10% is only the speed in spite of illness. In line with the balance of existent class power, and the consciousness level of disadvantaged group, we should not expect to fundamentally change the situation of unfair distribution in the short term. However, as long as the distribution tilts a few percentage points to the disadvantaged group, the consumption rate of residents will increase significantly. It is normal for the GDP growth rate driven by consumption to remain above double digit for decades. As soon as the GDP growth rate of 1% is converted for the social identity of rural migrant workers each year to enable them to truly enjoy the national treatment of urban people, despite the fact that the consumption level reaches only half of the current urban population, the China full employment rate, and actual investment rate will be enhanced substantially. GDP will not be lower than 10% simply by right of this measure. A variety of negative problems arising from the China current economic growth are not caused by the growth rate, so-called gross but quality, and structural problems, and are caused by the material-oriented development concept, severely unfair financial distribution system, and resident income distribution mechanism. Providing that reducing artificially the rate of development and growth does not start with the root cause of problem, more serious consequences will be generated. In no event shall we sacrifice substantial employment, and income for the sake of outer part like CPI.

In the next place we must re-understand the investment rate indicator in China. Supposing that the investment amount that realized the combination of labor, and means of production is regarded as actual investment, the present actual investment rate will be generally only about half of the nominal investment rate. A considerable amount of loans will be converted back into deposits in China, or that of money is moving among banks, enterprises, and different banks, and is not really converted into capital at all, neither variable capital for purchasing labor, nor constant capital for purchasing means of production. Not most of them are converted into cash flow, and entered ordinary people's wallets. At the same time bank management departments and financial experts make such a fuss about more or less M1 and M2, scissor or reverse scissor differences, viscosity. It is nothing more than a mere talk. Before the examination and approval economy is fundamentally transformed into market economy, none of these things plagiarized from the West can reflect the Chinese actual economic relationship, and economic structure under the condition of money, food and energy in setting price systems. It is only for the birds to regulate, and control the economic operation according to these indicators, inevitably calling white black, being poles apart, adding flour for more water, and water for more flour. Such hard work does a disservice for economic development.

Ultimately we must recognize the active force for this round of commodity price uptrend. When specifically analyzing the reason for commodity price increase, as everyone knows distinctly it is undeniable that the first driving force is the production cost, of which the largest proportion is the cost of living labor. In the first three quarters of this year, the wage of rural migrant workers was increased by 18.7%. This increase in labor price has nothing to do with increasing the money issuance amount. It is not that the boss' currency increases or depreciates but that wages are compensated, debts are repaid, and the extreme economic exploitation is reduced. Cost of living labor rises, demand does not fall, and increase in product price is quite normal. As the cost of industrial and commercial living labor enhances, the opportunity cost of agricultural products (17.61, 0.69, and 4.08%) will inevitably boost, and it is totally impossible for agricultural product prices without rise. Along with the reform of distribution system, it can be expected that the wage of rural migrant workers will continue to enhance, and the upward trend in production costs and commodity prices is irreversible. The rise in wages triggers the commodity price run-up, which in turn triggers the rise in wages. Such a cycle will unavoidably lead to the excessive increase in money issuance amount. We must distinguish causality. It is not the commodity price rise caused by the money issuance amount but the increase in money issuance amount is caused by the rise in wages and commodity prices. In this case, if the increase in money issuance amount is artificially suppressed, the consequence will be to hinder the adjustment of distribution relation and economic structure, and delay the transformation of social identity and the economic status of rural migrant workers. The strategic imbalance of economic structure is caused by the wrong policy in history. To achieve the strategic adjustment of economic structure, a strategic breakthrough must be made. Strategic adjustments include the transformation of social identity for rural migrant workers, and the elimination of extreme economic exploitation. For this purpose the benefit distribution structure must be changed again. Further variations in wages and commodity prices are included the adjustment of benefit structure with reshuffling nature. Stock problem is solved by virtue of increments. As long as the government increases continuously financial subsidies for the group whose income levels cannot withstand rising commodity prices, this trend of which needs not to be anxious about, and instead it should be treated as a market mechanism to change unreasonable and unfair property relations, and distribution relations. Source: Sina.com

Chapter 3

New Excess Money as the Source of Increase in Money Supply

According to media report, on the evening of December 15, 2010, a president of the central bank made a speech at the Peking University, first explained his "pool theory" "invented" in November, and expressed some standpoints on the money supply. Main views in reports from various media are combined as follows:

1. Typical pool is foreign exchange reserves with different modules, corresponding to different pools, wherein some guarantee for import and export payments, and some are prepared for dividends from foreign-funded enterprises or a "hot money", 100% of which is hedged by the central bank after entry. The gross should not have a negative impact on the national economy yet we have not prevented them from making some money from an individual point of view.

2. The president stated that on the one hand the broad money of high-saving countries and low-saving countries is different as a percentage of GDP. China is a high-saving country so the proportion of M2 to GDP is high. On the other hand, when the proportion

of indirect finance is high, the proportion of broad money to GDP is high. The United States is a typical developed country with direct finance while China has a large proportion of indirect finance. Therefore the contrast between Chinese M2 and American M2 is not appropriate. He discussed that the concept of "excessive issuance" must be clarified. The concept of money issuance beyond economic growth was from the traditional planned economy because the price was fixed, and price multiplied by physical quantity was money demand, and simultaneously there was no financial market and service market at that time. Thus the concept of that time is used now that is wrong. From the current perspective the criterion for measuring whether the money supply is more or less is the core CPI, considering that some prices are less connected to the money such as commodity price fluctuations caused by imported bulk commodity, climate, and the like.

3. The president said that we must face up to the apparent increase in the money supply in response to the global financial crisis in the past two years. Since 2008 we have adopted an expansive monetary policy, in other words "forceful steps and quick action". All these measures contain ineluctably overshoot. The key is to adjust, and turn timely once this cycle enters an inflection point so that it is not too excessive to achieve the purpose of successfully fighting the crisis without large side effects. In the face of large market liquidity this year, the central bank has repeatedly adopted reserve instruments. The president showed that the source of liquidity must be observed in the

entire economic system. Given that it is caused by recovery and the growth of trade surplus, or growths of capital inflow or FDI, we should increase hedging even if there is no higher commodity price increase at this time. Visibly this instrument has different roles.

In order not to misinterpret the president original intention as much as possible, his views are quoted in large. His first viewpoint is how to hedge the hot money, i.e., all kinds of foreign currencies entered China for speculation with the "pool" method. His second viewpoint is how to treat with the excess money issuance. He thought that the excess money issuance is just an outdated concept of planned economy. From the current perspective the criterion for measuring whether the money supply is more or less is the core CPI. His third viewpoint is how to use the money supply to increase or narrow down the problem in response to crisis. Are all of his viewpoints worthy and sustained after scrutiny, and understood and supported by the people again? It is a horse of a different color.

I. Whether His Viewpoints Can Persuade the People?

Judging from messages left by more than 1,000 people in just a few hours after his opinion reported by Sina.com, a minimum of 99% of net citizens oppose. The author excerpts several representative messages as follows:

Net friend Breeze from blog.sd.sina.cn/jinan

How can flowing or profit-seeking money form a pool? It cannot be anything but river or flood.

Merely still money or money for savings can form a pool.

But now the interest rate is negative, money is inclined to invest in reality.

So the pool is just "an imperatorial new clothing", or a fig leaf for wrong policies.

Net friend chinafive from blog.gd.sina.cn/gz

I am a common citizen. I have to make a living every day. My monthly salary has not been increased. Savings from my pinch and screw for many years have become increasingly worthless in current two years. I don't know what shall I do in the future? I had hoped that I can save some money through my hard work, so that my old age can ensure be supported. In the face of higher and higher commodity prices, please tell me how do I live? I have read a lot of economic books recently! President, you want for nothing yet how many people in China can have such status and treatment as you! If I were you, I would do better than you! You don't know how expensive the housekeeping is without being butler! Don't use your theory to make fun of our simple people! Actually I can debate theoretical things more than you. You are just lucky to get the opportunity given by the people!

Net friend Internet Content Provider from blog.ln.sina.cn/as

He said that high-saving countries can issue excessive money, the level is too low. I want to ask you, where is the money for savings, is it put and idled in the safe box? The money deposited also has flowed to the market through loans, doesn't it? Unexpectedly the level is so low.

Net friend bluestar from blog.sina.cn/area/bj

So-called "forceful steps and quick action" is a political slogan put forward by some politicians who do not understand economics, which is the direct cause of currency inflation today.

Net friend Old Moon from blog.gd.sina.cn/sz

Don't take the person majoring in economics too seriously. A great many of senior economic talents graduated from mathematics, and physics departments. The key is whether there is a problem with philosophical thought. The president insisted that the excess money issuance was a concept in the planned economy period. Something is wrong here: First output value and price in the market economy are relatively stable, or else there will be huge issues in economics. Second now that there is not the excessive money issuance, why is liquidity tightened? Don't you contradict yourself? Most importantly third the vast majority of the people don't want to hear his explanation about who is right and wrong but are concerned about the depreciation of own money, and how own income responds to high commodity prices!

From aforesaid net citizens' comments, they raise hard questions about the effect of "pool theory" against the hot money, the impact of excessive money supply on commodity prices and resident lives, and the harm of monetary policy utilized to stimulate economics. Seemingly it is necessary to listen to the voice of the people when the central bank executes monetary policy. Full name of the central bank is the People's Bank of China, and the central bank should listen to the ordinary people's opinions seeing that the signboard covers "People". Still the Federal Reserve (FED) as a private bank would like to listen to the opinion of Congress when it issues currency. Whereas we are the "the People's Bank", and should even more listen to the people's opinions. Your monetary policy should be adjusted accordingly in case your point of view cannot convince the people.

II. How the Money Supply Increases

Not to comment on his "pool theory" first considering that experts had stated briefly that the utilization of "pools" can hedge the growth of domestic money supply, and the hot money make a profit as before, whereupon the "pool theory" is nothing new, in any case his theory regarding the money supply is indeed appalling. Is the proportion of money supply to GDP necessarily high as China is a high-saving ratio country? Conversely is large money supply (M2) caused by that the Chinese is keen on the depositor responsibility? This seems out of common sense a little. Firstly whether the Chinese keen on deposits is good, and secondly how the money supply is created after all.

The Chinese are fond of deposits, the saving ratio is high, and so bank deposits are more. It should have been good for the bank. Seeing that there is no loan without deposit, in the final analysis the obscure and frugal people deposit their painstaking efforts and labor fruits from hard work to the bank, and then the bank lends them to companies, and entities that need money to promote the social economic development. We should thank ultimately tens of thousands of diligent and thrifty depositors who lend the wealth they can enjoy to such borrowers to fund their enterprises for entrepreneurship. Only by saving more money can the national economy be sustainable. Dissimilar to the Americans, who wouldn't like to deposit money except for borrowing money for consumption, and therefore the sustainability of U.S. economics is in trouble. President Obama often called on citizens to deposit money more.

Savings are a virtue. Correspondingly the central bank must treat kindly, and be grateful to these citizens who are on fire for savings, and ensure the maintenance of their money value. On the contrary borrowing intentions of the spender with loans such as local governments, real estate speculators, and developers should be strictly scrutinized in that they are bank opponents theoretically, and borrow or do not repay in all probability. Hence banks should adopt fundamentally different attitudes towards depositors, and lenders. The Chinese still prefer saving when the actual deposit interest rate is negative. It is a helpless choice considering that investment channels are limited. Nonetheless high savings are not the essential reason for the sharp increase in money supply.

How is the money supply created exactly? By way of illustration the total deposit of a country was 30 trillion in 2005, and reached 85 trillion by the end of 2011. How were 55 trillion deposits increased? It can be explained clearly though this process is extremely complex. First and foremost let us see how the total deposit of bank is increased from the common sense of life. On the assumption a person in this country called Tom had 100 yuan cash in his pocket, lent this 100 yuan to his friend Dick on January 1, 2012, who only put this 100 yuan cash in his cabinet. Tom reduces, and Dick increases 100 yuan. The debtor-creditor relation between Tom and Dick will not increase the total deposit of this country.

Instead Tom deposited the 100 yuan into a Bank A, and got a current deposit card with 100 yuan. Dick borrowed 90 yuan from the Bank A (at a 10% deposit reserve ratio), then deposited in a Bank B, and also got a current deposit card with 90 yuan. Here Tom's 100 yuan becomes 190 yuan, and monetary aggregates are increased by 90 yuan through the debtor-creditor relation between Tom, and Dick in the bank. Moreover the 190 yuan can be used to purchase any goods and services on the market. By analogy Tom's 100 yuan can produce up to 1,000 yuan deposits via repetitive deposits and loans midst banks at the deposit reserve ratio of 10%. In this way the money supply is increased by 10 times from 100 yuan to 1,000 yuan. Who leads to the increase in monetary aggregate at an exponential growth? Needless to say, it is not because Tom, who first deposited 100 yuan cash while the bank does not stop lending for profit. Supposing that the bank does not lend each yuan of Tom's 100 yuan cash to others, the money supply will not be increased. In any case such increase in money supply should just be temporary theoretically.

On the understanding that depositor Tom withdrew 100 yuan cash from the Bank A on January 1, 2013, did not deposit to any bank but put in his own cabinet at home, and nailed, not planning to use it within three or five years, what will happen? Consequently the Bank A must collect debts from Dick. Dick must withdraw 90 yuan from the Bank B, and repay to the Bank A. At this very moment Dick's 90 yuan deposit was written off. The rest may be deduced by analogy. Tom's 100 yuan cash corresponds to different borrowers' deposits in different banks such as 80 yuan, 70 yuan, 60 yuan, and 50 yuan, counting up to 1,000 yuan, all of which must be canceled. As a result the money supply of banks, to wit the total amount of deposits and loans, is suddenly dropped by ten times. Everything is restored to the total money supply in the first place.

Be that as it may the money supply of bank could never be restored to its original amount given that something went wrong in a part of bank loans. As an illustration the Bank A stipulated that the Dick's loan period was one year after the Bank A lent Dick 90 yuan. Yet the Bank A did not collect back the 90 yuan from Dick somehow after one year was expired, and Dick's loans will never be written off. The total deposit among banks outside the Bank A may increase forever by 900 yuan (at the deposit reserve ratio of 10%). Simultaneously the Bank A must take out more than 90 yuan from own capital fund, and then get back more than 10 yuan from the central bank (at the deposit reserve ratio of 10%, and interest accrued by the central bank) to amount to 100 yuan, and interest, which was repaid to Tom. Assuming that the Bank A capital fund has not redundant money (just satisfies the proportional requirement of central bank), and could not afford 90 yuan, how to do? The Bank A has only three countermeasures:

1. Borrows from other commercial banks or sells security assets held;
2. Absorbs a new depositor to repay the old depositor Tom;
3. Borrows from the central bank.

In the midst of three countermeasures, the first two will not boost permanently the money supply. Only by the third, videlicet banknotes newly printed by the central bank are lent to the Bank A will it permanently boost the money supply. This is because newly printed banknotes of the central bank are not recovered probably after lending to the commercial bank. The newly printed banknote is again the new asset as to the central bank, viz., the governmental debt to own people. 100 billion yuan will be newly added for total deposits midst commercial banks (according to the deposit reserve ratio of 10%) as soon as the central bank in the name of supporting economic construction prints more 10 billion yuan cash to lend to a commercial bank. On the assumption that 100 billion yuan deposits are generated by means of loans and deposits of different government agencies in commercial banks, the government will not be able to repay afterwards due loans, in the interim it is hardly possible for the central bank to recover 10 billion yuan of original loans from the commercial bank. From the above the new currency of central bank is only the pivotal reason for the increase in money supply.

[News Excerpt]

In early November 2010, remarks of a president from the central bank at the Caixin Summit, which introduced a "hot money" into the "pool", triggered a widespread speculation and discussion from market analysts. After more than a month, the bank president interpreted positively the "pool" for the first time on the evening of December 15th. He also pointed out that the money supply has increased significantly in current two years. The standard for measuring money supply is core CPI.

The president said, "Until now comments in the market hold that there is the excessive money supply in China".

The "pool theory" as a countermeasure against the hot money triggered a huge debate. On the 15th, the president, the concept "inventor" personally explained it. In his view the typical "pool" refers to foreign exchange reserves with different modules, some of which guarantee for import and export payments, and are prepared for dividends from foreign-funded enterprises or the "hot money", 100% of which is hedged after entry so that the total amount will not have a negative impact on economics.

The president thought that the core CPI can be used as the criterion to measure whether the money supply is more or less, considering that some prices are less connected to the money such as commodity price fluctuations caused by imported bulk commodity, climate, and the like. The money supply has expanded remarkably in past two years in order to cope with the financial crisis. We have to adopt expansionary monetary and fiscal policies during the crisis, in other words, forceful steps and quick action. In this process, it is ineluctable to overshoot. The key is to adjust timely policies after the inflection point is found in the cycle.

He commented that several different reasons for the rise in core inflation include the role of expansionary fiscal and monetary policies yet it does not mean that the policy during the crisis was overexerted. This can be argued by whether the policy is adjusted in a timely manner after the inflection point. The liquidity contraction of central bank did not start until the CPI reached 5.1%. In fact the deposit reserve ratio was heightened from the first week of January 2010, and up to six times throughout the year. It was once eased during the period since the impact of European debt crisis required observation time.

The president remarked that the source of liquidity in the entire economic system can be studied from another angle. In the event of the recovery and growth of trade surplus, growths of capital inflow and foreign direct investment, and other reasons, the hedging intensity should be extended even if there is no higher rising commodity price.

The president regarded that the proportion of M2 in GDP between China and the United States cannot be simply compared. First of all countries in the Asian region have a relatively high savings rate, particularly China, which easily leads to a high proportion of M2 in GDP; followed by the impact of financing structure, substantially China is indirect finance while the United States is direct finance. He emphasized that the concept of excessive money issuance was used by the planned economy period, and cannot be used under market economic conditions. Appropriate indicator is the money supply.

With respect to the concept of super-sovereign currency previously brought up, the president explained that it was a suggestion or assumption alone at the time. The international reserve currency is largely the US dollar-denominated asset holding, and the reserve currency may generate inconsistencies between domestic policies and international responsibilities. For this purpose I hope there is a better alternative upon the reserve currency. Aside from that the financial crisis at the end of 2008 and early 2009, some countries passed the buck to China, which has a largest surplus in global imbalances as a background for the concept. (Wen Tao)

[Concept Presentation 1]

The so-called core CPI stands for the consumer price index after excluding the price of products that are greatly affected by climate and seasonal factors. China has not as yet defined the core CPI in a distinct manner. The United States uses the consumer price index after removing fuel and instrument prices as the core CPI. It is generally acknowledged that the core CPI can more truly reflect the macroeconomic performance.

The methodology of relying on the core CPI to determine the price situation was first proposed by the American economist Robert J. Gordon in 1975. At that time there was a dramatic inflation, and the rise in consumption prices was largely affected by the rise in food prices and energy prices under the background of the United States suffered from the first oil crisis in 1974-1975, for which respectable economists considered major impact from supply factors and the minor impact from demand pull. Therefore the methodology was proposed to deduct the variation in food and energy prices from CPI to measure the variation in price level. Ever since 1978 the Bureau of Labor Statistics (BLS) of the United States of America has announced the increase rate after excluding food and energy prices from the consumer price index (CPI) and the producer price index (PPI).

Hereafter the core CPI has gradually become a common terminology in the macroeconomic analysis of the United States. In 1981 monographs with the title of core CPI appeared. At all events, even inside the American economics, whether the price of food and energy should be deducted from the CPI to judge the price level has been in dispute, and there is a strong argument midst plenty of opponents.

According to the basic principle of numismatology, a country or regional economic value grows every one yuan, the central bank as money issuance institution should also supply money of one yuan, in the event of more than one yuan, which is deemed as the excessive money supply. In emerging market countries, the process of resource commodification is intensified, and it is reasonable for the broad money supply to be moderately higher than the GDP growth for economic development due to market-oriented reforms, and other reasons. Nonetheless too high money supply readily brings about inflation.

[Concept Presentation 2]

On the whole direct finance signifies a capital market financing including the issuance of stocks, and equity financing through the transfer in equity markets. Indirect finance refers to bank financing, including private lending. In essence deposits are borrowed via the bank intermediary. Just that the bank procedure is added, it is known as indirection.

The standard differentiation between direct finance and indirect finance is the formation mode of credit and debt relationship. Direct financing activities are anterior to and base of indirect finance and indirect finance in turn greatly promotes the development of direct finance. In the modern market economy, direct and indirect finances are developed in parallel and promote each other.

Indirect finance is financing mode through financial intermediaries. Under this financing mode, the surplus enterprise deposits funds in financial institutions or purchases various securities issued by financial institutions for a certain period, and then these financial institutions provide the concentrated funds plus interest accrual to the fund demand enterprise for use. Both supply and demand sides of funds do not meet directly, and have no a direct creditor-debtor relationship. Instead financial institutions intervene as creditors and debtors to realize the adjustment between surplus and strapped funds. Compared with direct finance, indirect finance is distinguished by flexibility. Scattered petty cash accounts can be used for great things through the concentration of intermediaries such as banks. Simultaneously these intermediaries have more information and specialized talents, which have unique advantages in ensuring fund security and improving fund use efficiency. It is beneficial to both investment and financing parties.

[Viewpoint Collision]

The "pool theory" against hot money clarifies one view. On the premise of without changing the current foreign exchange management system, and train of thought, it is obvious that the overseas hot money entering China will be firstly absorbed in full by the central bank as foreign exchange reserves, and then the corresponding CNY amount of funds outstanding for foreign exchange will be recovered by the central bank bill issuance, that is, the CNY amount released which is caused by the increase in foreign exchange reserves of the central bank is hedged. The same is true of that the so-called hot money pool can only be managed by the central bank. What is the purpose of "pool theory"? This is not difficult to understand. To put it bluntly is to prevent the overflow of CNY liquidity caused by the inflow of hot money, and further prevent the hot money from impacting the stock market, property market, bond market, and credit market, and ultimately prevent new non-performing loans (NPL) from damaging domestic financial security. It seems that this is a good logic. Nevertheless, in case the pool cannot effectively prevent the CNY from significant appreciation, when the hot money flows back, it is inevitable to take generous exchange gains away, as a result of that the hot money will make a killing from the central bank. The loss of the central bank is that of finance, and manifestly that of wealth of domestic residents. Upsides, the hot money just impacts in a different way, as broad as it is long.

Chapter 4

Whose Pocket Were Low-Interest Loans in

[Note I] Numerous and complicated perspectives on the market will confuse your thought, make judgment lose your bearings, and you perplex and greatly painful.

[Note II] This article first and foremost reveals profoundly and thoughtfully the harm posed by Keynesianism governmental economic stimulus measures all over the world. The government deliberately lowers interest rates, increases money supply, and indulges loans making to stimulate the economic growth, bringing not only short-term prosperity, but also deeper crises and disasters, and shadowing inflation and debt crisis. As a consequence only if the government must make use of higher profits and tighten monetary policy at the expense of growth would the economy get on track.

I. Three-Year Low Interest Rate Policy Came to an End

Finally the second interest rate hike in 2010 came late on December 26 although it was urged repeatedly, and gave a glimmer of hope for countless people held deposits with a negative interest rate. In the long past people had suffered much in the difficult reality of negative interest rates. In 2010 the one-year deposit interest rate was 2.25% most of the time and meanwhile commodity prices rose by 3-5% year-on-year. This negative real deposit interest rate forced market liquidity to skyrocket, and asset prices rose in tandem with prices of commodities and services. In case the statistic commodity price is calculated according to a basket of samples and methods in the West, it is likely that the veritable inflation rate had been amazing high in China.

Maintenance of authentic negative interest rates to stimulate economic growth not only does not accord with the principle of fairness and justice, but also results in a huge harm to the China economy. More dangerously the bank sharp increase in uncollectible and bad debts will threaten the safety of financial system and seriously restrict the sustainable development in China. The subject absence of state-owned property rights in Chinese financial companies will inevitably lead to a rampant government intervention and power rent-seeking.

Needless to say the authentic negative interest rate gives the power rent-seeking and corruption a good opportunity. The central bank had gradually lowered one-year deposit and loan interest rates from 4.14% and 7.47% to 2.25% and 5.31% respectively since December 21, 2007. It had been as many as two years and ten months until October 20, 2010. **In the past three years of interest rate decline cycle, the money supply was increased by a full CNY 30 trillion, viz., from CNY 40 trillion in December 2007 to CNY 70 trillion in October 2010.** Various loans increased from about CNY 26 trillion in 2007 to about CNY 47 trillion in October 2010. Loans increased by a full CNY 21 trillion from 2008 to the first ten months of 2010.

Where did CNY 21 trillion loans go to? Whose moneybag did it flow to? Can it be recovered in accordance with the contract? This is an indefinite time bomb over the Chinese economy. Once accidentally "igniting the lead" of this huge loan crisis, China financial system will inevitably suffer a devastating blow as a consequence the entire financial system and Chinese economics will be completely collapsed. The subprime mortgage crisis in the United States was precisely because loans were so indulgent by the financial system that debtors could not repay their debts on time, which led to the bankruptcy of more than 90 banks to hit the U.S. economy hard. The Keynesian method, lowering interest rates or over-issuing monetary base was applied to stimulate economic growth by the government, as a matter of fact, was proved completely wrong by the example of President Nixon as early as the 1970s. The fact that Nixon's intervention policy had long proved that the government uses monetary or fiscal policies to force the economy out of the trough, which in the end can not make economics grow healthily, whereas will produce more serious problems than before stimulus.

II. The Central Bank Lowered Bank Interest Rates While Private Lending Interest Rates Skyrocket

In China the harm caused by this stimulus is far more severe than that caused by Nixon to the United States in that very year, nothing but has not yet been fully exposed. At present we analyze the internal reason why China loans have increased by CNY 21 trillion in the past three years.

There are obviously two different loan markets in China loanable funds. One is a lending market mediated by Chinese official banks, and deposit and loan interest rates are implemented in accordance with the central bank command under the planned economic model. The other is a private lending market, and deposit and loan interest rates are determined by both depositor and lender or intermediary. The private lending market is closer to the free market. What was the interest rate of private loans from the end of 2007 to 2010? Generally the **monthly interest** of one yuan is 1-5 cents, that is the **annual interest** of one yuan is 1.2-6 dimes, and namely the one-year loan interest rate is as high as **12-60%**! Loans within the collars are very popular in China and recognized by the market.

Plenty of Chinese enterprises have borrowed money from private financing at the collars for many years. In the meantime the one-year loan interest rate of state-owned commercial banks was only 5.31% or even lower after discounts. The difference between the loan interest rate of state-owned banks and that of private loans was about 6-55%. What a huge drop! For instance, a Person A borrowed CNY 1 million from a state-owned commercial bank in 2008 and only paid CNY 53,100 interest to the bank per year. On the assumption that the Person A lent it to another Person B who urgently needed funds in switch transaction, and the Person A can gain the interest of CNY 120,000-600,000 annually! Compared to huge returns, the Person A bank loans, as it were, have no cost.

III. Who Borrowed Bank Loans with Low Interest Rate?

Compared with high-interest private loans, who likely obtains low-interest loans from commercial banks?

Most of all in the context of Chinese government dominant economics, these low-interest loans are often issued local government-led railway, road and other infrastructure projects by mobilizing or instructing commercial banks in the name of supporting local construction under the governmental leadership at all levels. Frequently the investment amounts of such railways, roads and urban infrastructure projects reach tens of millions, billions or tens of billions in CNY. It is incredibly expensive, and far from the true cost of the market.

Why do local governments make the project cost prohibitively? That's the key! It involves the mature hidden rule that the Chinese construction market has long run, which is to reserve the power rent-seeking space for projects. As an illustration Enterprise A needs to launch a CNY 10 billion project, the Enterprise A must first protocol a plan internally, and then apply for approval. The leadership and staff of the Enterprise A will strongly support this works. After the internal consent of the Enterprise A the plan must be reported to the local development and reform commission. Only if the development and reform commission approves, would the project be established, and could the Enterprise A solve the funding source of investment. In condition that the project of Enterprise A is listed in key projects of the local government, all establishments, examination and approval, and they can enjoy loans of preferential interest rate much lower than the market.

Naturally operators of this project, including leaders of the Enterprise A, relevant examination and approval leaders, and the person in charge of bank loans, et al. can get a corresponding rebate from the CNY 10 billion. Without doubt there are unwritten rules about the proportion of this rebate. There are three possible approaches to operate this CNY 10 billion project:

1. The leader of the Enterprise A hopes own relatives to make a fortune by contract, must spend money to open all the joints of relationship network, that is, to buy out various examination and approval procedures at one time;

2. The leader of the Enterprise A cooperates with the superior leader to find a joint agent to undertake this project, therefrom making a larger profit;

3. The leader of Enterprise A lets the most powerful and influential company win the bid by the "open and fair" bidding, and waits for the opportunity to be promoted quickly in an official career; or lets the foreign company win the bid, and deposits directly the USD rebate into own overseas bank account.

As thus when this CNY 10 billion project is in mop-up, all parties benefit from their participation in power, and the money is not enough to share. What should the leader of the Enterprise A do? He will add another CNY 5 billion loan and borrow from the bank! Why does the bank dare to lend in the face of this bottomless pit? Given that the bank money belongs to the state, does the state need to ensure that the GDP growth rate is more than 8%? Does the central session require banks to support actively the economic construction? The leader of commercial bank knows that the loan cannot be recovered within the contract period, be that as it may, the loan is still granted.

CNY 4.5 billion before and after the CNY 15 billion loan directly becomes the profit of middle operators at a minimum 30% rebate. Therefore local governments, and relevant ministries and commissions are so keen on setting the *Twelfth Five-Year Planning*, doing large projects, and maintaining more than 10% of GDP growth! Right here the true intention is.

Unquestionably this does not demonstrate that railway, road, and other infrastructure projects cannot be carried out at all. Given that the CNY 10 billion of project may be as-built with CNY 5 billion, and the quality may be better than on the basis of the free bidding method in the market. The project investment and bank credit are all reduced by CNY 5 billion, and the loan repayment capacity of the Enterprise A is greatly enhanced on the due date. Consequently it is not impossible for the government to operate projects but increases costs and risks for commercial banks greatly. The project quality is always not guaranteed for the sake of the participation of power rent-seeking.

Next some of these loans with a low-interest rate flow to private enterprises, and **focus on real estate companies everywhere**. Another part flows to the people who bought a house on mortgage. The acquisition of loans with low interest rate by property developers is similar to that by local governments apart from differences. Acquisitions of property developer loans with a low interest rate from state-owned banks predominantly rely on tackling key problems with the bank leader. What is the key problem to be tackled? Undoubtedly after getting the trust of a bank president by virtue of 10-20% of the total loan as his rebate, allowing that the rebate is 10%, the loan interest rate is 5.31%, and one-year loan interest rate of the property developer will be 15.31% alone. Though it is close to the lower limit of 12-60% of private loans, and is still worthy of the property developer on the grounds that the loan interest rate for remaining years is only 5.31%.

In consequence the **actual loan interest rate** of China state-owned commercial banks has already reached 15% or more in addition to railway, road, and other infrastructure projects! Conversely how much one-year deposit interest rate does the commercial bank currently give for depositors? **Just 2.25%!** Only rose to 2.75% by 2010. Facts in reality show that the property of majority of depositors is risked by the minority of banks in support of railway, road and other infrastructure projects on the one hand, and is used by a small number of people to earn interest margin for personal gain on the other hand. The loan amount of railway, road, and other infrastructure projects, and the property developers is too large to recover on time by the bank so the bank must further adventure. This risk is to allow all potential home-buyers to get loosely loans at house purchase. Only when everyone is encouraged to buy houses with loans can the money that the bank lends to the local government and property developers be recovered.

On all accounts a large number of real estate property speculators who buy wantonly houses by using loans with the low interest rate may not even think of really paid-up their bank loans! They get low-interest loans with their houses, and then lend to the private lending market to earn high loan interest spreads.

Railway, road, and other infrastructure project loans, and real estate enterprise loans are closely linked to ordinary homebuyer on mortgage. Why do local governments borrow recklessly for the construction of railway, road, and other infrastructure? You see with half an eye about building advertisements of real estate brokers every city that the intention is to raise the housing price. Property developers use the public construction best to find excuses for the rise in housing price. Such as the information about infrastructure of subway, high-speed railway, and square in a certain place will be immediately utilized by property developers to raise prices. Therefore whether railway, road, and other infrastructure projects serve the general public or the building price increase of property developers should arouse attention from relevant parties.

IV. Harm of Low Interest Rates to Stimulate Economics

The emergence of above situation is created chiefly by the central bank regulation for interest rate. In the loanable funds market, providing that the central bank raises deposit and loan interest rates in a timely manner, the demand for loans will decrease, and deposits will increase. Instead the central bank keeps deposit and loan interest rates lower than the market price for a long time, merely **two consequences** will occur:

1. Depositors are increasingly reluctant to deposit due to actual negative interest rates but tend to buy goods, services, and assets with the money. Like this, deposit sources of commercial banks will be exhausted day by day. Banks cannot lend loans without deposits unless the central bank prints and issues the monetary base. As a result it is impossible for commodity prices in the market not to rise sharply. Once the monetary base is over-issued, inflation will be out of control. In time of war, inflation can also be understood by the people while in times of peace may be extremely reluctant to be accepted.

2. Benefits of loans with the low interest rate cannot be realized in economic growth at all but are used by the minority of personal for gain. More specifically in railway, road, and other infrastructure projects, seeing that stakeholders can obtain a large amount of loans, they will double the project cost, and charge rebates without restraint. Providing that a CNY 10 billion project is planned to loan at the market price with an annual interest rate of 10%, and allow bidders to bid openly. It may cost as little as CNY 5 billion with the annual interest of CNY 500 million. Whereas the government intervenes in bidding at a cheap interest rate of 5.3%, and the total cost may be greater than CNY 10 billion with the annual interest of CNY 500 million above on the score of power rent-seeking. Governmental public works will not reduce expenditures due to low interest rate loans. On the contrary the cost of government-invested public works or projects will multiply under loose credit conditions. The local government debt will jump sharply until bankruptcy, and in the meantime the bank can only collect debts nowhere. Another benefit is often taken by the person in charge of the bank in **the form of rebate** while the borrower does not get real benefits. It shows that the consequence of suppressing interest rates encourages tremendously corruption and speculation.

V. Express the Interest-Rate Hike Cycle and Imply Risks

According to the current situation, only by quickly raising the one-year deposit interest rate above 3.5% will the deposit be guaranteed not to be lost. **How does the central bank lead 1.3 billion people into the interest rate hike cycle?** This will indeed cope with pressures from international and domestic various interest groups. Such as local governmental debts are these days calculated by CNY 10 trillion, and the annual interest will be increased by CNY 100 billion every 1% loan interest rate hike. The annual interest will be increased by CNY 100 million every CNY 10 billion for property developer loans. Most importantly given that the long-term negative interest rate policy has been implemented, local governments, and property developers tend to be rascally, their loans will not be repaid to banks on schedule even if they have money, and **rather will be postponed via the relationship or even indefinitely.** In case **banks fail to collect such huge loans, they will always turn into the money supply to vastly promote inflation.** Thus the central bank must withstand the pressure from all sides, and maintain resolutely the provisions of the *Banking Law*, and the stability of CNY currency value. To do this, the CNY 21 trillion of new loans that have flowed into the market since 2008 must be recovered on schedule. The optimum strategy to recover the loan is to raise the loan rental price, id est., interest rate. The loan interest rate is getting higher and higher, and the borrower only tries his best to repay.

[Viewpoint Collision]
Two Views on China's Economics

An article on Steven N.S. Cheung blog praises his so-called theory better than Adam Smith! It is suggested that the article writer should really understand the essential signification of Adam Smith's Invisible Hand. Steven N.S. Cheung's Economic Theories on China have principally two views: 1. He has obdurately insisted, and supports that China needs currency inflation with various sophistries; 2. He opposes the governmental support for independent labor unions, and advocates the modern contract labor system. In 1988, when Milton Friedman came to China, he criticized the Steven N.S. Cheung's inflation view (M2 must grow at a rate of 25% in those days), and it was accepted grudgingly by Steven N.S. Cheung. In later time Steven N.S. Cheung in the name of senior Milton Friedman is opposed to the basic principles about currency of Milton Friedman. The China existent monetary crisis is likely related to the Steven N.S. Cheung's fallacy. [Source: Dong Fang Dao Blog]

Chapter 5

Loans of Power Support Unable to
Be Recovered on Schedule

Speaking of the interest-rate hike cycle, which makes China asset prices fall, talking in generalities from a macro perspective. Indicating provided that the central bank raises continuously interest rates, more and more money in the market will be deposited into banks. Accordingly loans also increase the rental price (interest rate hike) and no one will borrow too much loans. Banks increase deposits, and decrease loans as a result of the interest-rate hike. Money reduces in the market circulation, and commodity prices falls. This is the common principle of central banks all around the world: that is, raising interest rates curb inflation. The purpose of central banks to raise interest rates is not to let depositors earn more interest but curb inflation reluctantly.

Please allow me to further elaborate on the topic of interest-rate hike. According to Ms. Ye's article, she thought the raising interest rate helpless to curb market liquidity for the sake of the existence of loans of power support in China. This is the reason why bank loans are utilized by the finance company of local governmental platform, and by the railway, road, and other infrastructure projects. In this regard Mr. Dong Fang Dao made the most comprehensive discussion in the first place. This type of loan is called the loan for state-owned enterprises and institutions. Debtors and creditors are public. There is no clear credit for borrowing from this public ownership account to another one, to put it like this, the debtor still borrows without a repayment capability while the creditor still lends to the insolvent debtor. Operators in both sides can share completely benefits by borrowing and lending. In the end the debtor is in huge debts, and bank loans cannot be recovered on time.

Such phenomenon can be found everywhere in China so that China has to establish four major asset management companies (China Great Wall, China Cinda, China Huarong, and China Orient Asset Management Co., Ltd.) to deal with the bank non-performing loans, and dozens of people make a fortune by virtue of it. Since there is no clear responsible person for repayment of such loans, the debtor does not care about the interest rate level of loans, and still borrows in kind. Consequently, even if interest rates are raised, the liquidity of market loans will remain. This view finds out the issue of Chinese characteristics or a big loophole in our governmental functions. Contrary private banks have clear property rights, and no one will do such a loss-making stupid thing. If the borrower leader must personally bear jointly and severally economic responsibilities for the loan project, and no one will go about borrowing regardless of the actual situation. Therefore it is very important to manage bank loans appropriately so that money is not lent to public-owned enterprises and institutions as much as possible. Under the current system it is necessary to stipulate in the future: Local governments, state-owned enterprises and institutions apply for loans as little as possible, or even are not allowed loans. In case of loans, the legal representative of business entity must make personally jointly and severally economic responsibilities for the repayment clear.

To deal with currency inflation, the interest-rate hike cycle works. If the interest-rate hike cycle is not enabled, inflation will still be uncontrollable even if all commercial banks do not lend to railway, road and other infrastructure projects. Firstly the control of lending to state-owned enterprises and institutions can only be effective for the liquidity of loans but that of deposits. Secondly raising interest rate on loans restrains those debtors with sense of responsibility from state-owned enterprises and institutions. Thirdly interest rate without hike may lead to hyperinflation in the context of strong currency inflation, bringing disaster to the macroeconomic.

According to the data from the Central Bank and the National Bureau of Statistics of the People's Republic of China in January 2011:

A. At the end of January the balance of broad money (M2) was CNY 73.56 trillion, and the year-on-year growth was 17.2%, which was 2.5% and 8.9% severally lower than the end of and the same period of last year. The balance of narrow money (M1) was CNY 26.31 trillion, and the year-on-year growth was 13.6%, which was 7.6% and 25.4% severally lower than the end of and the same period of last year. The balance of currency in circulation (M0) was CNY 5.81 trillion at the year-on-year growth of 42.5%. M0 increased by CNY 1.35 trillion that month on account of the Spring Festival.

B. In January the year-on-year growth of CPI was 4.9%, specifically 4.8% in cities, 5.2% in villages, 10.3% in foods, 2.6% in non-food items, 5.0% in consumption products, and 4.6% in services.

Several important data is remarkable: The balance of currency in circulation (M0) was CNY 5.81 trillion at the year-on-year growth of 42.5%. Year-on-year growth of CPI was 4.9%. This shows that M0 at the year-on-year growth of 42.5%

has been transformed into sharp inflation. It is a severe signal for the CPI at the year-on-year growth of 4.9%! In January 2011, M0 increased by CNY 1.35 trillion at the year-on-year growth of 42.5%. Is it just caused by the Spring Festival? The Chinese New Year in 2011 was on February 3, and special festival purchase for the Spring Festival should be in January. Like that at the data of February 2010 on the grounds that the same Chinese spent the Spring Festival on February 14, 2010, and special festival purchase for the Spring Festival should be in February. The data between years of 2011 and 2010 is completely comparable.

A. The money supply increased by 25.52% in February 2010. At the end of February 2010, the supply balances of broad money (M2), narrow money (M1), and currency in circulation (M0) were CNY 63.6 trillion, CNY 22.43 trillion, and CNY 4.29 trillion at the year-on-year growth rates of 25.52%, 34.99%, and 21.98%, and the month-on-month decline rates of 0.56% and 3.97%, respectively. The cumulative net monetary issuance for the current month was CNY 210.7 billion, and the year-on-year excess was CNY 804.8 billion.

B. The National Bureau of Statistics of the People's Republic of China announced that CPI was increased by 2.7% year-on-year, and 1.2% month-on-month in February 2010. From January to February 2010 the total retail sales of consumer goods in China accumulated CNY 2,505.2 billion, and the year-on-year growth rate was 17.9%.

The data between February 2010 and January 2011 is compared. The balance of currency in circulation (M0) was risen from CNY 4.29 trillion to CNY 5.81 trillion, and the year-on-year growth of CPI was from 2.7% to 4.9%. This shows that the central bank and commercial banks over-issued 30 trillion currencies in the interest rate decline cycle from 2008 to the first ten months of 2010, which was gradually transmitted to the circulation field and the commodity price increase.

In case the central bank does not start the interest rate hike cycle, and leaves free to rising commodity prices, there will be panic purchases, and a large amount of deposits will be withdrawn in a short time to exchange no mater what commodities are. Contrariwise the central bank continues to raise interest rates. It will stabilize people's commodity price expectations to prevent panic purchases.

Nonetheless the interest rate hike cycle is adopted to deal with inflation, and the bank has two unwilling options:

1. Deposit interest rate must be increased;
2. Loan interest rate must be increased although the loan size may decrease.

Chapter 6

Logic among National Debt, Inflation and High Housing Prices

The increase in upper limit of debt by the U.S. government is criticized without a single redeeming feature by the Chinese media. The impression on more than 1.3 billion people is that the United States has to borrow money again, is embarrassed by debts, and will soon collapse. It is true that the U.S. government borrows, and owes a total of USD 18 trillion, which is definitely not a good thing. Just as Tom Family had owed CNY 1.80 million debts as of January 1, 2014, in spite of Tom loans from a domestic bank or private lending at home or a foreigner, surely it's not a good thing.

Conversely the Chinese have gone crazy in the past 20 years or so, thinking that it is a good thing and is glorious, and they are proud of borrowed money, in particular large-scale loans. In any case the money that Tom borrowed has to be repaid back on schedule. Tom will not go bankrupt only if Tom must earn more money than the principal and interest before maturity. For this purpose Tom must have a reliable pathway to make more money before borrows CNY 1.80 million. If not, Tom boldly borrows money, and will get into hot water sooner or later.

With respect to the same borrowing money, Chinese experts now often use different evaluation criteria. The American government is preparing to more borrow trillions of US dollars, and experts request unanimously to suppress it. While Chinese homebuyer slaves on mortgage borrow huge debts for 20 or 30 years due to high housing prices, and experts think it is a good thing and a guarantee for China economic development. No one can touch or reveal the expansive and false prosperity caused by Chinese debts. Once it is revealed, China is going to be in chaos, violent social upheavals, heaven and earth upside down, and is caught in hell or high water under the influence of seeming crack doom. Anyhow, when maintaining the bubble, they have forgotten all the huge loans of homebuyer on mortgage from the people. American government debts are not good business, and experts' train of thought is very clear. Is it a good thing that the Chinese people owe huge debts? Does their train of thought become all muddled once again?

Let's Take A Look at These Platitudinous Opinions:

1. Mortgage loans account for 30-40% of loans in China banking industry, and most collateral are land or house property. The value of collateral declines along with the decrease in house prices. In case house prices fall by 50%, the total assets of banks will shrink significantly. Systemic risks should not be underestimated;

2. Not only that 60% of the repayment of China local investment and financing platforms comes from the land leasing revenue. In case house prices fall by 50%, local investment and financing platforms will lose their solvency, and their non-performing loans will come out in the wash. The provision of CNY 1.3 trillion is far from covering its risks;

3. The real estate industry collapses, and real estate-related industries will inevitably be dragged down such as steel, cement, building materials, home

textiles, and others so that they will be unable to survive. These industries will have large-scale bad debts, and the bank credit to companies will in turn become a noose to tighten the bank "neck".

Since there are so many hazards of falling housing prices, whether the real estate regulation should be obsolete? Can China only return the old path to high energy consumption? In case house prices don't fall, what harm will be brought? China inflation bounces back! Letting house prices fall is equivalent to a doctor specific prescription for the pathological Chinese economy. There will be some bad debts from banks, some local governments cannot bear the burden to repay the debts, and real estate-related industries will be suppressed however this is the pain that must be experienced to cure the disease. Only in that way can the Chinese economic disease be cured.

Therefore in terms of the real estate regulation and control it is necessary to further carry out the differential housing credit policy to supervise and urge financial institutions to make loans in a timely manner for eligible indemnificatory apartment construction projects in accordance with the requirements of the central government on "unshakable determination of real estate regulation and control, constant direction, and strength without relaxation". Under the "three" "unshakable, constant and not slack" principles of the central government, house prices must be lowered to return to normal and reasonable prices. That is to say people can buy one suite of 90-square-meter commercial house with a family income of 4-6 years.

Only by returning to the reasonable price of average social profit may other industries flourish without squeeze in the realty, and social resources be shared equally. In actual fact nearly crazy high house prices are closely related to the banking industry in

China. Absolutely high house prices will grow in waves by right of the encouragement of real estate loans. Only if the central bank controls tightly inflation within 3% and M2 growth rate within 10%, would it be responsible to the people and the country. At all events house prices will still rise under this premise, and it is only the genuine demand in the real estate market.

How did American national debts of USD 18 trillion come? Undoubtedly the American government borrowed from domestic people and foreign governments such as China and Japan. The reason for borrowing money is that the American governmental expenditure is larger than income. Not enough to disburse needs loans. The U.S. government only has three revenue sources: Taxation, loans, and currency inflation. They dare not raise taxes or depreciate except for borrowing money to cope with expenditure. It is honest because how much money every session government borrowed, accounts are kept clearly, and can be used to trace and audit at least. In comparison, how does China deal with enormous governmental expenditures? With the exception of imposing a variety of heavy taxes and dues, it prints directly money for supply. From October 2008 to the end of December 2012, M2 increased by 55 trillion (from 45 trillion to 100 trillion) in less than 4 years! Over the past three years or so, China did not war, and the money stock in peacetime has soared so much that it is rare in all successive reigns and dynasties of China.

National debt inflation and high housing prices are inherently logical. There must be reasonable reasons for the national debt. Loans should be repaid in any case. Nevertheless currency inflation stands for printing paper money excessively. There is no borrower and honesty. It is a deprivation of the original currency holder's purchasing power. Additionally the more the higher house prices need money, the more the central bank often is forced in turn to print banknotes. In case house prices reduce by 30%, the homebuyer demand for money will decrease by 30%, banks will have money to lend SMEs, and the central bank will not need to print the new excessive money, currency inflation can be only fundamentally controlled. Once the central bank can not cope with inflation, treasury bonds could also be sold to the public to recover currency and control market liquidity. Be that as it may we have seldom seen the sale of treasury bonds in recent years. Is this a good thing?

Chapter 7

Ben Shalom Bernanke Art of Operational Money

Tips: According to expert research, China was the richest
country in the world during the Han and Tang Dynasties
(before Yuan Dynasty). This shows that the Chinese
with yellow skin, dark eyes, and medium height had the
highest social status, and were once vital under the sun.
Our contemporary Chinese should not let our ancestry
be ashamed of their progeny, and should make genuine
achievements in front of the people of the world. To that
end, do not torture the people of our country but learn
from Bernanke to safeguard the people benefits in own
country.

1. Bernanke Flies "Helicopter Dropping Money"

Ben Shalom Bernanke, the second most powerful man in the
United States with a full-faced beard, if grown, exactly like Karl
Marx, in the world after Obama, is indeed a true "master". Since
he served as the Chairman of the Federal Reserve (The *American
Constitution* does not allow the establishment of central bank so
the American government and bankers created such a public-
private partnership), his slogan "helicopter dropping money"
has been heard throughout the world. This day in the minds of

people all over the world Bernanke has become the so-called crazy inflation maker of United States banknotes: Operating a money-printing machine, and dropping greenbacks on the market. After reading this article almost all Chinese think so about him at any rate.

2. Is Bernanke the Chief Culprit of Chinese Inflation?

At present mad Bernanke printing greenbacks has become the main source of China domestic inflation and asset bubbles in Chinese experts and media investigation. Precisely China current asset bubbles and inflation are worst. In the China's stock market the Shanghai Stock Exchange (SSE) composite index reached a peak more than 6,000 points, fell to 1,000 points and rebounded to 3,000 points. In the China's house market the housing price had been surging to 8,000 CNY from CNY 2,000 and even CNY 20,000 per square meter by a factor of 4-10 higher in the first-tier cities since 2003 so that the housing price-to-income ratio, price-to-rental ratio and vacancy rate had already reached an alarming extent. Unfortunately as regards all these price increases, experts found a sufficient reason in most cases: Imported inflation.

What is the imported inflation? The price rise of imports drives up the increase in domestic commodity prices. Experts also found another reason, the more exports, and the more greenbacks enter China so the "passive exchange settlement" of the central bank also results in domestic inflation (the funds outstanding for foreign exchange of China yuan up to a staggering CNY 20 trillion above). According to experts, **import and export trigger domestic inflation in China**. In short, Chinese inflation and asset bubbles are caused by foreigner tricks, and have nothing to do with the People's Bank of China. Their logic is: considering that exports are priced in US dollars, supposing Bernanke did not overprint greenbacks, exports would not increase in price, and there would be not the "imported inflation" in China.

3. How Much Money Did the "Helicopter" Bernanke Print Authentically?

The trouble is that: How much money did the "helicopter" Bernanke print authentically? How was the money printed and issued? Only a few professionals are aware of breakthrough in so large China but remain silent in order to protect the benefit of interest groups.

How did Bernanke print money? In 2007-2008, the USA real estate bubble burst, a large number of banks closed down, and loans declined sharply. When the monetary aggregate began to decrease, Bernanke began his bold "quantitative easing" monetary policy.

Bernanke is an expert who studied the Great Depression of the United States in the 1930s. He is worried about the deepening crisis in the American economy due to the monetary deflation, and adopted thus a monetarist "quantitative easing" policy. In line with this fearful background, how much money did Bernanke print in 2008, 2009 and 2010 until the end of March 2011? How was the money issued? We need to analyze the United States monetary and relevant data in March 2011. As of the end of March, M2 or broad money stock was USD 8.98 trillion, and new loans decreased by USD 42.9 billion, of which real estate loans decreased by USD 38.9 billion, M2 increased from nearly **USD 8 trillion at the end of 2008** to **USD 8.98 trillion** at the end of March 2011. In about two and a half years, M2 increased by **USD 1 trillion** or about CNY 6.5 trillion (at exchange rate of 1 to 6.5 or so) in USA, which was printed by the "Helicopter" Bernanke in two and a half years.

4. First Reveal the Secret of Bernanke Money issuance

How was the Bernanke money issued? This is a whopping secret. Today his scientific research achievements are unselfishly contributed by Mr. Dong Fang Dao that may be used as a precious reference for China monetary policy, provided that the authority is not willing to listen, it beats a dead horse. The secret of Bernanke money issuance is his control over the growth rate of USD. In 2008, when the American subprime mortgage, viz., the real estate bubble burst, Bernanke **increased** directly the growth rate of US dollar supply to **11%** from 6% but in 2009 again **reduced** it to **a staggering 1.5 %** at a time, since 2010, steadily increased to 4.6% in March 2011. According to the preliminary estimation, so far the Bernanke's monetary policy has been successful. The American industry and commerce are recovering, the unemployment rate has been reduced to 8.8%, and the CPI has reached 2.7%. At the same time the real estate loan still decreases by 38.9 billion US dollars. It indicates that American economics transform successfully once again.

The mode of Bernanke money issuance displays that the growth rate of USD was only 6% on average in 2008-2009 actually! In consequence **Bernanke is a "liar"**! He declared in fanfare that he flied helicopter dropping money but the money supply of his excessive issuance was not much. It can be demonstrated by commodity prices in the United States in 2008, 2009 and 2010. The American CPI was almost negative throughout the year of 2009, and then slowly increased to 2.7% in March 2011. It expressed adequately that the American inflation is manageable.

There is nothing to worry about. However **why did Bernanke declare in fanfare that he flied helicopter dropping money? What is his purpose? According to Mr. Dong Fang Dao's courageous conjecture, this should be a well-planned early conspiracy of Bernanke.** From the analysis of China relevant data we can explore its essence.

5. China Tricked Practically by "Flied Helicopter Dropping Money"

Let us first examine how much money has printed and issued in all since the bailout policy adopted by the People's Bank of China in October 2008. It is said that the subprime crisis was triggered by the housing bubble burst in the United States in the fourth quarter of 2008, which led to a sharp decline in China exports at that time, and the annual GDP may drop significantly. In response to the economic crisis the authority adopted decisively three major bailout measures of lowering interest rates, increasing money supply and easing real estate loans.

Above all let's observe the most critical money stock, i.e., M2, how much had increased in total from October 2008 to March 2011. In October 2008 China M2 stock was CNY 45 trillion, and in March 2011 China M2 stock was CNY 76 trillion. In two and a half years China M2 increased as many as CNY 31 trillion. As mentioned above, during the same period, the United States increased by only USD 1 trillion, or CNY 6.5 trillion. **Simultaneously, the monetary aggregate increased of China is almost five times that of the United States.** Hard fact is that: **compared to China, Bernanke is actually a coward in printing money. He flied helicopter, and circled around the United States seldom dropping money while Mr. Tom from China is a master who flied helicopter dropping money.** Mr. Tom printed and issued CNY 31 trillion to rescue the market, and was not yet renowned as the "helicopter dropping money" worldwide. Such a superb art of money issuance, probably Bernanke trained as an economist is ashamed of his inferiority.

Secondly let's observe how **the CNY 31 trillion increased by the People's Bank of China** was printed and issued in 2008, 2009 and 2010 up to March 2011. The growth rate of China M2 was 17.8% in 2008, was soared to 27.7% in 2009 at the year-on-year of 10% with a rush, and was still 19.7% although there was slightly decline in 2010. The year-on-year growth rate of M2 reached 16.6% up to March 2011.

It can be seen that there is essentially different for the arrangement of monetary growth rate between China and the United States of America. Indeed the monetary growth rate was increased by 5% (from 6% to 11%) in 2008, at all events, and reduced immediately by 4.5%, and reached 1.5% by Bernanke in 2009. Overall the monetary growth rate is sternly controlled. Whereas in 2010 the M2 growth rate was not reduced to 7.7%, and the 10% additional increase in monetary aggregate in 2009 was not offset in time, unexpectedly the monetary growth rate of 19.7% was also arranged, and was 2.7% higher than the normal 17% again after China increased abruptly the M2 growth rate to 27.7% in 2009.

This is breakneck, just that the excessive money supply is not recovered right now, and inflation cannot be avoided. Precise control of the monetary growth rate is the key to country governance. On the one side the continuous high CPI in China economic operation also suggests the hazard of excessive money issuance that China has not recovered in a timely manner. China CPI had reached 4.4% in October 2010 and 5.4% by the end of March 2011. On the other side China has paid unusual costs due to the strategic error of "treatment head due to headache", "separation" or the "dogmatic" model without overall plan in response to the recent rise in commodity prices. Actually the excessive money supply is not hedged promptly that is only the root cause of such inflation, and is the ultimate secret of governing China inflation but no one accepts sincerely and solves successfully.

6. Bernanke Takes Advantage of China to Overcome American Crisis

Recalling the art of Bernanke monetary policy to this day, I feel that Bernanke is definitely the best one midst masters. He rescued the United States at a crucial moment while took advantage of China. The author believes that Bernanke is veritably the planner of money wars.

Thinking it over, how great he is: In 2008 USA economics was still running at a high inflation rate of 4-5.6%, when the subprime mortgage crisis broke out, the United States was caught in the quagmire of stagflation at any time, and cannot extricate itself. It is this cunning guy who built up the momentum of "helicopter dropping money" with the help of media to make the Chinese trust that the US dollar would depreciate significantly. At this time China exports to the United States just fell linearly in the last quarter of 2008, and Bernanke was most **anxious about a sharp decrease in imports from China**, considering that Bernanke was about to launch a "monetary stimulus" plan, once cheap and fine imports from China were reduced, inflation in the United States would arrive early, causing his monetary intervention policy to fail miserably.

In order for Chinese cheap and fine commodities to flow constantly to the United States, Bernanke should use tricks. He must find a way to devalue the practical exchange rate of CNY to USD. Only by the CNY depreciation or the increase in export subsidies from Chinese government (indirect depreciation) will Chinese products continue to be cheaply exported to the United States. Whatever happens, **Bernanke will never tell anyone about this core secret that devalues CNY.** He applied skillfully a psychological warfare.

In the first place he must declare in fanfare "his helicopter dropping money" to make the Chinese trust that the US dollar will depreciate greatly. After learn of this news, the Chinese worry that exports are affected owing to the appreciation of CNY to USD so China yuan banknotes are over-issued to devalue CNY. In practice it is exactly what the Chinese did further the American demanded strongly in the crisis concerning the actual devaluation of CNY on the grounds that the Americans cannot be separated from the Chinese products in a short time. As long as Chinese products are suddenly out of stock, the Bernanke's stimulus plan will worry about future.

In the second place Bernanke withdrew secretly after "helicopter" dropping a handful of money. Granting that he authentically used the "helicopter dropping money", the price of domestic commodities in the United States would have inevitably skyrocketed. The U.S. commodity price was just the opposite from 2008 to 2010, not only did it not rise, but the CPI was negative, and even up to -2.1%, commodity prices almost fell all through the year of 2009, and only reached 2.7% until March 2011. This shows that Bernanke is lying. He induced inflation in China, and contrary was firmly controlling the American monetary aggregate.

This can be confirmed from the press conference he held without precedent on April 27, 2011, and confidently pointed out, "The U.S. Federal Open Market Committee expects that the impact of rising commodity prices on inflation will be short-term. Since commodity prices have not risen much, inflation will move closer to the basic level. In particular colleagues at the conference predict that the central trend of inflation in 2011 will be 2.1-2.8%, higher than the forecast in January, will fall to 1.2-2.0% by 2012, and followed by 1.4-2.0% in 2013, consistent with the forecast in January". This paragraph expresses that Bernanke has controlled safely the U.S. inflation at about 2% in the next three years, which will not exceed 3% definitely. He won precious two and a half years for the American economic transition from real estate bubble by way of feint.

7. "Quantitative Easing" Turned Out to Be Aimed at China

From the end of 2008 to March 2010 China foreign exchange reserves were increased by exactly US $ 1 trillion from US $ 1.9 trillion to US $ 3 trillion. What an amazing thing this is! From 2008 to March 2011, Bernanke just overprinted and over-issued 1 trillion US dollars in the United States, actually which was full transferred to China accounts. This is the whole implication of "quantitative easing": **The quantitative stands for directional printing of 1 trillion US dollars to the Chinese; the easing stands for making the Chinese exchange easy**.

What did the Chinese use in exchange for the USD 1 trillion of excessive money supply? Goods and services were made by the Chinese at the cost of using own natural resources, destroying own environment, and sacrificing own health. China cheap and fine commodities that numerous low- and middle-income Chinese want to buy but resolutely cross the ocean for foreigners to enjoy, and are not willing to benefit to the Chinese people under the shameful mercantilist export subsidy policy.

Bernanke is veritably great, used a few tactics to exchange equivalent commodities made by the Chinese bleeding and sweating by 1 trillion US dollars of paper overprinted, allowing the Chinese to help the United States overcome difficulties. Further more he did not waste paper expenses, as long as he changed a few figures in the bank account of China, the cost is equal to zero! The main idea of American China is just as follows: The United States overprints money to the Chinese, and the Chinese provide honestly goods and services. Conversely assuming that we overprint CNY to Americans, would Americans like to provide goods and services to the Chinese? Before 2008 there might be such a possibility but currently the Chinese have overprinted and over-issued CNY 31 trillion in two years or so that the people all over the world discover, no one dares to hold the CNY - this rapid devaluation banknote for a long time. As a Chinese, would you like to put the paper money depreciated sharply in Brazil, Vietnam and Zimbabwe in your moneybag?

8. Impact of Bernanke Interest Rate Hike on Chinese Money Supply

The biggest problem up till now is how to use the USD 3 trillion in Chinese foreign exchange reserves. This is the wealth earned by the Chinese blood and sweat that must be returned to Chinese low- and middle-income earners. After all the US dollar is paper and it is reliable to buy back items from the international market. Allowing that items are purchased from the international market to give to the low- and middle-income people in China rural and urban areas, what a superiority of the socialist system this will reflect! Is this possible? Or the US dollars are given to the poor Chinese in batches, letting them also go abroad sightseeing tour, and widen their horizon, shopping by the way without influence on domestic commodity prices. How beautiful it is! Seeing that most of the US dollar wealth was originally created by the Chinese people, they should be returned to the people!

Now Bernanke is holding a press conference as a winner just that he knows thoroughly that industrial and commercial loans increased, real estate loans decreased, inflation was 2.7%, and the unemployment rate fell to 8.8% from the American data in March. These explain that the American economy has steadily revived. Sequentially these conditions lay the foundation for Bernanke to start the interest rate hike cycle in next step. Bernanke, this guy wearing with a full beard densely dotted in his cheeks, and around his mouth, if grown, looks like Karl Marx. He is an excellent master to deal with China in virtue of the sword of currency whereas it is not easy for him to deal with fault-finding Americans. Because he had set the nominal interest rate of US dollar to "zero" since 2008, it was for more than two years especially in the first three months of 2011, and the practical interest rate of US dollar had been negative, reaching -2.7% in March. He must save the American economy, and more urgently the USD credibility. Wherein, the optimal way is to raise interest rates so that the nominal interest rate of US dollar achieves above 2.7%.

The interest rate hike cycle of US dollars will have a great impact on the China domestic money supply. Given that US dollars in China outflow, the funds outstanding for foreign exchange that the central bank has repeatedly emphasized will not hold water. Foreign exchange goes, should the corresponding funds outstanding of more than CNY 20 trillion be withdrawn to the central bank treasury for safekeeping? If not, it nakedly plunders own people. If withdrawn, the Chinese money supply may drop from CNY 76 trillion to CNY 56 trillion all of a sudden, and all asset bubbles will expose their true situation upon falling tide. As for the housing price bubble in China it is bound to return to its standard price. Things soaked in foam look big but are actually small. You will feel it is not as stable as walking on sand when you walk by the river and walk in the waves. It is similar to the price.

Chapter 8

Hardly Scientific Decision of Central Bank

Central banks of various countries still defend their master benefits by the subreptitious to their kind-hearted clients. This essence did not change much, and instead became even more violent in the early 21st century. Those people who knew the inside story secretly wept for Presidents Thomas Jefferson and Andrew Jackson in the early days of the United States. It was these great men two centuries ago who had long found the deficiency of the Central Bank, and waged an indomitable struggle with greedy bankers.

Unfortunately bankers have triumphed, and the central bank advocates their belief on a large scale, making waves in countries all over the world, and disturbing the world economy since the 20th century. Several major economic crises in the United States and Japan, and ongoing economic crises in various countries around the world are not enough to remind contemporary elites to review the precise exposition of President Jefferson about the central bank.

Perhaps the contemporary people cannot accept the fact that could the world economy develop truly healthy only if the central bank is abolished to allow bankers compete freely, and businesses of buying and selling money open to all citizens. Although this was the normal state in the 19th century, the people were deceived for so long that they had forgotten that their ancestors had freely operated own money shops. In the history of China the mint industry and the money shop were completely free private trade activities, and created the prosperity of Han and Tang Dynasties. Today the Chinese are used to one central bank to monopolize, and control 1.3 billion people's moneybags, and this housekeeper decision never needs to explain the reason to the owner.

It is hardly scientific for the central bank decision, and also in line with public opinion. The central bank decision is frequently like a drunk who suddenly pushes the interest rate down with might and main, to rock bottom, so heavily until the end of the third year. Now the central bank awakes from that drunken situation, dose not push down, and releases slowly the interest rate. Stupid people appreciate its greatness. Sober people think this just suffers from its own actions. The central bank always thinks itself clever and makes decisions on behalf of the market. It seems that only it knows the money price, money supply in the market, and how much money required. In fact, it is these stupid measures that have led to economic crises in various countries. This is not the Mr. Dong Fang Dao's conclusion but the one that the U.S. Central Bank has admitted. The American crisis in the 1920s and 1930s had already been concluded that the Federal Reserve made a mistake. 2008 subprime mortgage crisis in the United States was concluded that the Federal Reserve was also wrong. The Federal Reserve doesn't seem to do anything properly, just is a bad boy but honest, like George Washington in his childhood, was a bad boy who dared to admit his mistakes.

The People's Bank of China **had increased a money supply by full CNY 30 trillion from CNY 40 trillion in December 2007 to CNY 70 trillion in October 2010 in the interest rate decline cycle of past three years.** Various loans increased from about 26 trillion in 2007 to about 47 trillion in October 2010, especially increased full by CNY 21 trillion from 2008 to first ten months of 2010. In less than three years the monetary inflation of CNY 30 trillion, to our surprise, was described as a courageous measure and great achievement to rescue the Chinese economy. However such achievements that were bubbled by overprinting money were soon dealt head-on by various interest groups, and the people by reason of soaring currency inflation. The central bank did not admit mistakes verbally but began to correct mistakes in reality. The posture to correct the mistake was shilly-shally, turning back half a step but it was correcting after all.

The People's Bank of China announced on the evening of February 8, 2011, "Since today the benchmark interest rates of CNY deposits and loans in financial institutions are raised by 0.25% separately for the one-year period and adjusted accordingly at other grades. After this interest rate hike, the one-year loan interest rate will be increased from 5.81% to 6.06%, and the one-year deposit interest rate will be increased from 2.75% to 3.00%. The People's Bank of China all raised interest rates twice, and increase extent was uniformly 0.25% on October 19, and December 26, 2010.

The most direct effect of interest rate hike is to increase the cost of loan homebuyer. The total interest of CNY 1 million loans will be double. Taking a loan of CNY 1 million in 20-year period as an example, in regard to the loan for first-time homebuyer, monthly installment payment is CNY 7,396.98 at benchmark interest rate of 6.4% before the interest rate hike, and is increased to CNY 7,514.72, and the accrual increment is CNY 117 after the interest rate hike. In regard to the loan for second-time homebuyer at the lowest interest rate of 1.1 times, monthly installment payment is CNY 7,777.02 at interest rate of 7.04% before the interest rate hike, and is increased to CNY 7,909.82, and the accrual increment is CNY 132 after the interest rate hike. According to bank regulations, the interest rate hike in 2011 for stock housing loans would not be implemented until 2012, and for new house purchase, especially after the Spring Festival, would be implemented immediately.

Chapter 9

No Free Lunch in the World

The People's Bank of China decided to raise the benchmark interest rate for CNY deposits and loans in financial institutions from July 7, 2011, of which one-year interest rates were hiked by 0.25% respectively. Benchmark interest rates of deposits and loans at other grades, and individual housing provident fund loans were adjusted accordingly. After the third interest rate hike current year, the one-year deposit and loan interest rates reached 3.5% and 6.56% severally.

What does the consecutive interest rate hike of the central bank illustrate? It explains no free lunch in the world. You lunch too good or too full, must have less or not dinner. Otherwise, you will be positively full, and fall ill or even need operation. This is the physiological law. In terms of economic laws your lunch uses the dinner money, and you overdraw, and must save dinner.

To be specific the original plan for lunch, and dinner was CNY 20 per person. Now your lunch eats CNY 60 on June 8, 2011, and you must save CNY 40 in the future. There are three frugal methods:

1. Don't eat lunch, and dinner to save CNY 40 on June 9;
2. In June 9-12, dinner costs merely CNY 10 for consecutive four days to save CNY 40 in total;

3. From June 9 to July 19, dinner eats CNY 19 per day to save CNY 1 per day and CNY 40 in 40 days.

The first method is called **hard landing**, the second method is called **soft landing**, and the third method is called **slow landing**. What is the **slow landing**? Let me tell you, there is never such a noun, and Mr. Dong Fang Dao makes up blindly it to **scare** those people who do not understand economics. Experts always talk about the "hard landing", and "soft landing", which are also made as bells and whistles to scare people. These people include foreigners, fake foreigners and semi-fake foreigners who have been walked to and fro throughout China in recent years, of which their country citizenship have been even changed, secretly enjoying capitalism, and overtly preaching socialism, extremely bad. They just want to make a killing again in China.

Why do I say no free lunch in the world? This is because our M2 increased full by CNY 31 trillion from CNY 45 trillion to CNY 76 trillion through October 2008 and the end of May 2011! In 2011 the growth rate of M2 should be controlled within 16%, and the task in the second half of the year is still very arduous. Anyhow 16% is the solemn promise of *Government Work Report* in current year. There is no "approximately" behind 16 this year so it must be honored. Or else, deputies to the National People's Congress (NPC) will not agree, and it will be meaningless to review the relevant data again next time. Provisions of the *Constitution* can also be discarded, standing for arbitrarily inflationary.

The **normal** eating method in our country is that M2 is arranged 17% every year. What does this mean? Given that GDP and M2 grow by 10% and 17% respectively, the government will confiscate 7% of the total income of the people as the governmental revenue through the currency inflation every year.

Governmental revenue has mere three sources: The first is taxation, including various taxes and dues under a multitude of items. The second is borrowing money such as the central government one called national debt, and local government one called local debt. The third is the income from currency inflation. Taxation, national debt and local debt are supported by vouchers. How much tax is levied, and how much money is owed? It is written in black and white, and there are accounts to audit. By contrast, currency inflation is an action of the government stealing money from the people's moneybags. There is no record when the government earns income, and the money in the people's moneybags is reduced. This is an unethical method to seize money from the people.

So does the United States Government, apart from less courage, no more than 3% of the American people's income is seized in the form of currency inflation each year. In China the annual growth rate of GDP is 10%, that of conventional M2 is 17%, and inflation rate is counted as 3% approximately. This symbolizes that the government merely obtains about 3% income from the people with the aid of currency inflation. In some experts' eyes, 3% is not considered as inflation, and has nothing to do with the people. Therefore foreign economists have not been able to understand when the growth rate of Chinese M2 reaches 17%, and why the currency inflation does not appear all the year round. To this day they do not figure out. Where is 4%? This is an enigma, I am afraid that the senior gentleman Steven N.S. Cheung can't explain it. Not to mention these let's discuss unceasingly there is no free lunch in the world.

From October 2008 to 2010, how have we "eaten"? The growth rate of M2 was 17.8% in 2008, 27.7% in 2009, and 19.7% in 2010. Supposing that 17% was normal, M2 should be increased excessively by 10.7% in 2009 and by 2.7% in 2010.

Money supply should be over-issued by 13.4% in the two years. The government plans to reduce 1% inflation income according to the growth rate of M2 of 16% in 2011.

Like this providing that the M2 growth rate is 16% per year later, the government need take 13 years to only offset the amount of excessive money issuance from 2009 to 2010.

Providing that the M2 growth rate still is 17% per year in the next few year, is it possible? The answer is: On no account! The new excess money of CNY 31 trillion will drown everything like a monstrous flood, driven by the M2 growth rate of 17%. Therefore the future M2 growth rate must be reduced to 15%, followed by 8%, and then maintained until 2020, we can only cure this currency inflation completely. Incentives for inflation are generally the need of politicians. Like the U.S. President, in the next election, he will order the Federal Reserve to buy national debts, and release US dollars on all accounts to stimulate the economy convenient for his votes.

Since October 2008 the new excessive money supply has reached CNY 31 trillion in China. Who did eat it? First CNY 10 trillion was "eaten" by local governments, and another CNY 10 trillion was "eaten" by property developers. In this way, CNY 20 trillion or so has been used by local governments and property developers in real estate and supporting projects. Recently CCTV reported that the annual interest rate of private lending has reached 60%, and SMEs have no way to borrow money. Why? In the new excess money of CNY 21 trillion, the local government has borrowed CNY 10 trillion, and buying and selling houses have spent another CNY 10 trillion. How can there be money to lend to pitiful SMEs?

Visibly the Chinese economy development is very troublesome in the future. On condition that the central bank prints new money to lend to SMEs, the currency inflation will skyrocket. If not, SMEs will be forced to death by usury. There are just two preferable strategies currently: One is to collect loans of property developers in advance to solve the financing difficulty of SMEs; the other is to use history as a mirror, learning from the emperor practice, emperor solved difficulty encountered that was to arrest corrupt officials commonly. The enormous fortune of corrupt officials was confiscated into the state treasury. The two strategies will not increase the money supply, and cause the currency inflation but solve financing problems of SMEs in the market. Only like this can three goals of the modern state governance, low inflation, high growth, and high employment rate be achieved.

[Reference Material]

Benchmark Interest Rate Adjustment Form of CNY Deposits and Loans in Financial Institutions, Unit (%)

The People's Bank of China decided to raise the benchmark interest rate for CNY deposits and loans in financial institutions from July 7, 2011, of which one-year interest rates were hiked by 0.25% respectively. Benchmark interest rates of deposits and loans at other grades, and individual housing provident fund loans were adjusted accordingly.

Interest Rate after Adjustment:

I. Deposits of urban and rural residents, and enterprises: (1) Current deposit, 0.50 (2) The lump-sum time deposit: 3.10 for three months, 3.30 for half a year, 3.50 for one year, 4.40 for two years, 5.00 for three years, and 5.50 for five years.

II. Various loans: 6.10 for six months, 6.56 for one year, 6.65 for one-three years, 6.90 for three-five years, and 7.05 for above five years.

III. Individual housing provident fund loans: 4.45 for below five years (including five years), and 4.90 for above five years.

[Reference Material]

First-Time Homebuyer on Mortgage Loan Interest Rate Sets the Highest Record in the Past Decade.

Interest rate hike of 0.25% represents that the benchmark interest rate above five years will exceed the historical psychological peak of 7%. Beijing Centaline Property Statistics shows that the increase in monthly installment payment is not large from the data. For example, calculation on the basis of CNY one million loans, the total accrual interest increases nearly CNY 30,000, and the monthly installment payment increases CNY 119.59 at the benchmark interest rate for the first-time homebuyer on mortgage loans. Monthly installment payment increases CNY 134.96 for the second-time homebuyer on mortgage loans. In any case the cumulative effect of several interest rate hikes has gradually reflected.

Dawei Zhang, the chief research officer (CRO) of third-level market at Beijing Centaline Property remarked, firstly this signifies that the actual loan interest rate cuts the record in nearly a decade. The data manifests that though the current benchmark interest rate is not the highest in history on the grounds that most of previous loans can enjoy a preferential interest rate decline of 15%, which makes the benchmark interest rate that can only be implemented for the first-time homebuyer become the highest housing mortgage loan interest rate in the past decade.

Secondly the cumulative effect of interest rate hikes is obvious little by little. In the past year the interest rate has been raised time after time. The direct impact of previous interest rate hikes is not obvious but the impact of this gradual cumulative effect on the market will change from quantitative to qualitative, and the result of interest rate hike becomes obvious inch by inch.

Thirdly so do the synergistic effect of policies. Compared with strict purchase restriction measures, main reasons in support of home-buyers still entering the market are currency inflation and the excessive money supply, and no better investment channels. Additionally interest rate hikes will significantly increase investment costs, and loans will be inevitably more difficult for investors.

Fourthly the interest rate hike channel is evidently opened. At present the interest rate increase will continue, in other words the cost of home-buyers will increase persistently. Especially for investment home-buyers who have bought house previously, the pressure of raising interest rates will add the holding cost of houses step by step, and force them to resell the house.

Part Two

Arcana of Economic System

Introduction

If you want to make a profit

First of all you need to find out the truth about governmental economic operation.

Actually it is easier to get rich within the territory of China than foreign countries! However those people who decoded the governmental information can only achieve. Foreign governments have not own economic plans so it is difficult to consider. While China sets the five-year planning, and has the annual *Central Economic Working Conference, Government Work Report*, and regular bulletins of various documents, and information. Much important information is enough for smart investors to make a fortune. This part tells you first and foremost:

How to read and analyze the *China Five-Year Planning*, the information in the *Central Economic Working Conference*, as well as the data in the *Report of the State Council on Government Work* uniquely so as to seek out the basis for future investment. As long as the Two Sessions continue to be held in China, you apply the principles offered by the author to analyze, and will make money probably;

Taking the Chinese real estate as an example, this part will tell you how local governments make a fortune with the aid of real estate (by monopoly), and how to control their making a fortune recklessly (regulation and purchase restriction), and that they want to make money by another new way (house property tax).

Key point of this part:

If you want to make a profit, first of all you need to find out the truth about the governmental economic operation!

Chapter 1

How to Direct the Economy with Government Planning

"Who can tell me the CPI trend in the next three years?" Well, it is excellent enough to predict the commodity price throughout the year of 2013, and who can predict the commodity price throughout future three years from 2013 to 2015? Who knows this, and can make a fortune. Particularly in China it is difficult to obtain timely and accurate information so as to more difficultly make predictions on the score of too many uncertain factors in real estate, and stocks. No matter what business is, there are clues that can be found, and predictive signs that can be used for analysis. The *Twelfth Five-Year Planning* announced by China can be read the basic trend of Chinese CPI in the next three years.

The *Twelfth Five-Year Planning* includes 14 parts and 62 chapters. What is the logical relationship within the entire planning? The first part focuses on main goals, the second part focuses on agriculture, the third part focuses on industry, the fourth part focuses on services, the fifth part focuses on regional development and urbanization, the sixth part focuses on resources and environment conservation, the seventh part focuses on scientific education and talents, the eighth part focuses on improving people's livelihood, the ninth part focuses on social management, the tenth part focuses on public cultural undertakings, the eleventh part focuses on structural reform, the twelfth part focuses on opening to the outside world, the thirteenth part focuses on democracy and legal institution, and the fourteenth part focuses on national solidarity and unity.

Contents directly related to real estate are included in the fifth part on urbanization, and the eighth part on indemnificatory apartments of improving people's livelihood. Before the analysis of these contents we need grasp the essence and goals of the *Twelfth Five-Year Planning* as a whole. That is to say what is the main task of our country during the *Twelfth Five Year Planning*? In the next few years it is necessary to ensure that a new and significant advancement is made in scientific development, and that substantial progress is achieved in transforming the mode of economic development. Most notably the transformation of economic development mode should be accelerated. How to transform the mode of economic development?

1. Adjusting the structure of economic growth as the main development direction;
2. Technological progress and innovation as an important support;
3. Guarantee and improvement of the people's livelihood as goal;
4. Resources conservation and environmental protection as the key point of strength;
5. Reform and opening up as a powerful driving force.

In short it is to transform the mode of economic development from five aspects of structural adjustment, emphasis on science and technology, service for people's livelihood, and sustainability and reform application. In the light of the guidance ideology of above five aspects four principal development goals during the *Twelfth Five Year Planning* were determined:

1. Economics develop steadily and rapidly. Average annual GDP growth rate is 7%, CPI is basically stable, and international receipts and disbursements tend to be basically balanced;

2. Significant progress is obtained in structural adjustment. The ratio of consumption to GDP rises. Agricultural foundation is further consolidated. Industrial structure continues to be optimized. Breakthroughs are made in the development of strategic emerging industries. Proportion of the added value of services to GDP is enhanced by 4%. Urbanization rate is increased by 4%, and the coordination of urban and rural regional development is further strengthened.

3. Remarkable efficiency in resource conservation and environmental protection. Quantity of cultivated land kept is 1.818 billion mu. Water consumption of the industrial added value per unit is reduced by 30%, and the effective utilization coefficient of agricultural irrigation water is increased to 0.53. Non-fossil energy accounts for 11.4% of the primary energy consumption. Energy consumption and carbon dioxide emissions of GDP per unit are reduced by 16%, and 17% respectively. The total discharge amount of major pollutants is significantly reduced, of which chemical oxygen demand and sulfur dioxide, and ammonia nitrogen and nitrogen oxide emissions are decreased by 8% and 10% severally. Forest coverage rate is increased to 21.66%, and growing stock is increased by 600 million cubic meters.

4. Continuous improvement in the people's livelihood. The overall national population is controlled within 1.39 billion. The average lifespan expectancy prolongs by 1 year, and reaches 74.5 years old. Average annual growth rates are above 7% for the disposable income per capita of urban residents, and net income per capita of rural residents. The new rural social endowment insurance system achieves full coverage. The number of people participating in the basic endowment insurance in villages and towns reaches 357 million, and the coverage of three basic medicare in urban and rural areas is increased by 3%. Urban low-income housing projects are built 36 million suites. Poverty population is decreased prominently.

How to understand deeply these goals and specific indicators is of great value for judging the commodity prices in the next three years. We above all focus on analyzing and interpreting the implication of Goal 1: The average annual growth rate of GDP around 7%, and basically stable CPI.

The average annual GDP growth rate of 7% is just an anticipatory target. According to past practices, it is likely to exceed 7% each from 2012 to 2015, namely, the average annual growth rate will reach a minimum of above 7%. During the *Tenth Five-Year Plan* (2001-2005), the average annual growth rate was set at 7% in the governmental target, and was 9.5% actually. The CPI target set was basically stable, and the annual average growth rate of actual CPI was 1.7%. During the *Eleventh Five-Year Planning* (2006-2010), the average annual growth rate was set at 7.5% in the governmental target, and was 11.2% actually. The CPI target set was basically stable, and the annual average growth rate of actual CPI was 4.04%.

The *Eleventh Five-Year Planning* (2006-2010) compares with the *Tenth Five-Year Plan* (2001-2005). According to Xianping Lang, the GDP growth rate announced by China is the nominal growth rate (Note: it is not necessarily right or wrong as China does neither release nominal nor real growth rate. How to calculate the actual growth rate is not stated). Providing that what Xianping Lang said is right, subtracting the currency inflation rate from the nominal growth rate, you will find a huge arcanum that the genuine growth rate of China's economy (GDP) declines actually. The actual annual average GDP growth rate was 7.8% (9.5%-1.7%) during the *Tenth Five-Year Plan* (2001-2005) and 7.16% (11.2%-4.04%) during the *Eleventh Five-Year Planning* (2006-2010). What important principle is found hereto? The larger the nominal GDP growth rate, the larger the real GDP growth rate does not necessarily demonstrate. The larger the nominal GDP growth rate, the smaller the inflation rate, the larger the real GDP growth rate can only be reflected, the faster a national actual GDP growth can only be described, that is, the more the actual domestic wealth increases.

Economic growth, viz., so-called development, is today regarded as the major core target of all state governments around the world. At all events to measure the growth rate of one state authentic wealth must calculate not only the nominal GDP growth rate in a certain period, but also the inflation rate simultaneously.

Supposing that any government agency wants to exaggerate achievements in own official career and deceive the people, there will be only two tricks: One is to increase the nominal GDP, and the other is to reduce the inflation rate artificially. Moreover the calculation of veritable GDP and CPI is inseparable from the price of goods and services. By way of illustration on the basis of prices of various types of goods and services in 2000, when calculating the real GDP of 2012, the quantity of various types of goods and services in 2012 must be multiplied by the corresponding price in 2000. The gross calculated hereby can be only applied to measure the practical increase in productions (wealth) relative to 2000. In the event of productions and prices in the current year only used, the GDP calculated is only the nominal GDP. From a certain perspective this value is meaningless. For instance, in the spring of 1949, the commodity price in April 1949 was increased by 51,000 times from August 1948 by the reason of money over-issuance in the Kuo Min Tang (KMT)-controlled district. Providing that the nominal GDP was calculated based on the commodity price of April 1949, and would definitely be a factor of 51,000 higher whereas the true GDP of April 1949 was calculated based on the commodity price of August 1948, and would be a factor of 51,000 lower. Hereby, the bubble drops the mask.

The calculation of authentic CPI is more closely related to prices of goods and services in the reference year used for comparison. If the price in 2000 is used as the benchmark, the typical quantity of various goods and services in 2000 is determined at first, and then is multiplied by the corresponding unit price, and then is summed to obtain the total price of typical goods and services such as 100. The CPI in 2012 is to be calculated, and quantities of types of those goods and services determined in 2000 will be multiplied by the current commodity price in 2012, and then aggregated to obtain another total price such as 1000. 1000 divided by 100 is 10, i.e., the CPI in 2012. The CPI in 2000 is that 100 divided by 100 is 1, and the CPI in 2012 is 10. The CPI rise rate is 9 (10-1 and then÷1), which stands for the inflation rate is 900%.

Therefore it is very momentous to find prices of goods and services in 2000 for the above example. Without the commodity price in 2000 as a measurement standard we cannot compare the level of the commodity price increase or decrease in 2012. These days China only announces the year-on-year increment of commodity price for CPI calculation, which is unscientific. Because the year-on-year numerical value is only generated by the comparison with the same period of last year, the people cannot learn ../../../Documents and Settings/Administrator/Local Settings/Application Data/youdao/dict/Application/7.5.2.0/ resultui/dict/about the level of long-term commodity prices. There is only a relative ratio, no an absolute ratio to make both the people feel insecure about commodity prices, and the governmental credibility lose. Unlike the United States, CPI data has been established since 1867, and until now, can be inquired every year. As long as the government offers the CPI data in good faith, ordinary people can calculate the inflation rate, and can believe genuinely the government.

Just like climbing stairs. The ground is regarded as the benchmark, and you keep climbing stairs step by step. Assuming that one step represented one year, you climb every step, only enhance by 1 foot compared to the previous step but when you climb to the 10th floor, looking out of the window, are already very high from the ground. Evidently you can't know exactly how high you have climbed without the ground as the base point of measurement. Unlike our current CPI released by the Chinese government, how much the commodity price increases per year that the government only announces year-on-year, and never announces the comparison ratio with the base year. Beyond all doubt, this will make the national people lose the judgment standard on commodity prices.

In summary the calculation of actual GDP and CPI is closely related to the commodity price in base year. In the event of always taking "that in last year" as the benchmark, "that in last year" has been passing, and there is no standard at all. The determination of the base year should be a right of the people, and should not be determined willfully by a few people because this is a vital matter related to national governance and people's happiness. Only after determining the base year of commodity prices can the country and the people have the foundation to measure economics, commodity prices and incomes, and become truly prosperous country and wealthy people.

For example, the commodity price in 1990 is used as benchmark. All kinds of commodity prices in this year are fixed, and can be queried that no one can change or falsify them, and then they are adopted to calculate the GDP and CPI of subsequent years. You can have real data to compare. Provided that someone wants to exaggerate GDP nothing but productions since the price is fixed, it will be difficult to fake productions. It is easy to see through the imagination production. Just that the production of each industry follows rule, and there are simple and convenient computational methods for productions within the industry. Evidently the counterfeit production is easily penetrated by peers. So does the CPI calculation. The commodity price was fixed and open../../../Documents and Settings/ Administrator/Local Settings/Application Data/youdao/dict/ Application/7.5.2.0/resultui/dict/ed in 1990, no matter who wants to hide or deceive the commodity price increase, and it is very difficult in that the people are familiar with the commodity price in 1990. As long as the commodity price in current year is divided by the commodity price of same classification in 1990, you can calculate how many times the commodity price has increased. There is a tendency in present academic circles to analyze alone the year-on-year and month-on-month commodity prices, compare with the same period last year or last month, and never mention the comparison with the base year. What a major pity it is in academic circles! The commodity price in current year and month should be comparable to the commodity price of any year and month in history, especially of the base year. Year-on-year and month-on-month commodity prices are applied to analyze alone the nearest variation except for the long-term. From a certain perspective, year-on-year and month-on-month data has no large value.

Also taking climbing stairs above as the example, you have climbed to the 10th floor, at this height of which, each stair only elevates one foot in spite of year-on-year or month-on-month growth. When you stop and stand on the first step of the 10th floor, videlicet, the year-on-year, and month-on-month growth rate is zero. What is its significance? How astounding it is! In any case you cannot deny the fact that you are already at the height of 10th floor. Therefore only with the ground as benchmark is comparison truly valuable.

In this day and age, monetary authorities headed by the Federal Reserve are playing this game of climbing stairs across the world. Since the separation of banknotes and precious metals, central banks in various countries have over-issued continuously banknotes like clockwork to make commodity prices rise step by step every year. Where is ceiling? Won't the commodity price reach the upper limit forever? This is impossible. The ladder diagram of M2 growth in the United States shows that the paper money supply also increases step by step. Obviously the year-on-year and month-on-month growth are very small. Dissimilarly in some countries, M2 is striding upwards, and has caught up with the height of the United States only in a few years. Contemporary governments of all countries have never considered whether commodity prices should come down from a higher level, and return to a position closer to the ground.

Chapter 2

How to Operate the Economy with Governmental Reports

Nowadays taking the 2011 *Government Work Report* as an example, this Chapter will illustrate how to analyze the genuine significance implied by the main data in the *Government Work Report*.

On the forenoon of March 5, 2011, as soon as the State Council *Government Work Report* was enacted, media and experts began a variety of interpretations, however their basis (data) entirely centers on the protocol submitted to delegates of the National People's Congress (NPC), and the Chinese People's Political Consultative Conference (CPPCC) under examination and review, it is seemingly not too solemn. Seeing that the relevant data in this report is only from the protocol of the State Council, and is submitted to delegates for deliberation, becomes an accomplished fact that experts interpret, which is obviously disrespectful to deputies and members. As is well-known the *Government Work Report* is of great importance. From the relevant data and policies bulletined by the state, you can absolutely discover business opportunities or make money. Therefore experts should interpret the official text of the report as a criterion after the NPC approval by vote.

Seeing that the report is used to prepare for review, media should cover how **deputies and members** express different opinions, unify their cognition and determine the basis on the source and target of report data. Only like this can the connotation of "**examination and review**" be met. **The content of *Government Work Report* is still in the stage of deliberation, and examination and review by the delegates, and will not make the official vote until the closing ceremony of Two Sessions on March 14.** When experts and the media interpret the report protocol, the content and data equate that in the official report voted by NPC deputies and the CPPCC members. Whether this is not too solemn, and does not too respect the intention of delegates? This problem should arouse attention from relevant parties.

In that everyone regards the protocol under consideration as the official text for interpretation, the author will analyze the relation between the data in the report and the commodity price in 2011 through the investigation for the full text of report. **The commodity price trend is decided by three sides: The first is the monetary policy of the central bank; the second is the supply-demand relationship in the market; and the third is policy measures of the central government and local governments.** Among three influential factors the first one is the most basic, to wit, the monetary policy of the central bank is foundation. Then let's analyze the first factor foremost.

Generally speaking there is one regulation in ancient, modern Chinese and foreign countries: The more the state prints and issues money, the more the asset price rises; the state tightens the deposit reserve, and the asset price falls. This regulation has played a role in China since the Han Dynasty. At the beginning of the Han Dynasty, in order to fight against the Huns, the Queen Lu minted and issued excessive copper coins, and reduced the weight of copper coins to remint them. As a result commodity prices rose by more than 300 times. In the reign of Emperors Wen and Jing in the Western Han

Dynasty, Emperors Wen and Jing knew deeply how to govern the country, developed production, weighted copper coins, and implemented a policy of deflation. Therefore the state was ruled in an outstanding order.

The fact that the reign of Emperors Wen and Jing in the Western Han Dynasty educated contemporary economists a serious lesson, and refuted vigorously their lies: **Deflation would lead to economic depression, and people unemployment.** The deflationary policy in the reign of Emperors Wen and Jing proves that economic prosperity is not inevitably related to the level of money supply. As another example, the United States put the deflationary policy into practice for most of the 19th century, and commodity prices were basically stable for nearly one century. Thus the prosperity and technological progress of the United States in the 19th century were unmatched in the 20th century. In contrast the so-called quantitative easing or loose monetary policy is actually currency inflation, which is beneficial to a small number of people at the beginning, and harmful to everyone at the end. Han, Tang, Song, Yuan, Ming and Qing Dynasties, and Republic of China all lost to currency inflation, which was the most fundamental economic reason though there were corruption, centralization, and other reasons for their extinction. The essence of inflation, just as the originator of inflation and government intervention, John Maynard Keynes said, "Currency inflation is a means for the government to deprive secretly the people's wealth but no one in one million people knows what happened".

Back to the subject, after the bulletin of the *Government Work Report*, the monetary policy can be basically unfolded: **A prudent monetary policy is implemented. Social financing scale is maintained reasonably, and the broad money growth goal is set at 16%. Macro-prudential policy framework is perfected, and price and quantity tools are comprehensively** utilized to improve the effectiveness of monetary policy. The proportion of direct finance is increased to give full play to the role of stocks, bonds, sector funds, and other financing tools to better meet the needs of diversified investment and finance. Credit structure is mainly optimized to guide commercial banks to enhance the credit support in key areas and weak links, and control strictly loans to "high contamination and high energy consumption", and overcapacity industries. The Central Economic Working Conference held at the end of 2010 did not confirm the target for monetary growth, and nowadays finally determines. Hereby, what does the digit 16% symbolize? Without doubt, only by comparison do we know.

One is longitudinal comparison. The broad money growth rate was 27.7% in 2009, was 19.7% in 2010, and 16% proposed in 2011. Judging from the gradual decline in the year-on-year growth rate of the money, China is entering **a relatively deflationary cycle.** On all accounts the monetary base is too large, is already the first in the world, and deflationary pace is too small so inflationary pressure is huge.

The other is horizontal comparison. The horizontal comparison shows the internal cause of inflation. According to the proposal in the report, main prospective targets for 2011 are that: **GDP growth rate is about 8%. Economic structure is further optimized. CPI growth rate is controlled at about 4%. The Report mentions** that the target of broad money growth rate is 16% in a positive mood, and there is no expectation word. While 8% GDP growth rate, and 4% CPI growth rate are "prospective targets" in a consultation mood.

The problem is that the three digits are contradictory. According to the formula of Milton Friedman, the originator of numismatology, and the winner of Nobel Prize in economics, the growth rate of money is equal to the sum of growth rates of GDP and CPI, i.e., 8 + 4 = 12, however why does our government arrange 16% for the growth rate of money? Where is another 4% of the growth rate of money? The calculation is on the basis of M2 balance of CNY 72.6 trillion at the end of 2010, 4% of the growth rate of money should be the order of CNY 3 trillion of new excess money supply. Assuming that it was calculated at the 16% growth rate, the money supply would be newly increased by approximately CNY 11.6 trillion in 2011. **By the end of 2011, the Chinese money supply would reach about 84.2 trillion.** Xiaoling Wu, the former deputy president of the central bank, also conveyed in an article in 2010 that the monetary growth rate should be equal to the sum of GDP and CPI growth rates in order to maintain the commodity price stability. Therefore I wonder why the drafter of work report protocol arranges 16%? What is the basis for scientific decision? Can the answer be found in all economic theories around the world?

In addition, whether 4% of the excess money supply arranged contradicts the work focus of 2011, which is to keep basically stable CPI? The report stated that: At present commodity prices are rising fast. It is predicted that inflation trend is enhanced. This problem involves people's livelihood, is related to overall situation, and affects stability. **On the one hand steady commodity prices need to maintain, and on the other hand so much money should be over-issued, isn't it that you are getting yourself in trouble?** The size of money supply is a major event for a country, as well as for the government and the people. This is related to the wealth of 1.3 billion people, and should be scrupulous. Stable monetary value has been written into the *Constitution* of the United States while the *Chinese Constitution* does not make regulations with regard to the function of the People's Bank and the stability of monetary value. **Constitutional provisions of China keep silent about money in blank.** Although China has several laws on banking and money, and cannot find their foundation in the *Constitution*. Therefore it is hoped that the relevant person could make a request to amend the *Constitution*, and the maintenance of CNY monetary value stability is regulated as a constitutional provision so that CNY can benefit the economy, and the people.

Although the monetary growth rate of 16% is arranged, compared with last year, is more moderate. What the original text of 2010 *Government Work Report* stated that: **The broad money M2 growth target is set at 17% or so, and CNY 7.5 trillion or so of new loans is added.** What the *Government Work Report* in this year stated that: **A reasonable scale of social finance is maintained, and the broad money growth target is set at 16%.**

There is huge difference between these two sentences! The two words "or so" were added behind 17% last year, and a full stop is followed behind 16% this year. Last year, just on the score of the addition of "or so", the actual growth rate of money reached 19.7% in 2010, unexpectedly higher 2.7% than the target. The money supply was increased excessively by CNY 1.64 trillion in 2010 based on the money supply of CNY 60.6 trillion at the end of 2009. Where was so much money? We can find an accurate answer from soaring housing prices in 2010. I also hope that the full stop followed behind 16% can achieve the purpose of restraining the irrational monetary growth. If so, the growth rate of money can be reduced by 3.7% from 2010, and the decline rate is also acceptable.

[Reference Data]

Interpretation of the Key Data in the 2012 *Government Work Report*

Two sessions are held every year, and there is also different in this year. Several key data in the Government Work Report on March 5, 2012 appeared to be of essence. The two or three data are related to not only the well-being of 1.3 billion people, but also that of future generations. Unfortunately most people don't realize the power of these digits. They can make a nationality either prosper for a century or collapse.

I. Above all Analysis of the First Digit: 14

Premier Wen's Report put it this way: We will unceasingly implement the prudent monetary policy. In accordance with the moderate monetary aggregate, prudent and flexible requirements, we must also take into account the promotion of smooth and steady, and rapid economic development to maintain the commodity price stability, and prevent financial risks. We should apply comprehensively various monetary policy instruments to adjust the supply and demand of monetary credit and loan, and maintain a reasonable growth in the scale of social finance. It is expected that the broad money growth rate will reach 14%. As everyone knows the Government Work Report proposed that the broad money growth rate was 16% in 2011, and dropped to 14% in 2012 again! This decline in the broad money growth rate is mainly to control the source of inflation.

The central bank said in the Announcement in 2012 that the growth rate of broad money (M2) in 2011 was 13.6%. In reality, the data for 2011 is particularly unusual. The sum of GDP growth rate and CPI growth rate was 14.6% while the growth rate of money supply in the year was 13.6%, which is almost untenable. It turned out to make a mistake in calculation by the central bank. The money supply was CNY 72.6 trillion at the end of 2010, and was CNY 85.2 trillion at the end of

2011. The year-on-year growth of money supply was CNY 12.6 trillion, and that of broad money should be 17.3% instead of 13.6%. However the goal proposed by the 2011 Government Work Report was that the year-on-year growth rate of money supply did not exceed 16%!

During the Twelfth Five-Year Planning, whether China can develop sustainably in a mode where the money supply growth rate is 7% higher than the economic growth rate (i.e., the growth rate of M2 is more than 14%). It is worthy of discussion and investigation of people with conscience. If the M2 growth rate maintains the previous 17% or so, the China's money supply would reach CNY 160 trillion, CNY 349 trillion, and CNY 1,677 trillion by the end of 2015, 2020, and 2030 respectively! By then (just two decades), every Chinese will have CNY 1.23 million on average, and be a millionaire! Hence this digit, M2 growth rate implies the secret of a national life and death. The reason why the demise of Chinese successive reigns and dynasties is that this digit was not well grasped to trigger domestic conflicts, and plunge the people into an abyss of misery! In the end the dignitary, the rich and the poor perished together, and immense social wealth was written off in each dynasty.

II. Next Analysis of the Second Digit: 4

Premier Wen's Report said that the rise in CPI is controlled at around 4%. It is necessary to understand accurately. What is around 4? It should be correct between 3.5 and 4.5 such as less than 3.5, like 3.3, should belong to around 3; such as larger than 4.5, like 4.7, should belong to around 5. Obviously around 4 should be some numbers between 3.5 and 4.5. Provided that the currency inflation in 2012 was controlled within this interval, the goal of government work should have been reached. In 2011 the year-on-year growth rate of CPI was 5.4%, which greatly exceeded the original target. For that reason the Director of National Development and Reform Commission (NDRC) apologized. This is a good sign!

Speaking of CPI, I want to talk about another few words. The Chinese now stress including CPI as a control indicator alone, which is biased. CPI is important just as PPI. Producer procurement and ex-factory prices should be monitored as key point in that investment price and consumption price are interrelated. The price of investment product is not well controlled, neither is the price of consumer goods produced. Further the key of whether the price of investment and consumer products nationwide is controlled is to master the growth rate of M2 correctly. According to the monetarist theory, if GDP growth rate is 7.5% in 2012, M2 growth rate will be 7.5%. Only like this can commodity price stability be authentically maintained, only by which can the people have confidence. The rich will not emigrate and transfer their wealth to capitalist countries. Seeing that experts all say that zero currency inflation is not well, then about 4% is all right! However, the government is also like a greedy child as usual. In case you give him CNY 5, he will ask CNY 6, and CNY 7. Similarly you allow about 4% of the inflation rate, and he will increase to about 5%.

III. Final Analysis of the Third Digit: 7.5

Premier Wen's Report expressed that GDP growth rate is 7.5%. It should have been the most important number and puzzles most 1.3 billion people. This GDP growth rate is 7.5%. Is it nominal growth rate or real growth rate? Whenever the National Bureau of Statistics announces the growth rate, data all are selected. It is normal for a modern country to have both nominal growth rate and veritable growth rate. Why not announce the nominal growth rate? This is a science, and no luck or impatience is allowed! Additionally the target is set at 7.5, is it too high? In the Twelfth Five-Year Planning, it is clearly stipulated that the average annual growth rate is 7%. I don't know why those experts request 8% every year, and even every day. Is it useful for 7% of the Twelfth Five-Year Planning? Such people preach seemingly the governmental merits, and hide really the purpose of excessive money issuance, and supply.

Because there is an unwritten convention in China that the growth rate of money supply must be 7% larger than that of GDP. The GDP growth rate hike implies the M2 growth rate hike such as the growth rate target of GDP was set at around 7.5%, and that of M2 was around 14% in 2012. At all events such an arrangement cannot find a basis in economics. Keynes never said so, and Milton Friedman was resolutely opposed to such an arrangement. Only Steven N.S. Cheung by himself, an American citizen in Hong Kong China, frequently offered such a bad idea of rapid M2 growth.

Since it is very dangerous that M2 exceeds the GDP growth rate for 7%, it will definitely lead to fearful currency inflation. Despite, the fact, that inflation rate was just 5.4% in 2011 and food prices rose nearly 12% year on year. For example, the unit price of some vegetables is now double. Peppers increased from CNY 4/kg to CNY 13/kg. Cuttlefish rose from CNY 96/kg in early 2011 to about CNY 200/kg in the Spring Festival of year of 2012. Essentially the core CPI is the Chinese food price most importantly. People do not buy durable consumer goods such as washers, refrigerators, and televisions every day but 1.3 billion people must eat foods every day. Distinctly the Chinese inflation has given a very dangerous signal in the matter of foods.

On all accounts from the three big data of M2 growth rate adjusted to 14%, and CPI and GDP growth rate reduced to 4% and 7.5%, China should enter a relatively contractionary cycle. Otherwise house prices keep rising without falling to promote the irrational rise of M2, as long as 20 years or so, M2 will reach the CNY 1,677 trillion mentioned at the beginning of the article. This is "a blind alley" that other countries had undergone long ago.

Why M2 has been annually running at the 17% growth rate over the past three decades in China? The key is that various interest groups push M2 to run at this speed. Why do they so? Just that they operate tens of billions and hundreds of billions of large projects to "make contributions to the country" through the local government and monopoly state-owned enterprises. These large projects cost huge loans but benefits are very low. As a matter of fact a tacit purpose hidden in large projects is that the operator can gain a rebate of about 20%. What is the relation between loans and M2? Loans are the main component of M2. At all events, why are these large projects with low benefits always available? This is as a result of the operation of interest groups. If someone is disobedient, the interest group will change him, which is very powerful. In the United States various interest groups act on the national president, and the central bank president but the latter will not easily bow. Whereas the power of appointment in China comes from superiors, and some people have to succumb to interest groups! Obviously only by the advancement of political restructuring reform in the top-level design can this M2 high-speed running problem be completely solved. (Source: Dong Fang Dao Blog)

Chapter 3

How to Set the Economy with Central Session

After the announcement of *Central Economic Working Conference*, experts are interpreting the significance of being **active, steady, prudent and flexible**. Anyhow such a **partial** interpretation is very one-sided, and will draw surely the wrong conclusion. Provided that we interpret from **six major economic tasks for 2011** determined by this conference, agriculture, manufacture and new energy industries only are new growth points that are supported vigorously by the government in 2011.

What are such six major economic tasks? I. Strengthening and improving macroeconomic regulation and control maintains smooth and steady, and healthy economic operation. II. Promoting the development of modern agriculture ensures the effective supply of agricultural products. III. Accelerating the economic structural strategic adjustment enhances the coordination and competitiveness of economic development. IV. Perfecting basic public services innovates social management mechanisms. V. Increasing reform efforts pushes the transformation of the economic development mode. VI. Adhering to the mutual-benefit and win-win open strategy expands the space for international economic cooperation.

What is the first task? Smooth and steady, and healthy economic **operation** is kept principally. Before the conference the theme that the major media and economists guessed was **steady growth**, and it turned out to be wrong after the announcement of this conference. **The predominant task is to keep the economic smooth and steady, and healthy operation rather than steady growth!** Another comprehension, that is to say, the problem to be solved is not **whether economics grow** but whether economics can operate smoothly and steadily, and healthily in next year. More clearly the Chinese economy already gets sick, awfully severe. What is the disease in reality? The first clause stated clearly, "We shall make up our mind to reduce regular expenditures and make every penny count, and **strengthen the local government debt management to resolutely prevent from blindly preparing for a new entity or carrying out a new job or launching a project by virtue of the commencement of** *Twelfth Five-Year Planning* **period.** We shall implement the prudent monetary policy, and manage properly liquidity as the master valve, and invest more credit funds in the real economy, especially the "agriculture, rural areas, rural residents", and SMEs in accordance with the requirement of overall stability, moderate adjustment, and structural optimization".

Why do they say like this? They chiefly aim at local governments and commercial banks, and must control local government expenditures, including regular expenditures such as public spending on government cars, overseas trips, and official receptions, and blind investment projects. The local government debt has reached to such an extent that the mandatory management must be executed. According to the expert estimation, local governments are currently in debt of around CNY 8-9 trillion, which is not small. Should government debts be repaid? What if they don't repay the bank? **Don't confuse the concept of wealth and banknotes!** Wealth can automatically neither fall from the sky, nor grow from the ground, and must rely on work and creation by both hands. Have you seen that goods and services automatically fall from the sky? No, everyone has not! The money the local government owed, in any case, is the genuine money of banks, what if they cannot repay the debt? Does the bank also depend on overprinting banknotes to fill it again?

Overprinting banknotes are currency inflation, and in fact, it is levying a coinage tax. This kind of unclear taxation is at all events more dangerous, and worse than the flagrant national tax, and local tax, which generally leads to a disorder in the production of one country. Firstly as the price system is completely useless, producers and operators are at a loss, and are greatly distressed in the face of turbulent prices. Secondly such inflationary taxation is often beneficial to the dignitary and the rich, and harmful to the poor as the rich have purchased goods, services and assets before commodity prices rise while the poor can only buy after commodity prices rose. In consequence the rich get richer, and the poor get poorer. On all accounts the normal taxation is generally to impose the rich income to subsidize the poor. Probably because the central government realizes this, and then requires that: **We must implement the prudent monetary policy, and manage well liquidity as the master valve in accordance with the requirement of overall stability, moderate adjustment, and structural optimization.**

What does the prudent monetary policy mean? Do not overprint and over-issue randomly banknotes in infinite again! It is impossible, and not allowed to excessively print, and issue nearly CNY 10 trillion and CNY 8 trillion like 2009 and 2010, and that the growth rate of money supply reached 28%. The prudent monetary policy is also strictly required in Western countries, namely the growth rate of money supply can only be the same as or up to 3% higher than the growth rate of GDP.

While the growth rate of Chinese GDP has been 10% in the past decade, and the average growth rate of money supply has reached more than 17%.

Keynes advocated that the government should use fiscal and monetary policies to stimulate the economy when the economy is at a low point but he is firmly opposed to the currency inflation. So does the senior Milton Friedman besides he advocates that the growth rate of money is synchronized with that of GDP. Seeing that only if commodity prices are steady, would the government have credibility, the economy grows, and the people live and work in peace and contentment. **Whatever happens, it is probably more difficult to perform a truly prudent monetary policy in China.** Since 2001, the central bank has always over-issued banknotes, and money supply is about 7% higher than the GDP growth rate every year. According to the past practice, provided that the GDP growth rate in 2011 was 8%, and 7% of the excess money issuance was added, the growth rate of money supply in 2011 should be 15%. This is also the standpoint held by almost all domestic economists.

Be that as it may the author wants to ask that how many the GDP growth rate is in 2011 veritably? This is an unknown! **Is it 8% growth rate? Who can know the actual GDP growth rate in the coming year?** May I ask experts: most of all how do you know that the Chinese economy will inevitably grow by 8% or higher in 2011? What is the basis? Are you God? Why is the growth rate of money supply 15% in 2011? Now the monetary aggregate has reached CNY 71 trillion in China, being far ahead in the world. China still keeps at the growth rate of 15%, won't there be a problem? Next whereabouts should be the credit increased? This *Central Economic Working Conference* gives the answer: First, the agricultural investment ensures the effective supply of agricultural products; second, the investment in SMEs involves manufacture, services, and green economy, etc.; third, the investment in people's livelihood or public services involves education, employment, security, and culture.

[News Excerpt]

Economists Predict House Prices in the Light of Conjecturing Conference Report.

On the evening of December 12, 2011, as soon as hearing of the closing of Central Economic Working Conference in news, Bocheng Yin browsed deliberately the report on the conference online. However after reading all of the full relative texts, he did not find a word with regard to the real estate regulation, which made him not sure.

"Although conferences at this level will not mention too many details, current house prices are risen again everywhere, at this very moment, the bulletin should still mention the statement of real estate regulation and control so as to turn around current market expectations", said Bocheng Yin, the director of Fudan University Real Estate Research Center.

Last weekend the National Bureau of Statistics released the national real estate operation in November. The data showed that the sales area of commercial houses nationwide in November was 101.13 million m^3 at the year-on-year growth rate of 14.5%. The absolute amount increased by 8.34 million m^3, and was 9.0% higher than that in October month-on-month. In the matter of prices, sales prices of houses in 70 large and medium-sized cities throughout the country rose by 7.7% year-on-year and by 0.3% month-on-month in November.

This situation of "both volume and price increase" puzzles the public: Why do house prices still rise even after the government introduced so many regulation and control policies?

"We will further boost the resource tax reform next year, and the current currency inflation is also rock-ribbed. Although we will continue to tighten liquidity next year, it will take a while until the appearance of substantial effects. These factors will lead to more severe increase trend in housing price expectations next year," believed Bocheng Yin. Allowing that the government does not introduce new control measures now, and the possibility of retaliatory rebound in house prices will be not entirely non-existent next year.

Chapter 4

How to Develop the Economy with Land Transaction

The Nationwide Land Price Statistics for the year of 2013 were released by the Ministry of Land and Resources of the People's Republic of China on February 11, 2014, showed that the total amount of land leasing revenue across the country reached CNY 4.1 trillion last year, breaking the historical record of CNY 3.15 trillion in 2011. The robust year-on-year growth rate was 44.6%. From 1999 to 2012, the total land leasing revenue throughout the country was close to CNY 15 trillion, and an annual average surpassed CNY 1 trillion.

Is it good for the government, especially the local government to collect money? We first analyze the phenomenon of CNY 19 trillion of land leasing revenue in 1999-2013. From 1999 to the end of 2013, local governments in China had received a total of CNY 19 trillion in the land leasing revenue. What is **the land leasing revenue?** Foreigners don't understand this elegant noun because the land ownership in most foreign countries is sole private with clear property rights, and the land is privately owned plot by plot. More specifically Citizen A sells a plot of land to Citizen B, as long as both parties negotiate a price on a voluntary basis, they can conclude a transaction, and alter the Land Title Deed, and hereby the plot of land of Citizen

A will always belong to Citizen B. The income of Citizen A is called the **land sales income,** which but is called the **land leasing revenue** in China.

Should this CNY 19 trillion be taken away by local governments? Obviously it shouldn't. Since local governments sell land, and collect money in violation of three major principles:

I. **In violation of the principle of establishing the market economic system in China.** The goal of this market economic system is that the government should withdraw from market operation, merely manage the macroscopic readjustment and control. This is the goal set by the *Fourteenth National Congress of the Party* in power, and should be implemented. Whereas the local government sold land and collected so much money, which then is personally invested in some projects to the market as a sportsman. This obviously returns to the planned economy, and already forgets the goal of market economy.

II. **In violation of the spirit of the *Constitution.*** The *Chinese Constitution* stipulated that the state can only requisition the land where farmers and citizens live for the sake of public interest, which refers to the project that must benefit the common people and be non-profit. For example, the government plans to build a road and park, and provides them to the general public for free use, and such project can only be called for the sake of the public interest. For another example, a local government cooperated with domestic and foreign capitalists to build an expressway. It needs land requisition for construction, and the toll is very expensive after completion. Such project cannot be called for the sake of the public interest. At present capitalists take advantage of the public right of local governments to requisition some lands, such project is completely used for money making after manufactured products with the land. How can it be called for the need of public interests? Therefore it is illegal, and unpopular for local governments together with domestic and foreign capitalists to requisition land for the construction of commercial houses in the name of public interests. Demolition households in some cities are very smart, and have long understood exactly details of property developers. When the property developer instructs the local government to force the demolition, they put the party flag and the national flag on the house. This idea practically works, and sometimes the compulsive demolition comes off second best.

III. High-price sales land pushed up house prices. It is well-known that currently local governments sell land, and actually auction land at the price of commercial houses per floor area. By way of illustration one mu of land is 666 m2, plot ratio is 3 to obtain the order of 2,000 m2, the area of commercial houses planned is allowed for property developers to build, and then the unit price per square meter for the floor area is calculated, and called as the land price. Why does the sales land push up house prices? For instance, a plot of land in Chaoyang District, Beijing in 2009, when the auction was completed, and the land price, unit price of floor area per square meter was CNY 27,000/m2 while the selling price of commercial houses next door was only CNY 26,000/m2. This is a weird thing that flour is more expensive than bread. At all events there is a reason why property developers dare to buy land at so high price regardless of consequences. An unspoken trick is that as soon as a record-breaking high-price land is auctioned, the media hype it, and the news about the house price increase spread, surrounding commercial houses are quickly bought by the law-abiding ordinary people. Undoubtedly the record-breaking high-price land is sometimes just used for property developers to play a hype trick. As for the security deposit paid for the auction, they don't mind too much.

The above analysis is concerning whether the local government should sell land for CNY 19 trillion in 15 years. The ordinary people understand easy this sense. At present economically we analyze the harm of local governmental revenue of CNY 19 trillion to the long-term growth of our economics, merely highlighting the long-term growth.

What is the long-term growth? Its authentic name should be known as the long-term veritable growth for national economics. For example, a Factory produced 100 vacuum bottles, and sold at CNY 10 each last year, and produced another 100 vacuum bottles, and sold at CNY 20 each this year. Output value was CNY 1,000 last year, and was CNY 2,000 this year. Evidently the nominal output value has increased, and the actual output value has not increased. It is still 100 vacuum bottles. **Long-term economic growth depends on four factors:**

1. Material capital stands for production equipment, tools and factories;

2. Human capital stands for human ability and technology;
3. Natural resources stand for minerals, matters, and raw materials provided by the natural world;
4. Scientific and technical knowledge exist in the society.

It is inseparable from these four factors for a product manufacture, and one condition for manufacturing commodities by right of these four factors. The condition is money! Thousands of private enterprises need money without a break every day to maintain production, expand production, and improve technology. Where does their money come from? They borrow from either banks or private usury. The government collects CNY 19 trillion in land sales to make government expenditures more increase CNY 19 trillion. This CNY 19 trillion of sales land revenue is collected from the people through the property developer as an intermediary. That is to say citizens have handed over CNY 19 trillion to the local government in the past 15 years. Accordingly national savings are reduced by CNY 19 trillion. In the market of loan-able funds it is much more difficult for private enterprises to finance. In desperation private enterprises in veritable manufacture have to borrow a private usury, and the annual interest rate of which is from 12% to 60%. So that high financing costs force Chinese manufacture and production enterprises to profit hardly, and even nowhere to go.

Although the CNY 19 trillion is taken by the government to build roads, squares, and railways, and has some output value however the crowding out effect on private enterprises, and agriculture is disgusting. What is more worrying is that the road exactly as a bottomless pit the government invests in. Some high-speed roads are completed and opened, next repaired and maintained every year. Digging a piece for maintenance in the east today and in the west tomorrow, and the maintenance cost is prohibitively expensive. As long as unnecessary maintenance costs on these highways are saved, private enterprises and farmers can be funded to do good deeds. Thus it is not something good for the increase in governmental land sales revenue.

On the one hand the high-price land pushed up house prices makes houses that are necessities for residents bring huge profits to property developers, real estates like a sponge, absorbing capital flows from other industries continuously, making the emerging industries ischemia or blood loss, and even the entity economy unprofitable. On the other hand the real estate bubble is enlarging to threaten the national financial security, and economic operation. As a consequence the Chinese economy will have no vitality at all without falling house prices. This is also the ultimate reason for the USA to puncture resolutely the real estate bubble in spite of the risk of bank failures.

[Reference Data]

"Abstinence" for Land Dependency of Urban Development

According to the data released by the National Land and Resources Work Conference in 2011, the Chinese land leasing revenue exceeded CNY 7 trillion during the Eleventh Five-Year Planning. In "the most stringent real estate regulation and control without precedent" for the year of 2010, the total price of land leasing transactions nationwide was CNY 2.7 trillion at the year-on-year growth rate beyond 70%. "An urban developmental dependence on land has increased unceasingly to make the benefit distribution unreasonable and social contradictions prominent, and the land leasing system needs to be further reformed and improved", said Shaoshi Xu, the minister of Ministry of Land and Resources of People's Republic of China, including multiple concerns of multi-level harm about the "land dependency disease" of urban development in China.

The urban developmental dependence on land has continued to increase, and the key is the "unreasonable benefit distribution" indicated by Shaoshi Xu. First of all the distribution of urban and rural land interests is unreasonable: Taking land from farmers in CNY 10,000 as unit, and auctioning in the land market in CNY 100 million as unit, the measurement unit is a factor of 10,000 different. Second the time distribution is unreasonable. The current mayor can sell lands on behalf of next three mayors, which overdrafts not only the urban development potential, but also rights and interests of future generations. Unreasonable profit distribution also includes unreasonable input and output of different industries. Reliance on extensive land use and low-efficiency industries makes real estates like a sponge absorb capital flows from other industries and fields continuously, the emerging industries ischemia or blood loss, and even the real economy unprofitable, and instead the real estate bubble is enlarging to threaten national financial security, and economic operation.

Urban developmental dependence on land has increased continuously to trigger prominent social contradictions. First and foremost the dependence on land makes rural land look like the meat of Tang Monk of various interest groups (Tang Monk or Monk Xuanzang in the Chinese classics of the Tang Dynasty, describing one master and three apprentices that went on a pilgrimage for Buddhist scriptures to the Western, whose meat can make men keep youth forever or obtain the most profitable). Rental instead of land requisition, illegal land use, and others emerge endlessly despite recurrent prohibition. Farmers' rights and interests have been suffering from violation, endangering the rural social stability, and urban and rural harmonious relation. In the meantime, the real estate becomes a fertile ground for excess monetary speculation for profit, less land and more money push up land prices, and house prices, and ordinary citizens merely give a sigh of disappointment, gasping for air due to sky-high house prices. Consequently the majority of farmers and ordinary citizens are dissatisfied. The unbalanced industrial structure has spread to the field of social life. Hence the accountability system for cultivated land protection should be extended to the evaluation of rewards and punishments for optimal and intensive land use, and even the accountability of steady land prices and house prices.

"Abstinence" for the land dependency of urban development must accelerate the reform of rural land management system, and further innovate and improve the land leasing system.

During the Eleventh Five-Year Planning the Chinese rural land acquisition compensation standards increased by more than 30%, which can be described as an unprecedented effort, be that as it may it is still not enough. During the Twelfth Five-Year Planning, we must strictly implement the compensation policy for farmers whose land has been requisitioned, speed up the reform of land requisition, gradually reduce the scope, approach and method of land requisition, and improve the land acquisition compensation, and resettlement mechanism on the basis of the supply of land for people's livelihood, and land for indemnificatory apartments should be guaranteed as far as possible according to the requirement of central government, in order to make the mayor not dare the land approval disorderly, and make the property developer not dare the land use arbitrarily.

"Abstinence" for the land dependency of urban development must also increase the cost of land use, and practically solve the problem of secondary development of inefficient land use, and improve the land bid invitation, auction, listing and leasing systems in cities. During the Eleventh Five-Year Planning, the construction land consumption per unit GDP fell by 29% in China, and however was ranked the highest class in the world compared with developed countries, and even most emerging economies. Under the basic national condition of more people and less land the most stringent farmland protection system will not become an empty talk only if the implementation of the most stringent land-saving system. Meanwhile it is necessary to promote the transformation of land supply from a single goal of "success of highest-price-bidder" to the multi-goal management such as market improvement and protection of people's livelihood, and strengthen the binding force on the real estate market, house prices, operations of property developers, and "land finance" activities of local governments. To be specific, more than 30% of the land revenue must be used to build indemnificatory apartments, and more than 50% of that must be used to repay governmental debts, and so forth. Front blockage, back pursuit, and intermediate management are used in order for the "abstinence" for land dependency disease of urban development.

Chapter 5

How to Control the Economy with Specific Economic Indicators

The first *Government Work Report* was promulgated on March 5, 2014, and was highly praised by all deputies and members. Throughout the report content this present government had indeed made great achievements in both simplifying administrative procedures, and instituting decentralization in office for one year. Various contributions cannot go unnoticed. Whereas with reference to the work expectation, and arrangement for 2014, goals, and approaches in this report are often debatable, and seemingly contrary with the spirit of the *Third Plenary Session of the Eighteenth Central Committee of the Communist Party of China* in terms of economics, and the sustainable development of Chinese economics in medium and long term.

As we all know, about three months ago, the *Third Plenary Session of the Eighteenth Central Committee of the Communist Party of China* made a major decision on November 12 last year, viz., the *Decision of the Central Committee of the Communist Party of China on Several Major Issues in Comprehensively Deepening Reform*, in which the market plays a decisive role in the allocation of resources.

The original text is as follows: Restructuring the economic system with comprehensively deep reforms as focus and controlling successfully the relationship between government and market as core make the market play a decisive role in the allocation of resources to exert better the governmental function. Market determining the allocation of resources is the general rule of market economics. Likewise a sound socialist market economic system must abide by this rule, sparing no effort to solve the problem of imperfect market system, excessive government intervention, and inadequate supervision.

We must advance actively, steadily and properly market-oriented reforms in breadth and depth to reduce significantly the direct allocation of resources by the government, and promote the resource allocation in accordance with the market rule, market price, and market competition for the maximum benefit and optimal efficiency. Moreover governmental responsibilities and functions are mainly to maintain the macroeconomic stability, and strengthen and optimize public services, ensure the fair competition, strengthen the market supervision, safeguard the market order, drive the sustainable development, promote the common prosperity, and make up for market failures.

According to the above author understands that the government must abide by following three principles in practice to manage successfully the relationship between government and market:

The first is to abide by the principle of the market playing a decisive role in the allocation of resources. This sentence states clearly that three basic economic issues of what to be produced, and how and for who to produce in the market should be left to private enterprises and state-owned enterprises outside the government in order to freely solve and invest, i.e., allocate their resources according to the market.

The second is to abide by the principle of significantly reducing the direct allocation of resources by the government to promote the maximum benefit of resource allocation. Bluntly this principle means that the governmental income and expenditure should be greatly reduced, only by which can the allocation of resources by the government be decreased dramatically. If not, this principle will fail.

The third is that the government should abide by three aspects of maintaining macroeconomic stability, ensuring fair competition and optimizing public services to remedy for market failures, in another word the government can only intervene in the market from such three aspects.

The essence of the *Third Plenary Session of the Eighteenth Central Committee of the Communist Party of China* was the proposal of three principles above on the market economy to lay the foundation for Chinese economic boom as the most innovative and popular root cause. Did the 2014 *Government Work Report* meet these principles just three months later yet? The author now elaborates objectively from the four fields of economic growth, commodity price control, monetary stock growth and government expenditure to judge whether our government marches onwards either market economics or intervention.

In his 2014 *Government Work Report*, the Premier Keqiang Li pointed out primary anticipatory goals of economic and social development in this year. They are as follows: GDP growth rate is set at 7.5% or so. Rise in the CPI is controlled approximately at 3.5%. New jobs are more than 10 million and unemployment rate registered is controlled within 4.6% in cities and towns. International balance of payments is kept basically. We make efforts to achieve the synchronization between resident income and economic development.

I. Anticipatory goal of GDP growth rate is at 7.5% or so. Whether the establishment of this goal is scientific, and conforms to the principle of market playing a decisive role in the allocation of resources?

Since the foundation of the People's Republic of China we had been implementing the five-year plan in the economic field, which was later changed to the five-year planning. Today it turns in the term of the *Twelfth Five-Year Planning* (2011-2015). The people have lived six decades in the governmental plan and planning. In addition the goal of GDP growth has been stipulated in every five-year planning and every year since the reform and opening up.

Should the government propose a uniform goal of GDP growth? Annual GDP growth of one economic entity should be determined by its entrepreneurs under the principles of market economy because the prospective growth of annual output value is a major decision and cannot be predicted by outsiders in regard to each enterprise. It is unimaginable that the government orders the enterprise to reach a certain growth rate regardless of state-owned enterprise or private enterprise. In addition the confirmation of corporate development goal is a significant right within the enterprise to determine its resource preallocation. Market (entrepreneurs) cannot play a decisive role in the allocation of resources if this right is taken away by the government. Therefore the anticipatory GDP goal set by central government is unscientific, and has not a constraint force for enterprises. In the past practice the entrepreneur did not take it seriously.

Whereas the anticipatory GDP goal suggested by the central government is efficient for and is very popular with local governments at all levels because their interventions are justified in the economy just like getting an "imperial edict". Firstly local governments plan numerous large projects or engineering in the name of the government each year to invest in economic projects as sportsman in person. Secondly they have to raise money to invest in these projects, and borrow money or even usurious loans if fail to constitute a huge government debt without designated payer. Thirdly a small number of governmental officials get benefit through the government intervention in economics and projects, leading to a rampant corruption. As a result the anticipatory GDP goal proposed by the central government in the form of commands every year is essentially an ideological model of planned economy. Obviously it is inopportune to suggest again such goals after the spirit of the *Third Plenary Session of the Eighteenth Central Committee of the Communist Party of China.*

In the past practice the anticipatory GDP goal set by the central government was also fraught with drawbacks. For instance, the anticipatory GDP goal determined by the central government was about 7.5%, would be immediately changed to about 9.5%, and even up to 10.5% or 11.5%, and be increased at every level by the local government after the plenary session was ended and they went back. In this way the major economic goal almost becomes a digital game without seriousness. In the statistical circle everyone knows that the GDP in a place is inauthentic, and is calculated in the light of the intention of local leaders. Privately no one believes.

II. CPI is controlled approximately at 3.5%. Does it contradict the anticipatory goal? Rise in the CPI, in other words, the control of currency inflation, is an event of central governmental macroscopic regulation and control, and local government cannot interfere fundamentally.

This target should not be merely included in the anticipatory goal still should tell explicitly the people the value of CPI in the next few years. Similarly the Federal Reserve (FED) tells clearly the people how to arrange the money supply, and what the inflation rate will be in the coming years so as to stabilize popular sentiments. While the calculation of China CPI is somewhat not serious, showing that the historical data and the base year of CPI are neither disclosed to the people in statements and the original commodity price data in base year may nor be queried. So whenever the National Bureau of Statistics releases CPI data, a barrage of questions and criticism is provoked.

Furthermore the CPI cannot hold running water by other methods after bulletin, as stated in the 2014 *Government Work Report*: GDP reached CNY 56.9 trillion at the year-on-year growth rate of 7.7%. Rise in the CPI was controlled at 2.6%. At the end of 2013 the balance of broad money (M2) was CNY 110.65 trillion at the year-on-year growth rate of 13.6%. Computationally the growth rate in 2013 was 7.7% higher than that of 2012, which should refer to the actual GDP growth rate, plus the CPI growth rate of 2.6% to sum 10.3% while the year-on-year growth rate of M2 was 13.6% in 2013. Whereabouts was the monetary difference of 3.3%? In line with monetarism theories in international practices, M2 should be equal to the sum of CPI and GDP in long term. The GDP in 2013 reached CNY 56.9 trillion, which obviously refers to nominal GDP. The GDP reached CNY 52 trillion in 2012 (the *Government Work Report*) was quoted, we can calculate the nominal growth rate in 2013 to obtain 9.4%, minus CPI growth rate of 2.6% to then obtain the actual growth rate of 6.8% (our calculation) but 7.7% (the *Government Work Report*) in 2013. There are only two possibilities for such a contradiction, either the rise in the CPI was underestimated or the nominal GDP in 2013 was overestimated by the National Bureau of Statistics.

In order to be more logical, the government should bulletin simultaneously nominal GDP, actual GDP, nominal growth rate and actual growth rate as bulletins GDP in the future. Accurate calculation and announcement of the CPI have a significant influence on the entrepreneur decision in the market because they often cannot figure out whether product price is risen by the increase in genuine market demand or inflation in their decision making. In case the rise in product prices caused by inflation is misunderstood or misjudged as the increase in genuine demand, decision to expand reproduction will allocate resources wrongly, leading to losses and bankruptcy. Hence CPI viz., consumer price index can only convey accurately the market price information in favor of the allocation of market resources.

Moreover the *Government Work Report* stated that the anticipatory M2 growth rate was approximately at 13% in 2014. According to the data of *Government Work Report* last year, what was the total amount if M2 was increased by 13.6%? The total M2 set was increased sharply by CNY 15 trillion. The benchmark was too large although the growth rate of M2 was controlled. It is also a practical monetary stimulus to the economy, and will certainly accumulate more energy for future inflation outbreaks.

III. 2014 *Government Work Report* stated that: A fiscal deficit of CNY 1.35 trillion is planned to arrange in current year, and the increase is CNY 150 billion in year-on-year, of which CNY 950 billion is the central government fiscal deficit, and CNY 400 billion of debt is issued by the central government on behalf of local governments.

In recent years more and more money was issuing, and deficit was expanding year by year. The behavior of monetary and fiscal policies to stimulate the economy was more and more severe. The *Third Plenary Session of the Eighteenth Central Committee of the Communist Party of China* required reducing significantly the direct allocation of resources by the government and promoting the maximum efficiency of resource allocation. In the specific annual administration the total money supply, and governmental revenue and expenditure were increased significantly. The governmental expenditure was more and more, demonstrating that the governmental intervention in the economy was getting severe. CNY 1.35 trillion is also increased on the premise that the total Chinese government debt reached CNY 30 trillion. Does it accord with the principles of reform and opening up, and simplifying administrative procedures and instituting decentralization?

According to the website of Ministry of Finance, the data released by the Ministry of Finance indicates that the national public fiscal revenue was CNY 12.9 trillion in total, and the increase was CNY 1.19 trillion or the growth rate was 10.1% year-on-year. Among them, central and local fiscal revenues increased by 7.1% and 12.9% respectively. The national public fiscal expenditure was CNY 13.9 trillion in total, and the increase was CNY 1.38 trillion or the growth rate was 10.9% year-on-year from January to December 2013.

The national government-managed fund income was CNY 5.2239 trillion, and the increase was CNY 1.4704 trillion or the growth rate was 39.2% year-on-year cumulatively from January to December. Among them the income of central and local government-managed funds (at this level) was CNY 423.2 billion, and CNY 4,800.7 billion, and growth rates was 27.5% and 40.3% year-on-year respectively. The leasing income of state-owned land use rights was CNY 4.125 trillion, the increase was CNY 1.2732 trillion, and the growth rate was 44.6% year-on-year via the main increase in transaction price of land leasing contracts.

From January to December the national government-managed fund expenditure totaled CNY 5.0116 trillion, increments were CNY 1.3786 trillion or the growth rate was 37.9% year-on-year. Expenditures of central and local level government-managed funds were CNY 276.1 billion, and CNY 4.7355 trillion, and growth rates were 26.9% and 38.6% respectively year-on-year. Among them the expenditure for state-owned land use right leasing income arrangement was CNY 4.060 trillion, and the growth rate was 41.9% year-on-year via the main increase in cost expenditures such as land acquisition, demolition and compensation.

In conjunction with the aforesaid fiscal revenue and fund income (land use right sales income), the total revenue and expenditure of Chinese government in 2013 were CNY 18.1 trillion and CNY 18.9 trillion respectively. The local governmental income and expenditure from land use right sales were CNY 4.1 trillion and CNY 4 trillion respectively. Governmental expenditure accounted for 33% of GDP. It manifests that the government spent CNY 33 every CNY 100, and the allocation of resources by the government accounted for 33% in 2013. Deficit, governmental expenditure, and allocation proportion of resources by the government are further increased in 2014.

If we believe that market economy will bring about a pervasive prosperity, the market decisive role must be kept in configuration resources, and the government can only rectify market failures. In the government work every year, this principle should be implemented to cut down gradually the government expenditure including not only regular expenditure, but also all other expenses. Like this China can only become veritably powerful in the 21st century.

Chapter 6

Rich Country and Poor People in Violation of What Economic Rules

Ever since the Han and Tang Dynasties, China GDP has always been at the forefront of the world, but why have the life of the poor never improved? Why are the poor in China always so impecunious? In 1776 (around 230 years ago), Adam Smith made an amazing and profound analysis on the Chinese situation.

I.Adam Smith Pointed out That the Chinese Economy Had Been Stagnant for a Long Time since the Yuan Dynasty

The Chinese is proud of the 41st year of Emperor Qianlong period in the Qing Dynasty (1776 AD), viz., the Kang-Qian Flourishing Age. At this time China was one of the richest countries, and the Chinese GDP ranked among the leading countries across the world. Just the reverse, in the face of this legendary "prosperous age", an Englishman, Adam Smith, who lived thousands of miles away, clearly pointed out that China at that time was not in a prosperous age but a "stagnation" period for hundreds of years just by some travelers' records. Adam Smith used his broad and profound economic theories to analyze deeply the essence of the "Kang-Qian Flourishing Age" so far it has been amazing. 64 years later (1840), the Qing Dynasty was forced to accept the *British Treaty* under the bombardment of British solid ships and advanced cannons. Further it was also proved in practice, how profound and accurate the Adam Smith's analysis of China was!

More than 230 years ago, Adam Smith showed clearly that China had long been one of the richest countries, and had the most fertile land, hard-working people and population, and the best cultivation all over the world. Whatever happen Adam Smith made a judgment from all sorts of beautiful descriptions of travelers, "China seems to be in a stagnant condition for a long time". Adam Smith further demonstrated, "Today the Report Concerning Chinese Tillage, Industriousness and Dense Population in the *Traveler* is almost the same as the record, so does the observation description in the *Les Voyages de Marco Polo* for the country five centuries ago. China perhaps had reached the limit of sufficient affluence allowed by its law and regime before the era of Marco Polo (the Yuan Dynasty in Chinese history)". The sole basis of that Adam Smith deduced this conclusion is, "Chinese toilers' incomes are too low to support their families".

He also enumerated the tragic life phenomena of ordinary Chinese people in the Qing Dynasty to support his argument:

1. The farmer works in the field all day, and is satisfied when a small amount of rice can be bought at night;
2. Unlike European craftsmen, they can stay leisurely in their workshops to wait for customers, and instead Chinese craftsmen continue to peddle carrying their tools like a beggar;
3. The poverty of the lowliest people far lags behind that of the poorest country in Europe. Thousands of families neighboring Guangzhou have no houses on land, and can only live on small fishing boats. Their

foods and clothes are extremely scarce, and eager to pick up the dirtiest garbage thrown away by European ships. All rotten and smelly meat such as dead dogs or cats is also their favorite nutriment;

4. In major cities some babies are abandoned in streets and lanes or drowned in the water like puppies every night.

II. The Reason for Chinese Economic Stagnation and Worker Poverty Is That Laborers Are in a Disadvantageous Status.

Just that the country was so wealthy at that time, why the people's livelihood were so meager and his income could not sustain a family life? The key is that we must distinguish the relation between wealth scale of one country and worker's income. Adam Smith's uppermost insight includes:

1. The rise in labor wages cannot be caused by the actual size of national wealth but its continuous growth.

2. In case a country has a huge wealth but has been stuck for a long time, the number of workers hired each year will easily meet the number needed for the next year, and even be surplus. Thus employers will not compete with each other to obtain workers.

3. The increase in the number of workers exceeds the number required by the employer, and workers will feel that employment opportunities are insufficient, and will have to compete with each other for obtaining jobs.

4. Wages of workers depend on the labor contract between employers and employees. Workers hope to earn more while employers hope to pay less. Workers want to unite to raise wages while employers want to

unite to reduce wages. However employers often are in a favorable status with the help of the intervention of governmental officials in the game between employers and employees.

We in this day and age objectively analyze the economic situation in the Emperor Qianlong years to judge if the Adam Smith's analysis is in line with the situation at the time. Unquestionably we must grasp three key points:

1. In the age of Emperor Qianlong, total wealth (GDP) was very large in China;
2. During the Emperor Qianlong age, ordinary laborers got little income, and were insufficient to support their families;
3. In-depth analysis of the reason for Chinese economic stagnation during the reign of Emperor Qianlong from law and institution was not thoroughly conducted by Adam Smith at the time it stands to reason that he could not understand the institution of the Qing Dynasty in China.

Qianlong was the fourth emperor after the Manchu troop entered the strategic pass of Ming Dynasty, and founded the Qing Dynasty, reigning from 1736 to 1795 AD. The Emperor Qianlong, like his grandfather Emperor Kangxi and his father Emperor Yongzheng, attached great importance to the development of agricultural production. He commanded local officials to pay attention to planting trees for forest, and soil and water conservation. He encouraged land reclamation and expanded planting area. The arable area across the country was increased from about 45.76 million hectares in the second year of Emperor Yongzheng period to about 49.65 million hectares in the 31st year of Emperor Qianlong period. He was concerned about the water conservancy construction to make water conservancy projects play a role in preventing floods, and protecting agricultural production. The Emperor Qianlong focused on the development of commerce and granted a lenient policy, which stipulated that merchants selling grain in places of crop failure can exempt domestic customs and rice tax, and allowed the people to traffic a small amount of table salt (sodium chloride). Financial institutions (money shops operating exchange, deposits and credit) began to appear during the Emperor Qianlong age.

In the development of production mainly because China was a great power with a large population in vast territory, GDP was always huge but per capita was very small. National fiscal revenue had increased year by year since the 28th year of Emperor Qianlong period. The annual financial revenue was 30-40 million silver liang previously, reached more than 47 million silver liang in the 28th year, and reached the maximum point of 82 million silver liang in the 42nd year, and was lowered slightly to 60 or 70 million silver liang later. The Emperor Qianlong stressed the social stability, and cared for the people suffered from the disaster. During his reign the government exempted money and grain taxes (tax breaks) five times throughout the country, and the tax of grain transported to the capital by water three times from eight provinces, reducing the burden on farmers. According to statistics during the reign of Emperor Qianlong he reduced and exempted the official tax amount of 200 million silver liang plus the tax amount exempted due to disaster, and others over years of 100 million silver liang or more, totaling more than 300 million silver liang.

Although the Emperor Qianlong took some measures to develop production, the people's livelihood not only did not improve but they were even poorer than his grandfather Emperor Kangxi years. According to historical records in the 10th year of Emperor Qianlong period the rice price per shi rose from 2-3 silver liang in Emperor Kangxi years to 4-5 silver liang in Emperor Yongzheng years, and then to 5-6 silver liang in Emperor Qianlong years. The flour price per bowl increased from 10 copper coins during the Emperor Kangxi time to 16 copper coins in early Emperor Qianlong years. Commodity prices were rising while the income of working people was very low. The wage of river channel porter was 4 silver cents (i.e. 32 copper coins), which could buy 4 liters of rice per day in the 9th year of Emperor Kangxi period, and was 10 copper coins, which could buy 1 liter of rice for the porter wage of the Yongding River in the 15th Emperor Qianlong year. In the 18th year of Emperor Qianlong period, the wage of charcoal-burning, fire-burning and firewood-cutting workers was also 15 copper coins daily. Significantly the authentic wage for worker was only 1.5 liters of rice per day in Emperor Qianlong years, which was far behind the Emperor Kangxi time. In the last year of Emperor Kangxi period, Kangxi himself admitted that families had not adequate supplies, and people did not lived in contentment, and the Emperor Yongzheng also admitted that the Han nationality people was down and out. During the Emperor Kang-Qian age wealthy families that ate meat every day were scarcely ever, and poor families that worked every day were hand-to-mouth. Some farmers relied on selling their croplands to survive.

At the same time the income of British people was higher than the Chinese people. In the 24th year of Emperor Kangxi period, the wage of British peasants was equal to 2.7 silver liang monthly or 9 copper coins daily, that of skilled worker was equal to 4 silver liang monthly or 13 copper coins daily. At that time, half of the British civilians ate meat twice a week, and the other half ate meat once a week. By the end of Emperor Qianlong age British middle-class farmers had ample foods and clothes as evidenced by the description in the Austen's novel *Pride and Prejudice*. Conversely from the beginning of Qing Dynasty to the last year of Emperor Qianlong period, the official management was degenerated. Governmental officials at all levels led by Heshen, who was a powerful minister in the middle period of Qing Dynasty, were so corrupt that the people's labor income was concentrated in the hands of a few people.

III Real Incomes of Governmental Officials and the People Present an Anti-U Shape in Han, Tang, Song, Yuan, Ming and Qing Dynasties

Adam Smith's judgment that the Chinese economy had been in a stagnation state since the Yuan Dynasty is very consistent with China's historical facts. Actual incomes of peasants and workers in all previous dynasties of China had not increased much from the Qin and Han Dynasties to the Emperor Qianlong time of Qing Dynasty (during 2000 years). The average monthly income of farmers per household was equivalent to about 2 shi of rice in the peaceful period, and dropped significantly in wartime or disaster years or heavy land tax and other taxation, resulting in the phenomenon of "Whole country has no idle fields, farmers still starve to death". Each worker's wage from the Han Dynasty to the Qing Dynasty was equivalent to the order of 1-4 shi of rice monthly.

Under all circumstances the income of government officials had changed greatly in the past dynasties of China. It also reflected the trend of the Chinese economy. From the perspective of actual incomes of ranks of Chinese government officials and scholar-bureaucrats began to rise in Qin and Han Dynasties, and reached the peak in the Tang and Song Dynasties, and began to decline in the Yuan Dynasty, showing a parabolic shape. Prime minister, imperial senior official and grand commandant, known as millionaire, their monthly income was equivalent to 200 shi of rice in the Western Han Dynasty, and less than 100 shi in the Eastern Han Dynasty. In the prosperous age of Tang Dynasty the income of the highest-ranking government official was equivalent to 360 shi of rice monthly. During the Northern Song Dynasty the income of civil grand preceptor, military grand preceptor, and bodyguard as well as according deputies was equivalent to 800 shi of rice monthly. In the Yuan Dynasty the income of the highest-ranking government official was only equivalent to 220 shi of rice monthly so did it in the early Ming Dynasty but the income gradually declined due to the currency inflation. Entering the Qing dynasty the income of the highest-ranking government official was only equivalent to 80 shi of rice but the corrupt income of government officials was not easy to calculate. However the Chinese national strength rose from the Qin and Han Dynasties to a peak in Tang and Song Dynasties, and then declined since the Yuan Dynasty in accordance with the regular salaries prescribed by every dynasty. In 1776 AD, Adam Smith did not understand the data of Chinese dynasties, and concluded that the development of China wealth (GDP) began to be in stagnant since the Yuan Dynasty only based on the Marco Polo's records, and subsequent travelers' records but it is sufficiently precise.

Why did the Chinese wealth not grow after the Yuan Dynasty? This is a great topic, and the Chinese need to study earnestly. This article analyzes the reason for poor living standards of the working people during the Emperor Qianlong age on the grounds of the supply and demand relationship with regard to labor force in Adam Smith's theories. At the beginning of the Qing Dynasty, in order to increase the population the Emperor Kangxi announced, "People who are born in the prosperous age will never be levied capitation tax". Besides the Chinese population surged due to social stability, and the introduction and promotion of high-yield crops such as corn, and potatoes, which were intensely cultivated during the reign of Emperor Kangxi. A demographic census in the age of Emperor Qianlong showed the national population was 140 million in the fifth year, exceeded 200 million in the 27th year, and broke through to 300 million in the 55th year.

Be that as it may the increase in the number of arable land was far behind that of the population. The farmland per capita in the last year of Emperor Qianlong period was only 3.5 mu. Economic achievements were correspondingly offset by a large number of populations, and the people lived in a hunger and poverty. During his visit to China, the British ambassador George Macartney found that there were many beggars on the street of Beijing. Numerous people were unkempt and ragged. The food they threw as garbage was robbed by beggars to eat. The series of peasant uprisings that broke out in the late Emperor Qianlong period also had a lot to do with this. For the reason that the feudal emperor over-rewarded population growth in order to provide labor forces for the agricultural economy, it was caught one and lost another. The feudal emperor did not understand the calculation of exponential population growth, and the population had doubled within a few decades, and in the meantime agriculture did not expand on a large scale, and there was no technological innovation in the handicraft industry, resulting in insufficient employment opportunities, and a large number of labor force competition for fewer job opportunities. Thus the price of labor force had decreased dramatically.

IV. The Deeper the Extent of Dictatorship, the More Backward the Economy

Factually the first and foremost reason is not the oversupply of labor force but the autocracy and backwardness of China's political and legal institutions. Further analysis reveals that it was the extremely authoritarian political rule of Chinese dynasties, and the moral manner to maintain this institution, namely, the so-called the doctrine of Confucius and Mencius, which firmly controlled all generations of the Chinese people's thought to inhibit their innovation, and the increase in productivity.

Compared with Qin, Han, Tang and Song Dynasties, control mechanisms of Yuan, Ming and Qing Dynasties were more autocratic, backward and ran counter to the contemporary global trend, and even reached almost heinous anomaly regarding centralization and monarch dictatorship. During the Sui and Tang Dynasties the central administrative organization established Three Councils: Central Secretariat, Chancellery, and the Department of State Affairs. Its mode of operation was proposed by the Central Secretariat, and submitted to the Chancellery for deliberation, if was not passed, would be refuted and corrected, and if was passed, submitted by the Department of State Affairs to six ministries to carry out. In the Yuan Dynasty, six ministries only were controlled by the Central Secretariat that was the emperor commanded the crown prince who acted as the head of the Central Secretariat, and then six ministries carried out the emperor's order. The Emperor Taizu of Ming Dynasty canceled directly the prime minister, approved and issued orders to the six ministries for everything such as 3292 memorials to the throne all over the country for approval from September 14th to 21st, in the 17th year of Emperor Hongwu of Ming Dynasty, 411 ones needed to handle daily. Because of the heavy burden, power was often mastered by eunuchs.

The Qing Dynasty inherited the system of Ming Dynasty, and was even worse than the Ming Dynasty in the monarchy. All human rights in the Qing Dynasty were determined by the emperor. The monarch and ministers of the Ming Dynasty discussed affairs of government, and the minister only needed four worships while but had to kneel thrice and bow nine times, all officials reported to the emperor that they must claim to be minion in the Qing Dynasty. During the Emperor Shizong age in the Qing dynasty, spying on the country into full swing and sending countless spies, spreading the local government and people, made the government and the people feel uneasy on pins and needles as if treading on thin ice throughout the country, and dare not make jokes even in private rooms. Also the Qing Dynasty went in for literary inquisition in a big way, suppressing freedom of speech and association. Political autocracy and dictatorship are particularly harmful to the economy. During the Emperor Qianlong age, Heshen embezzled family properties were numbered to 109, of which the serial number of 26 were estimated, there were 223 million silver liang apart from that farmland was 53,360 hectares. By contrast in the 56th year of Emperor Qianlong period (1792), the fiscal revenue was 43.59 million silver liang, and the expenditure was 31.77 million silver liang. It does show that Heshen is a powerful minister of taking bribes. With the corrupt official controlling politics and economics, where is the enthusiasm of the people for production from? What's more the offspring of "Eight Banners" in Qing Dynasty, rode roughshod over the Han people, plundered their land and ruled the civilization with barbarism. As a consequence China's productivity was unprecedentedly destroyed, and China was getting poorer.

Emperor Qianlong's biggest mistake was self-important, immobilisme and self-seclusion, save and except for his extreme autocracy, which resulted in China to lose the good opportunity to keep pace with the world, and become a laggard country. After the Emperor Qianlong the Qing government began to implement a foreign policy of comprehensive isolationism, early had four treaty ports, later only one foreign treaty port in Guangzhou. Thirteen-hongs in Canton monopolized its import and export trade, and there were many restrictions on the type of export cargo. The Qing governmental isolationism policy blocked China contact with the Western world, and made China lose the optimal period of simultaneous development with the world, which foreshadowed subsequently an accumulated declining tendency for century in China. Thus the Emperor Qianlong should bear the largest responsibility.

V. The Fact of Century from the Revolution of 1911 up to Now Also Shows That a Small Number of People Impose Their Individual Will on the Chinese, Always Confuse the Chinese Economy, and Harm to the Chinese.

Even to this day it has passed above 230 years since the Adam Smith's evaluation on Chinese economics, and China has always struggled through the twists and turns. After being ruled by the Manchu it was first hit by the Taiping Uprising, and the Qing Dynasty was finally overthrown by the 1911 Revolution led by Sun Yat-sen. After the brutal dictatorship of the Qing Dynasty was collapsed, the people were not fully awakened. Because the Chinese ideology had been imprisoned for thousands of years, the people invariably cannot confound with who will protect authentically their interests. Moreover those who truly and thoroughly defend the interests of all the people do not regard any class as their special interests, and cannot gain mighty support from the people. Precisely because of it, Sun Yat-sen failed. Yuan Shikai, Chiang Kai-shek, et al, a series of "pretenders" restored the autocratic, totalitarian and authoritarian way of ruling the people.

After some rulers claiming to be democratic came to power, their desire for power far exceeded that of the Emperor Qianlong in the Qing Dynasty. The Emperor Qianlong only ceded the throne to the Emperor Jiaqing several years before his death. On the contrary, to this day some unreasonable Chinese people still praise for authoritarian rule, and "honest and upright" sage officials without business in the Qing Dynasty who but maintained feudal autocracy, and paralyzed the people. They pick up, and prettify the so-called enlightened monarchs from the pile of historical old paper, and vigorously hymn. They use the people's hard-earned money to chant ceaselessly Kangxi, Yongzheng, Qianlong, and other emperors' "great achievements" in the name of historical dramas other than these emperors cruel plundering people's land, oppressing people, creating literary inquisition, and other authoritarian and monolithic crimes, that were not mentioned at all. Why can these behaviors that blatantly violate the *Constitution*, celebrate the emperor's autocracy, and propagate its belief on a large scale?

Chinese practices show that the totalitarian and dictatorship of Yuan, Ming and Qing Dynasties for 600 years will only worsen the actual living standards of Chinese officials and people increasingly. Regardless of whether the authoritarian is a corrupt official or upright official in the Qing Dynasty, they will not do anything ultimately conducive to the people. It's nothing but that the bad things done by corrupt officials are easy to manifest while by upright officials in the Qing Dynasty only are discovered after a long time. The Emperor Qianlong is the cleverest, most hardworking and talented upright official, at all events ruined the China great future in the end. Starting from 1776, economically penniless and culturally blank United

States advocated the Adam Smith's free market in one hand, and Jefferson's democratic politics in the other hand. The USA must be regarded with special esteem due its remarkable development in fifty years, became one of powers century later, and the most powerful country in the world 200 years later. Isn't the arcanum of American success worth pondering of all people from China with long history?

Chapter 7

Political Restructuring Reform and Economic Issues

At present the Chinese are very concerned about and hate corruption, as well as unfair distribution on income, education and medical resources however how to change these prominent problems, and how about their goals are not so clear. It is indeed a unique feasible solution to reform various shortcomings hated currently by the people with democratic method.

I. Inequality of Income Distribution Is the Primary Cause for Unaffordable House Price

Why can't many people afford it even after the high housing price drops by 50%? Beyond doubt one side house prices are still too high, other side the people's income is too low. Besides no increase in income is also an important reason for high housing prices. Why the people's income doesn't increase? The main reason is unfair income distribution. In advanced countries there is also the problem of unfair income distribution, and it is at all events caused by different individual abilities independent of the entire system. That is to say the mobility of the poor and the rich in Western countries is very large within a few years. As long as the poor work hard in a few years, they absolutely have a chance to become the rich. In case the rich do not work hard, they will easily become the poor. On all accounts this is not the case in China. The majority of Chinese dignitary and wealthy rely on power to obtain stable income. Further the inordinate concentration of power is caused by the patriarchy of the planned economy inherited by the political system or the governance system.

Suppose there is a Section C in Enterprise B in City A. We start to analyze the primary cause of unequal income distribution, and so forth with the Section C. There is 20 staff in the Section C, consisting of 1 director, 1 deputy director, 8 workers with officially authorized strength (including director and deputy director), and 12 contract workers in the Section C. How is the monthly income of this section distributed? According to the principle of fair distribution in foreign countries, the distribution is based on labor effect, in other words labor capacity and time, the more the staff finishes work workload, the more the staff earns income in unit time, and vice versa. This manifestly reflects the natural justice of distribution. Whatever this is not the case in China, and income is distributed according to the size of power.

Taking the income distribution of Section C at the beginning of March 2011 as example, how to distribute all the income from February in the Section C? **The first is to allocate salaries. The first step of salary distribution begins inequality.** The salary card of per person is paid by CNY 3,000 for 8 permanent workers with officially authorized strength while CNY 1,000 for 12 contract workers recruited monthly in the Section C. The salary difference between the permanent worker and contract worker is the order of 2-3 times. The director, deputy director and worker with officially authorized strength in the Section C have not large salary gap so do contract workers. However the salaries between permanent worker and contract worker have large gap, and this kind of inequality is completely unreasonable, and violates the principle of fairness and justice. Seeing that like the Section C of such enterprise, contract workers are usually the main labor force, videlicet all of the income is created by contract workers while the income is mostly distributed to permanent workers with officially authorized strength. Hereby this is unequal distribution for the first time.

Distribution of gray income is unequal for the second time. For example, there is also a very important income, viz., gray income, which is to be secretly distributed save and except for the distribution of salary and bonus in the Section C. However the distribution of gray income is very popular in China, which makes the Chinese people morally corrupt, intrigue, and widespread resent and discontent. When the Section C allocates the income from February at the beginning of March, a director receives salary of CNY 3,000 and bonus of CNY 3,000, a deputy director receives salary of CNY 2,600 and bonus of CNY 2,600, each permanent worker receives salary of CNY 2,300 and bonus of CNY 2,500, and each contract worker gets salary of CNY 1,000 and bonus of CNY 2,300. Such distribution inequality is particularly reflected in the salary distribution of contract worker and permanent worker with a gap of about CNY 2,000 per month, and more than CNY 20,000 per year.

Yet for all that, this gap is not large. The largest one is the distribution of gray income. For instance, the gray income of CNY 80,000 in rebates, and the like comes totally from February in the Section C, how to distribute? This is distributed by the director of the Section C according to the level of power. The director of the Section C firstly distributes CNY 30,000 to himself upon the receipt of CNY 80,000, CNY 20,000 to the deputy director, CNY 5,000 to each permanent worker, and never to the majority of contract workers. As thus we can calculate the monthly income and annual income of staff in the Section C.

1. **Director:** CNY 3,000 salary + CNY 3,000 bonus + CNY 30,000 gray income = CNY 36,000 monthly income, CNY 432,000 annual income.
2. **Deputy Director:** CNY 2,600 salary + CNY 2,600 bonus + CNY 20,000 gray income = CNY 25,200 monthly income, CNY 302,400 annual income.
3. **Permanent worker:** CNY 2,300 salary + CNY 2,500 bonus + CNY 5,000 gray income = CNY 9,800 monthly income, CNY 117,600 annual income.
4. **Contract worker:** CNY 1,000 salary + CNY 2,300 bonus + CNY 0 gray income = CNY 3,300 monthly income, CNY 39,600 annual income.

Though the above-mentioned income distribution ratio assumed is not accurate, it does reflect the current income distribution ratio, and principles of certain administrative agencies, public institutions and state-owned enterprises in China. This distribution mode has existed for decades, has been deeply ingrained, and has generated severe social problems in China. Evidently some have gray income while others have not. Sometimes distribution of gray income is open or secret.

For another example the average price of commercial houses in the City A is CNY 10,000/m², and the house of 90 m² needs CNY 900,000 after drops by 50%. In the Section C one house is bought by the director with only 2 years of income, by the deputy director with 3 years of income, by the permanent worker with nearly 8 years of income, by contract worker with nearly 23 years of income. Contract workers account for the majority of Section C. So most people cannot afford a house!

Extremely few people can purchase houses every year. This mode of income distribution will make society more and more dangerous. Since China abolished the national guarantee job assignment system for graduates from colleges and universities, and technical secondary schools, all state-owned institutions, undertakings and enterprises in China have recruited contract workers. The number of permanent workers has decreased, and that of contract workers has increased gradually. Whatever happens, the income distribution system is centered on the power of permanent workers. It widens artificially the gap between the rich and the poor so that practical workers do not get enough income. A handful of people who are in power are reluctant to abdicate in order to gain greedily huge amounts of income.

II. Lagging Political Restructuring Reform Is the Root Cause of Unfair Income Distribution

Xirong Liu, a member of the Standing Committee of the National People's Congress, deputy chairman of the Law Committee of the National People's Congress, and the former deputy secretary of the Central Discipline Inspection Commission, pointedly indicated in his deliberations on the work report of the Standing Committee of the National People's Congress:

We need both incorruptible and clean government, and inexpensive government. Currently some leaders request to change offices with cars, drivers and secretaries on assumption of duty, which increase a lot of work costs. Additionally problems such as banquet, recreational activities, consumption, and travel at public expenses, most of "three public consumption" funds are extra-budgetary. Extra-budgetary funds are not easy to be supervised, and it is no wonder that they are so corrupt.

The author believes that sharing the gray income should also be counted as extra-budgetary funds in the case of the Section C. The state should stipulate by law that publicly-owned revenue must be included in the budget, and distributed openly and equally. Where an enterprise includes publicly-owned revenue in the extra-budgetary private distribution, the main person in charge should be sentenced to 2-200 years of imprisonment. Then too many corrupt officials there are should be imprisoned. The prison is not enough, and they may be imprisoned to the farm for exercise through manual labor. The best way is democracy anyway because the director freely elected by the staff of this enterprise must be accountable to the masses. The masses of this enterprise can dismiss jointly him at any time if corruption or bribery.

Why can a director of small Section C enjoy alone the authority to distribute income in reality? This is because the director of the Section C is appointed by the superior. The top leader of the enterprise B has the absolute power to appoint the director of the Section C. When the employees of the Section C oppose as a result of unfair distribution, the director of the Section C joins with the top leader of the enterprise B to disorganize, and retaliate against the opposition to protect their vested interests. The director of the Section C also conducts lip-deep democratic elections. Every once in a while their employees will get a table with only 1 or 2 candidates for election. This is essentially a designated democracy and a pseudo-democracy through and through, and as a matter of fact the will of few people is imposed on most people, which are beguilement in violation of the provisions of *Constitution* on the people mastering their own affairs.

In case the Section C is truly democratic, and everyone free nominates candidates, the fair person who is supported by the masses will be elected as the director of Section C. After the person publicly elected comes to power, he must distribute the income of Section C equally. At First the gray income of CNY 80,000 must be disclosed as a reasonable income, and then equally distributed. Each contract worker can share CNY 4,000 per month, monthly income is CNY 7,300, and annual income is CNY 87,600. One house of CNY 900,000 is affordable for contract worker with a decade of income or immediately is bought with a bank loan. From the effect of changes in income distribution, open and equal distribution actually has a little impact on the permanent worker with officially authorized strength. The major consequence is that the monthly income of the director of Section C is reduced by CNY 20,000, i.e. from CNY 36,000 to CNY 10,000. It is obviously that the key to the reform of income distribution is to dig the money from the corrupt leader, and then distribute to veritable working masses. Only in this way can we grasp the key point of Chinese income distribution. Principal leaders of some enterprises any way have racked their brains to prevent the masses from elections of truly free nomination candidates due to the deep beneficial temptation, and in most cases the masses are disintegrated by authoritarian corruptors and resign themselves to their fate. Therefore the Premier Wen said that the independent thinking and enthusiasm of citizens are a solid foundation for democracy. How significant it is!

This case study of the Section C may be suitable for one section, one village, one township, one county, one city, one province, and one country. To grasp this key: really lets the people be the master for their own affairs, especially from top to bottom, implementing the provisions of the *Constitution*. Corruption, collusion between governmental officials and businessmen, unfair income distribution, unaffordable house, medical expenditure, and tuition fee or whatever can be solved in one day, when the people will be truly the master for their own affairs, nominate freely the candidate, political restructuring reform will be restarted, and 1.3 billion people are eagerly looking forward to!

[News Excerpt 1]

Extra-Budgetary Funds Are One Major Source of Corruption

(Beijing Times journalist Hang Deng) Yesterday, Xirong Liu, a member of the Standing Committee of the National People's Congress, deputy chairman of the Law Committee of the National People's Congress, and the former deputy secretary of the Central Discipline Inspection Commission, revealed in his deliberations on the work report of the Standing Committee of the National People's Congress that the Budget Law is scheduled to launch amendment in April. He said that extra-budgetary funds are one major source of corruption, and the budget proposal must be reformed to prevent the phenomenon of "unit-owned exchequer".

Extra-Budgetary Funds Trigger Corruption

Xirong Liu revealed that the Budget Law is scheduled to launch amendment in April this year. "During the amendment process we must pay attention to how to eliminate the 'unit-owned exchequer'". He believes that to safeguard the fundamental interest of overwhelming majority of the people, we must prepare the financial budget in real earnest, and currently some funds are not included in the budget, and are not subject to supervision, which is also the reason for the existence of "unit-owned exchequer".

Xirong Liu also said that the Budget Law must be in line with the relevant anti-corruption laws. In the past, budget violations were mostly combined with the punishment of party discipline and political discipline. The revised Budget Law should stipulate explicitly where the funds that should have been in the budget are listed outside the budget and this action must be severely punished by law considering that this is highly possible the source of corruption. "Extra-budgetary funds are not easy to be supervised, and it is no wonder that they are so corrupt".

Requisite../../../Documents and Settings/Administrator/ LocalSettings/ApplicationData/youdao/dict/Application/7.5.2.0/ resultui/dict/**Inexpensive Government**

Xirong Liu indicated that the budget proposal also needs to be reformed. "Some budget items are now intersecting with each other so that it's hard to understand". Therefore it makes the supervision difficult.

"We need both incorruptible and clean government and inexpensive government". Xirong Liu believed that currently some leaders request to change offices with cars, drivers and secretaries on assumption of duty, which increase a lot of work costs. Additionally problems such as banquet, recreational activities, consumption, and travel at public expenses, most of "three public consumption" funds are extra-budgetary.

He expressed that in case the National People's Congress can manage thoroughly all the extra-budgetary funds, its authority will not be reduced, and will be greatly improved. "The National People's Congress controls comprehensively the money, and everything is at peace".

Appeal to Control the Number of Civil Servants

Xirong Liu considered that there are also problems in the current budgetary allocation method. "Whoever requests more now will get larger cake, as a result of that 'the child who can yell will eat more milk'". "More budgets are not always better, the key is to distribute appropriately it, and the budget should be used for the place where the people need most".

He also suggested that relevant laws and regulations such as the National Income Distribution Law, and the Authorized Strength Law should be promulgated as soon as possible. "The reason why thousands of persons participate in civil servant test is that they can obtain a secure job without the dismissal risk". He insisted that the authorized strength of civil servants should be reformed to control their number. "The larger the authorized strength is, the higher costs of support, education, supervision, and investigation and treatment take".

■ Scene
Taking Jiangxi Huge Corrupter Section Chief as Case Requests the Introduction of Corruption Prevention Law

"Supervision is not enough for leaders nowadays", Xirong Liu cited the "huge corrupter section chief" in a national poverty-stricken county in Jiangxi Province as case, and "one section chief can embezzle CNY 94 million, and then fled to Canada".

Xirong Liu discussed, currently there are some laws and regulations that require governmental officials to declare their property, and so on, on all accounts a perfect system has not been formed, and the legislation is still inadequate, "the regulatory system must catch up with".

Xirong Liu affirmed that the Corruption Prevention Law must be promulgated as soon as possible to supervise the property, family members and other situations of governmental officials. "Don't let these people escape to Canada as soon as something goes wrong, otherwise others will say persuasively or eloquently, 'there is a Canada in the world (Jia Na Da), and everyone takes in China (Da Jia Na)'".

[News Excerpt 2]

Reform of the Economic System Cannot Succeed without Political Restructuring

WWW.CHINANEWS.COM messages on March 14. In this morning, Jiabao Wen showed in response to media questions about political restructuring that reform is the eternal theme in history. The reform of political system and economic system should be harmoniously promoted because everything in the world will not be everlasting. Only by investigating in time and never stopping can we maintain vigor like the classics in the past. Only through continuous reforms will the party and the country be full of evergreen and vitality.

An American reporter asked, "You advocate political reforms on many occasions. In consideration of current challenges and problems in China, what kind of reform do you think should be implemented to enable the Chinese government to address more effectively the concerns, problems and dissatisfaction of the people?"

In this regard Jiabao Wen replied, "Reform is the eternal theme in history. The reform of political system and economic system should be harmoniously promoted because everything in the world will not be everlasting. Only by investigating in time and never stopping can we maintain vigor like the classics in the past. Only through continuous reforms will the party and the country be full of evergreen and vitality."

Besides political restructuring is the guarantee for reform of the economic system. Without political restructuring, reform of the economic system cannot be succeeded, and the achievement already made is in danger of being lost.

Jiabao Wen involved the political restructuring in three aspects:

-- The biggest danger at present is corruption. Reforming institutions and systems are the key to eliminate the breeding ground of corruption. The destiny of the country is decided by the will of the people. To solve the people's grievances, and realize the people's aspirations, it is necessary to create conditions for the people to criticize, and supervise the government.

-- Fairness and justice are the essential characteristics of socialism, and the foundation of social stability. China must not only achieve the fair income distribution to reduce gradually the phenomenon of widening income gap in distribution, but also resolve the unfair distribution of resources such as education and medical care to allow the people to share the fruit of reform and opening up.

-- Everyone should be given an educational opportunity in order to give full play to their independent thought and creative spirit. Considering that only people have enthusiasm, Chinese reform and construction have a solid foundation. In this sense, it stands for the veritable connotation of democracy really.

Jiabao Wen concluded that it is not an easy task to boost political restructuring in an enormous country with a population of 1.3 billion. It requires a stable and harmonious social environment, and an orderly progress under the leadership of the party.

Part Three

Arcana of Real Estate System

Introduction

When everyone makes a million

Monetary value will be reduced greatly.

In many countries house property is the largest part in the household income. However when the house property is converted into actual monetary income, its amount is large, and sometimes small! Evidently to make a fortune by virtue of real estate, must above all:

1. Pursue the maximization of nominal income, we must grasp in detail the information of supply and demand to determine the price, and should apply various information that affects both supply and demand to analyze price trends. Government regulation and control affects either supply or demand, if not, does not work. Its effect is subject to the implementation but the official document! You can grasp affirmatively the tendency of real estate, and earn the maximum nominal income when making the relation between supply and demand clear.

2. Simultaneously in case the CPI increases several-fold such as three times, the nominal income earned will be only one third! To be specific, you bought a house in 2003, and sold it to gain one million CNY in 2013 whereas your actual income earned was only CNY 200,000 providing that the CPI of 2013 was 5 times that of 2003! The reason is simple that: money value is reduced!

In 2013 the Chinese were calculating nominal income so that many persons' wealth reached to hundreds of millions, known as billionaires, anyway divided by 5, would they really be so rich? No, high house prices make you become a nominal millionaire or multi-millionaire, however your nominal income seems to be just a digital game, needs over the corresponding multiple of the rise in CPI if converted into real income.

You are so as smart to buy low and sell high, you can just earn nominal income, or else buy high and sell low, the nominal income will be downed the drain. In any wise, when all the home-buyers have made a lot of money, the money is worthless! Where was your money earned? The money was transferred to the real estate, and then was transferred by the rise in CPI! Obviously real estate is precisely a tool for wealth transfer!

Chapter 1

Real Estate Interest Groups Manipulate Inflation for Profit

Reporter asks, "What is your basis when you predict house prices? Could you explain the reason?"

Dong Fang Dao answers, "Three principles I studied are my basis: One is the currency inflation law, two is central policies, and three is the supply and demand relationship in the local market. The first principle is actually the research on monetary matters, namely the regularity between money supply and commodity prices. In recent years many experts have insisted that inflation, and house prices should rise, which is misleading the market. When inflation is at an all-time high, house prices should fall relatively. Why is this? Just that inflation control is one of the most important goals of responsible government for governing country in modern society. Nowadays the vast majority people don't understand inflationary dangers, and think that more money is better. This is completely wrong. Apart from foreign examples, Chinese dynasties were all wiped out by currency inflation such as Qin, Han, Tang, Song, Yuan, Ming, Qing, and the Republic of China".

"Certainly the cause is not just currency inflation, but also authoritarianism and corruption. But the main reason for eruptible contradictions is inflation. Just like the Emperor

Wu in Han dynasty, he was the first person who really made, and managed inflation in Chinese history. In the reign of the Emperor Wu, he abolished half of liang coin to three zhu (weight loss, inflation and depreciation), and then ceased three zhu coin to half of liang (weight increase, deflation and appreciation), and then canceled half of liang to mint three zhu (depreciation), and then ceased three zhu to five zhu (appreciation). These methods of the Emperor Wu in Han Dynasty are very similar to that of the contemporary Federal Reserve, and that of contemporary central banks of various countries. Suddenly excessive money supply, and then deflation back and forth fluctuates commodity prices incessantly. The Emperor Wu in Han Dynasty more than 2100 years ago was struggling to explore the law of money and commodity prices at that time. In the end he succeeded and laid a splendid foundation for the Han Dynasty of more than 400 years".

"Hence researches on numismatic laws are numberless as the sand in the Chinese history. Americans and Europeans can not understand deeply the Chinese linguistic cultural and historical background. They think their nummary experiences are really something. In fact they make a huge mistake. Milton Friedman doubted somewhat that the banknote was first invented, and used by the Chinese. In the Tang and Song Dynasties of China, especially the Yuan Dynasty, banknotes existed everywhere, and later were prohibited to circulate because the Yuan Dynasty suffered from the inflation of paper money in depth. At all events these may be a long time ago, and can't make people deeply aware of inflation dangers. Now let's discuss the Chiang Kai-shek governmental inflation in the Republic of China of modern times, and can recall the memories of seventy or eighty-aged elderly people who had experienced hyperinflation. Further you will understand clearly how terrible the inflationary danger is so that governments of different countries now regard inflation control as the major goal of administering country!"

Reporter traces, "Isn't Chiang Kai-shek defeated by Chairman Mao? How does it have to do with inflation?"

Dong Fang Dao insists, "Yes! Chiang Kai-shek was chased away by Chairman Mao. But why was the Chiang Kai-shek Government of the Republic of China, which had so many armies armed by foreign advanced guns, artillery, and other weapons with the assistance of so numerous ministers held foreign doctorate who once studied in the United States, Britain and France, rushed away at a stroke by Chairman Mao who only had behindhand guns, and other weapons in the short period of one or two years? Military science is one reason, and the hyperinflation in the KMT - controlled district of the Chiang Kai-shek Government takes a decisive role".

"Since 1937 the Nanjing National Government had been heavily indebted, and nowhere can borrow money had to rely on the excessive money issuance to compensate for the fiscal expenditure directly, resulting in hyperinflation. **In order to manage inflation, the Kuo Min Tang (KMT)** made a decision to issue Gold Yuan Notes in 1948. The ratio of the Gold Yuan Note to the original fiat money was set as 1:3 million, in other words, **1 Gold Yuan Note can be exchanged 3 million yuan fiat money**. According to the protocol of the foreign scholars at that time, the domestic monetary aggregate can be reduced to one three millionths, and the commodity price was correspondingly reduced to one three millionths. Seemingly the commodity price can be stabilized".

"On August 23, 1948 the Gold Yuan Note entered officially the circulation field. Since the Government of the Republic of China stipulated that the ratio of fiat money to Gold Yuan Note was 3 million:1, daily necessities and small commodities were impossible to buy and sell by Gold Yuan Notes, on one side only by fiat money at prevailing market commodity prices, on the other side fiat money was constantly redeemed to lead to make difficultly small changes, affecting normal transactions, and incurring continuous civil disputes, the closer the fiat money redemption period, the more serious the problem. Consequently respective vouchers were issued for small moneys all over the country, and Gold Yuan Notes caused chaos in the currency circulation field. By November 10, 1948 the Gold Yuan Notes of 1.7 billion yuan net amount was put into circulation, **equivalent to the fiat money of 5,100 trillion yuan, and 8 times of the total amount of fiat money (660 trillion yuan) issued in the thirteen years of the Republic of China (1935-1948),** with the addition of 200 trillion yuan unrecoverable fiat money in circulation, namely, **monetary aggregate of hundreds of trillions was increased** in short 70 days of **the KMT - controlled district."**

"The KMT put these stupid economic doctors held foreign academic degree in an important position carrying out numismatic reform, it is bound to collapse. **The practical economic knowledge level of these stupid scholars is worse a factor of 100 lower than the Emperor Wu in Han Dynasty 2100 years ago. Their educational diplomas of Harvard, Oxford, and other famous foreign universities are all in vain. It is a serious problem triggered by indigestible foreign economic theories introduced at home that pushed completely the President Chiang and the Government of the Republic of China to the opposite of the people, and their last trust was completely lost, and reputation was thoroughly discredited.** On September 4, 1948, the 15th day of the issuance of Gold Yuan Note, the commodity price rose by 21% in Hankou, 40% in Chongqing, and 83% in Guangzhou, as well as 300% in Beiping (Beijing), 34% in Shanghai, and 294% in Chongqing from the end of August to October. By February 1949, commodity prices in the KMT - controlled district had skyrocketed: Rice rose to 13,000 yuan, Wuxi rice was 13,400 yuan, and wheat was 13,500 yuan. Suzhou rice was 13,700 yuan, and wheat was 15,500 yuan per catty in Hangzhou city. The diary of a person named as Qi Zhu recorded that he had a haircut, and paid 15,000 yuan in the evening of April 9, 1949."

"At that times the KMT also carried out CPI. Taking the CPI at the end of August 1948 as 1, the commodity price increased 77 times by January 1949, 546 times by February, 2,470 times by March, 51,000 times by April, and 1.28 million times by the first week of May. (According to the *Old China Inflation Information* in archives of the KMT Central Bank, page 162). This led to the general rejection of Gold Yuan Notes from place to place since April 1949, instead silver and copper coins were used as a currency in circulation. In fact it was declared that the Gold Yuan Notes completely collapsed. Did the people living in the KMT - controlled district where commodity prices risen by 1.28 million times within eight months, really want the Communist Party to liberate them? After Chiang Kai-shek and senior KMT officials were rushed to Taiwan, they have been unable to figure out the reason for the failure so quickly, that is the danger of inflation has been never understood".

Reporter questions, "I heard that the Republic of China should have not used silver and copper coins? Why was Chiang Kai-shek so stupid to overprint so much paper money to hurt himself?"

Dong Fang Dao says, "Chiang Kai-shek was not stupid just confused, and did not understand economics. From the analysis of international reasons **he was mainly hurt by the U.S. President Roosevelt.** In 1933 in order to stimulate the American economic depression, Roosevelt began to implement an American **Silver Purchase Plan,** which promoted the growth of high-powered money in the United States in 1932-1937, and that the commodity price level of the United States increased by 14% at that time, and was a disaster for the Chiang Kai-shek Government of the Republic of China that implemented the silver standard in the 1930s anyway."

"The soaring price of the U.S. silver dollar forced the outflow of Chinese silver coins in the silver standard, leading to a severe deflation in China from 1934 to 1936. **More importantly the Chiang Kai-shek Government of the Republic of China lost monetary savings, and could only abandon the silver standard to use the dishonored fiduciary standard.** Therefore Roosevelt's Silver Purchase Plan in the 1930s laid the groundwork for the collapse of the Chiang Dynasty. In 1937-1945 the banknote issuance was a factor of 300 higher after the government of the Republic of China gave up the silver standard. Furthermore the growth rate of commodity prices was faster than paper money. By the time of the victory over Japan in 1945, the commodity price of the KMT-controlled district had risen by 1,600 times. Afterwards the monetary reform of the Gold Yuan Notes failed due to the KMT-the Communist Party war in 1948, which led to further hyperinflation in the KMT-controlled district. **Monetarism originator Milton Friedman once lamented, the KMT may be in power longer for a couple of years because of lower inflationary rate without the Silver Purchase Plan.**"

Reporter asks for an explanation, "What you said so much, and are these related to house prices?"

Dong Fang Dao replies, "Of course! Old time has past by, the world has been changed but the truth is the same for some things. Just like the harm of currency inflation, I did not explain in detail, could you understand thoroughly? Is it absolutely impossible? You don't understand but this does not mean that high-level policy decision makers do not understand! They are clearly aware of the inflationary trend, which is also the basis for their monetary policy formulation. Therefore the top priority of governments of all countries is to control the currency inflation towards a hyper development. To control inflation must deflate and suppress house prices."

Reporter inquires, "Doesn't the 2012 *Central Economic Working Conference* put stability growth first? What the conference presented is, "To finish economic work in next year, we must stick to overall planning and consideration, and effectively grasp the balance among goals and tasks to progress in stability. It is necessary to better integrate stabilizing growth, controlling commodity prices, adjusting structure, benefiting the people's livelihood, grasping reform, and promoting harmony. How does this have to do with house prices in 2012?"

Dong Fang Dao speaks, "Before the conference was announced, experts and media guessed: steady growth, structural adjustment and commodity price control while the order is steady growth, commodity price control and structural adjustment after the announcement. Commodity price control moves forward one level in the order. This shows that the commodity price increase in 2012 may still recur at any time. According to the law of currency circulation, the Chinese money supply increased from 45 trillion in October 2008 to 85 trillion in December 2011. The excess 40 trillion of monetary aggregate only used more than three years, and the currency inflation cannot be controlled entirely in 2011. **On the contrary the money supply in 2011 still grows at a 16% growth rate (scheduled) to lead to further inflation in 2012 or later. So the commodity price control will be inevitably the top priority for decision-makers in the next few years.**"

Reporter makes a detailed inquiry: "In case the monetary policy is not eased, how about the economic growth? Whether it is connected with house prices?"

Dong Fang Dao explains, "As a matter of fact the economic growth is not necessarily related to the growth of monetary aggregate. Some local governments and state-owned enterprises, especially speculative-type enterprises, want to catch a whale by throwing a minnow, will always feel that the loans are not enough, viz., they are hard up. Like those speculations for land, real estate and stocks, they borrowed 1 million, also want to borrow 10 million, borrowed 10 million, and also want to borrow 100 million, borrowed 100 million, also want to borrow 1 billion, borrowed 1 billion, and also want to borrow 10 billion, and others so that bank presidents all worship such debtors as gods, and send security guards to major debtors for protecting their personal safety. Today it is a common occurrence. They are none other than these people who are driving the irrational increase of Chinese monetary aggregate. In the event of entity enterprise of independently engaged in production and business activities, they dare not take loans casually, seeing that there is no a good project to generate profit, and the loans increase purely the burden to harm the growth of the enterprise."

"At present Chinese real estate enterprises are essentially speculative, and all want to catch a whale with a minnow by virtue of loans. Likewise house speculators and home-buyers on mortgage, feel that they are out of money, and then there is a voice in the society demanding easy monetary policy, undoubtedly threatened by the sounding slogan of economic growth in order to achieve their respective speculative goals. If this happens, these people are allowed to let their demands, and then the collaboration of internal and external public ownership banks will walk up step by step on the old path of the original KMT hyperinflation. By the moment the whole people will suffer disaster. The fact of Chinese dynasties indicates that it is purely nonsense for economists who held a foreign doctorate consider that the viewpoint of current moderate inflation is beneficial to economic growth. Economic prosperous dynasties in China such as the reign of Emperors Wen and Jing in the Western Han Dynasty, the Zhen Guan control of Emperor Shimin Li, they were the results of attaching great importance to the inflationary management, and applied all moderate deflation."

Chapter 2

Compressing Bubbles with Housing Price Bubble Indexes

In accordance with the *China Housing Development Report (2010-2011)* bulletined by the Chinese Academy of Social Sciences (CASS), it disclosed that their average housing price bubble is 29.5% by the comparative analysis of concentrated transaction prices with regard to ordinary commodity houses in the second-tier urban general lots (including 35 large and medium-sized cities across the country in September 2010).

Herein **top seven cities with the highest bubble index** are respectively: Fuzhou (0.703), Hangzhou (0.669), Nanning (0.668), Qingdao (0.558), Tianjin (0.542), Lanzhou (0.534), and Shijiazhuang (0.520). The bubble component in these cities accounts for more than 50% of the actual price.

Cities with **higher bubble indexes, and bubble component** accounting for 30-50% of **the actual price** include Beijing (0.496), Shenzhen (0.485), Wuhan (0.481), Changchun (0.473), Ningbo (0.444), Harbin (0.417), Dalian (0.400), Guiyang (0.369), Shanghai (0.365), Zhengzhou (0.346), and Chengdu (0.300).

Cities with certain bubbles, and bubble component accounting for 10-30% of the actual price include Nanchang, Jinan, Hefei, Xi'an, Guangzhou, Kunming, Xining, and Changsha.

What is the essence of this report? It maintains virtually the bubble under the cover of exposing the bubble signboard! If you are an office worker in Beijing, Shanghai, Guangzhou or Shenzhen, it is estimated that there will be an indescribable sense of being fooled as looking at such a bubble index ranking. To our surprise all of bubble indexes of the most expensive housing prices in Beijing, Shanghai, Guangzhou and Shenzhen are uniformly in the second echelon of 30-50% and while that of Fuzhou, Nanning, Qingdao, Tianjin and Lanzhou, which were not known before, rank first now. I wonder why these cities are put into the first echelon of bubbles, how do you feel? Isn't it so strange? It turns out that why did largest and highest housing price bubbles of the Beijing, Shanghai, Guangzhou and Shenzhen go backward behind the second-tier cities overnight? Obviously this is wrapped in a profound mystery.

We can't just consider, and believe in the results but must evaluate how their results are calculated. How was the result of CASS calculated? The writer of this part in the report, Dr. Linhua Zou, Doctor of the Institute of Finance and Trade, CASS, said in an interview with the *China Business News* that the index cannot represent the future trend of house prices, and the data is not completely accurate, in any case it has certain guiding significance for market analysis. Linhua Zou introduced that the housing price bubble index here was obtained through a certain calculation procedure. Specifically the bubble index = 1-benchmark price/actual price = (actual price-benchmark price)/actual price, which represents the proportion of price bubbles in actual house prices. For example, the bubble index is 0.5, which indicates that there is a 50% bubble in the actual house price. Taking the value interval of bubble index is between 0 and 1, the larger the bubble index, the larger the bubble component of housing price in the city.

After reading the Dr. Zou's introduction I find that **their method of bubble calculation is worthy of careful consideration**. Their calculation has a presupposition that the bubble index cannot be greater than 1, that is, the bubble should be controlled within 100%. The bubble index calculated like this is extremely not rigorous, and is contrary to the actual situation. For instance, you blow a balloon. The volume of balloon is blown to 1 liter at the start, and then is blown to 2 liters, and unceasingly to 3 liters. What is the expansion rate of the balloon? We use 1 liter as benchmark. When the balloon is blown to 2 liters, the expansion rate of balloon is (2-1)/1 = 100%; when the balloon is blown to 3 liters, the expansion rate is (3-1)/1=200%. Analogously the expansion rate calculated is the bubble index, only in that way is it matter-of-fact, that is to say the bubble index may be both less than and larger than 100%.

Where is the error of CASS report? CASS applies improperly the formula of bubble index= (actual price-benchmark price)/actual price. Considering that there is a benchmark price, **the calculation of bubble expansion rate should use the benchmark price as measurement standard, and be many times on basis of the benchmark price, which only is correct.** It should be bubble index = (actual price-benchmark price)/ benchmark price. In the light of the original calculation method of CASS it is calculated at the Beijing benchmark housing price of 13,316 CNY/m², and the actual price of 26,446 CNY/m², 1-(13316÷26446)×100%=49.6% is the housing price bubble in Beijing while the scientific calculation methodology is (26,446-13,316)/13,316 = 98.6%. Distinctly the latter calculation methodology is more scientific, and is also true.

The calculation error in the CASS report is to use the changing real house price as the denominator or the measurement standard of house prices, which is vividly

conducive to maintaining the housing price bubble. That is to say they admit furtively that rising real house prices are reasonable. In this case what is the significance of benchmark house price so painstakingly calculated? The result calculated like that will severely mislead central governmental monetary control policies, and real estate policies, harming others, and themselves eventually.

Chapter 3

Maintaining Bubbles by the Reduce in New House Supply

I. Two Kinds of Truthful Words with Different Essences

The Voice of http://www.wyzxwk.com: In this morning the National Bureau of Statistics released the Chinese economic and real estate data for 2011. Many net citizens doubt. May I ask Mr. Dong Fang Dao, how do you think about the authenticity of these data? Could you tell your research findings frankly to masses and leaders who are anxious to know the truth?

Dong Fang Dao: Do you want to listen to the real word or adulatory word? If the real word, do you want to hear full or partially?

The Voice of http://www.wyzxwk.com: It is the veritable real word! Is it divided into comprehensive real word, and partial real word?

Dong Fang Dao: Partial real word is to tell people only a part of the true things while hide others. The essence of partial real word is lie. It is a common weapon used by most politicians to fool the people. By way of illustration, blind men touching an elephant, a person who touches an elephant ear says that the elephant is a fan, taking a part for the whole. It is called the partial real word, but the fan and the elephant are completely different in nature.

II. How Many Is Housing Supply in 2012 in the Final Analysis?

The Voice of http://www.wyzxwk.com: Well, please tell full real words about the China real estate in 2012! These are that the people are most eager to know, especially home-buyers.

Dong Fang Dao: I investigated the data published by the National Bureau of Statistics several times. Assuming the data is analyzed alone, it seems to be very authentic, but analyzed comprehensively, and there is inconsistency. Above all one of the most important numbers in 2011 was the total construction area of houses throughout the country, the proclamation of the National Bureau of Statistics stated that the housing construction area of real estate development enterprises nationwide was 5.080 billion m^2, which can't not hold up to closer inspection!

The Voice of http://www.wyzxwk.com: This figure is really of great importance, and relates to the housing supply in 2012! Why it can't hold up to closer inspection?

Dong Fang Dao: This need investigate until 2010 in that the National Statistics Bureau said in the announcement about 2010 that: In 2010 the housing construction area of real estate development enterprises across the country was 4.055 billion m^2, and the completed area of houses was 760 million m^2. That is to say, 4.055-0.760 = 3.295 billion m^2 in 2010 (the prior period of 2011) entered for the continuous construction in 2011, plus the new construction area of 1.901 billion m^2 in 2011. It is concluded that the total construction area in 2011 should be 3.295+1.901=5.196 billion m^2 instead of 5.080 billion m²! Where was the 116 million m² in 2011? There are only two possibilities: One is that someone missed it in statistics, and the other is that fake numbers were reported everywhere. In any wise this is not a small number but a big problem! This 116 million m² will be confused, which will greatly mislead the real estate decision in 2012! In 2011, the total construction area of 5.196 billion m² minus the completion area of 0.892 billion m² is the intertemporal construction area of 4.304 billion m² in 2012.

In case the construction area of 5.196 billion m² is not delayed or suspended, they will be supplied to the market before the end of 2012, minus 1.099 billion m² sold in 2011, and there will be a quasi supply of 4.1 billion m² in 2012 (except for the new construction in 2012). Equivalently about 40 million houses can be built, and put on the market at a suite of 100 m². 160 million persons can live comfortably at four family numbers per suite. How huge this bubble is? On condition that property developers do not slow down or stop construction in 2012, and will bring them to market as scheduled, house prices will fall definitely in 2012. Some of developers postpone and stop construction in 2012, how long can it be delayed and stopped? Isn't it until most of them turn into suspended and abandoned towers? Other bubbles such as the financial bubble in the U.S.A, and the stock market bubble in China burst, that virtual assets disappear merely, having impact largely on individuals, and slightly on the country. Whereas the real estate bubble is different, plays games with money in hard cash and real resources. Like a huge waste in the ghost town of Inner Mongolia, is a crime against the people and the earth, and is unforgivable for our posterity!

The Voice of http://www.wyzxwk.com: Mr. Dong Fang Dao, don't you scare me? Many well-known experts in China believe that there is no bubble in the Chinese real estate. In 2012, 40 million suites of houses were built, including residences, and commercial and office premises. As though they can't be called the bubble broadly?

Dong Fang Dao: In line with the announcement of the National Bureau of Statistics, the housing construction area of real estate development enterprises nationwide was 5.080 billion m², of which residences were 3.88 billion m², office buildings were 160 million m², and commercial and operational houses were 560 million m², namely office buildings, and commercial and operational houses were 720 million m² totally in a small proportion. Except that office buildings cannot live, overwhelming majority of Chinese commercial houses such as shops, are funny architectures of commerce in combination with residences. Almost all residential building properties of Chinese property developers contain a large number of shops. So-called commercial and residential amphibious funny architectures are generally residences on upper floors, and shops on the lower floors. Therefore actually 560 million m² of commercial and operational houses are largely residential but are counted in the area of business houses. It may be almost the same that there are 4.3 billion m² of residential construction area in 2012 because some new house construction in the first half of 2012 can be sold in the second half. In 2012 a 5 billion m² of residential supply will be formed at least. It follows that property developers do not slow down or stop construction in large numbers in 2012, the huge supply comes into the market, which will pose inevitably a severe oversupply.

III. Will Chinese Real Estate Crash?

The Voice of http://www.wyzxwk.com: China is different from foreign countries. Didn't Steven N.S. Cheung affirm that the high housing price bubble is made of "steel" in China, can't it be broken? Did Xianping Lang also express that real estate is the rich investment choice? Is it possible for the Chinese real estate bubble not to burst?

Dong Fang Dao: Don't blindly follow so-called experts and scholars. Mainly you best understand about own economic and investment issues. Only by own independent thought can you get rich. Blindly following experts and scholars is likely to lose own investment principal. For a notable example, when the stock price was around 3000 points in 2011, experts believed that it would grow above 4000 points, and actually fell to 2700 points. Also experts firmly believed that it reduced down to the bottom, and actually kept falling to 2500 points, experts still believed that it reduced the lowest point in history, as a result broke through 2200 points in 2011. In 2011 countless experts preached the stock market had the opportunity so people invested one after another in the stock market, and consequently disappointed greatly. For that reason you have to think independently. It is a rational investment manner. Like some people, who write articles gracefully and profoundly, however strictly speaking, they are not the Chinese, mainly doing business in China. They show off knowledge to Chinese compatriots, who pay some money to them. They are also part of businessmen. Money is your own event in the final analysis. Don't be fooled by anyone whether he is a governmental official or a scholar, and who though seems to be smarter than you.

Besides I now answer your main question earnestly: Is China different from foreign countries, and won't the real estate bubble burst? To be honest there is a possibility that Chinese real estate bubble will not burst in 2012! This involves how the Chinese government and people assess two most important governance goals of GDP and CPI in 2011.

IV. Is the Housing Price Bubble Related to GDP and CPI?

The Voice of http://www.wyzxwk.com: Is the housing price bubble burst in 2012 related to GDP and CPI? Judging from the two data released by the National Bureau of Statistics today it is not only very good, but also excellent! The growth rate of GDP is 9.2, and the CPI drops to 5.4. Is there anything to worry about?

Dong Fang Dao: Seemingly it is precious for rational people to pursue comprehensive authenticity! When the director of the National Bureau of Statistics delivered a speech on TV in a rising and falling cadence but his face was not so natural, and his expression was not so calm, seemingly too solemn. Certainly the director's job may not be easy. Rongji Zhu warned formerly, we cannot make fake accounts since he knew that doing fake accounts will be a real headache for accountants. An artful fake account is to make only part of the veritable account, and another part is not recorded into accounts.

Regarding the 2011 GDP and CPI, the director's original words were: According to preliminary estimates, the annual GDP was CNY 47.156.4 trillion and the year-on-year growth was 9.2% at comparable prices, and others. The year-on-year growth of annual CPI was 5.4%. The director tells the people about these key data in this pattern, and visibly there is something debatable.

Firstly the annual GDP of CNY 47 trillion should be nominal GDP considering that CNY 47 trillion is educed by the measurement of current price in 2011, and is nominal, not actual. He should tell the people strictly according to the fact;

Secondly he connected immediately that "the year-on-year growth was 9.2% at comparable prices" after this sentence. This sentence is so sudden that many people, even economists and famous scholars believe mistakenly that the year-on-year growth rate of nominal GDP was 9.2%. Some well-known experts, including someone, Mr. Lang, also thought that it was the nominal GDP growth rate announced regularly in the past. In a TV show, Mr. Lang once suggested that this growth rate should deduct the inflation rate. In reality they have not figured it out, and the year-on-year growth of 9.2% at comparable prices refers to the growth rate of real GDP.

What was the actual GDP data in 2011 and 2010? The National Bureau of Statistics has never directly disclosed it. Their website published indirectly GDP anyway. Under this index anyone can calculate the annual practical GDP value, and further calculate the practical CPI index.

V. Burst of Housing Price Bubble Depends on Whether the Government Faces up to Currency Inflation

The Voice of http://www.wyzxwk.com: Mr. Dong Fang Dao, your research is so fruitful. The first time I hear, and it enlightens the benighted! Is it related to whether the Chinese housing price bubble breaks in 2012 on all accounts?

Dong Fang Dao: In fact I already have told you the answer! On the basis of the sales of national commercial houses of CNY 5.9 trillion in 2011, sales area of 1.1 billion m^2, and the average price of CNY 5,374 per square meter, allowing that the price is not reduced, it will cost CNY 22 trillion to sell 4.1 billion m^2 in 2012. The authority considers that all the houses are sold based on 70% of the loans, and CNY 15 trillion overprinted, and over-issued will be enough as long as the inflation rate can be controlled in next few years.

Provided local governmental officials and property developers collude with banks to ease monetary policy, two or three decades of loans of the majority of house slaves can be converted absolutely into CNY deposits in moneybags of a few people by the "tool" of commercial houses, and then converted into US dollar assets to splurge abroad.

Presuming China government can regard the currency inflation as exploitation for ordinary people, and the growth rate of money supply should be kept firmly within 3% like the U.S. government, and European countries. The government would rather borrow debt than dare not categorically money over-issuance. The Chinese real estate bubble is bound to squeeze out in some time like so. Currently relevant documents of central government focus on the transformation of development mode, to put it bluntly, the money is utilized to develop other substantial industries. However whether this transformation of development mode can be implemented in practice, the people have to doubt because the Chinese government has changed the development mode since the 1990s but has not succeeded 20 years later. We can only wait, and see what happens in the future.

Chapter 4

How to Analyze Prices with Economic Tools

What is the trend of house prices in the Chinese future? This problem will trigger definitely the majority of home-buyers to toss and turn, puzzling over. In China, to answer this question must learn three aspects of knowledge:

First, documents of the Central Government and the State Council,

Second, the central bank monetary policy,

Third, the local supply and demand relation

This knowledge is the foundation for judging the future trend of house prices (also known as share price). At this critical moment when the house transaction volume plummets, and house prices are currently locked in a stalemate, let's analyze the standpoint from some famous professionals at first.

I. Two Typical Standpoints on Future Housing Prices

On May 19, 2011 Lujiazui Shanghai held a forum where experts and senior governmental officials from various fields gathered to reveal some momentous information. Therein views of the notable economist Mr. Guozhong Xie, in his dialogue with Sina Finance at the Lujiazui Finance Forum, expressed: House prices will fall by 25% at the end of this year, and by 40-50% in three years. At all events the bank risk is not large for the decline in house prices on the grounds that the valuation of Bank of China project loans is only lower than a half of actual value. Even if house prices fall by 50%, banks can still survive the risk. This is an opinion.

However Mr. Guozhong Xie's opinion was immediately opposed by someone, Mr. Ren, a famous real estate developer and expert in China. Mr. Ren responded in a lecture at Fudan University, "This Jinx talks on forever (the house price is going to fall), and what he said was not realized in the end. The reason is that he always revolves around the real estate bubble instead of analyzing the relation between supply and demand. In the case of economic rise I have never seen the downward trend of real estate market in such countries. Chinese economy maintains a high growth rate of above 9%. Under this background, it is unrealistic to fall housing prices".

II. Nuances of Two Housing Price Views

One opinion is that house prices will fall by 25%, and plummet by 50% in three years from Mr. Guozhong Xie. The other opinion is that it is unrealistic to fall housing prices from Mr. Ren. They are diametrically opposed. Who is right in the final analysis? We need distinguish carefully. This actually involves in two levels of problems:

The first is whether house prices should reduce, namely, how should the house price develop?

The second is whether house prices will reduce, namely, how will the house price develop?

Two problems with different characters are precisely economists' mission. When economist studies how an economic problem will develop, his identity is the character of so-called scientist. When economist answers how an economic question should develop, his identity is the character of policy consultant. However there are many disputes in the Chinese real estate industry in chaos, there is not a consensual opinion at all, and it is unable to decide which is right. In truth these two problems with different natures are not distinguished. The primary cause is that when economists aired their opinions, two problems of different natures were neither expressed separately, and the majority of net citizens nor distinguished two problems.

We carefully investigate Mr. Guozhong Xie's opinion. Primarily house prices should fall by 25% at the end of this year, and by 50% within three years, and the reason that banks can still survive the risk. In other words, how should the house price develop? How should the problem be, which is moral, and is a proposal to the government based on the interest of entire economy or interest groups. We now carefully investigate Mr. Ren's opinion. Actually how will the house price develop, from the aspect he made a conclusion, that is he believes that the Chinese economy maintains a high growth rate of above 9%. Under this background it is impossible to fall house prices.

How should the house price develop, and how will the house price develop? These two problems must be distinguished, otherwise each says he is right, and there is much to be said on both sides. For all the world it is not so easy to distinguish in the practical supply-demand or purchase-sale relationship. How should the price develop often affects how will the price develop, and vice versa. In order to let the people all over the world for the first time in human history investigate the difference, and connection between these two issues economically, Mr. Dong Fang Dao now walks in the street to tell dear readers some amazing discoveries with a shoe shine as an example.

III. Connection between How Should and How Will the Price Develop

One day in May 2011, Mr. Dong Fang Dao took a walk on the street in the bright early summer. He was stop-and-go along the streets and alleys whenever he met peddlers, asked prices, and met shoe-shining women as usual on the corner of sidewalk. There are a great many of these women in southern cities wandering the streets and alleys, almost forming an industry. When your shoes are dirty in northern cities, you can't find a shoe shiner on the street; you can only go home, and polish them by yourself.

When Mr. Dong Fang Dao was about to pass by two middle-aged, shoe-shining women sitting on the stool, heard a familiar hello. "May I ask, do you need your shoes shined?"

Mr. Dong Fang Dao stopped and asked, "How much?"

The shoe-shining woman replied, "Two yuan."

Mr. Dong Fang Dao sat on the stool opposite her, and fixed the shoe of his left foot on her shoe-shining workbench. The woman then started the shining procedure: Cleaning, waxing, and polishing. Taking advantage of his free time, Mr. Dong Fang Dao brought the problem of price confusion to this aunt in her fifties, "Wasn't the original shoe shining price one yuan? Why is the price two yuan now?"

"The price rose to two yuan in 2009," the woman replied.

"Why did it rise to two yuan the year before last?" Mr. Dong Fang Dao asked.

"Since rent, rice, and vegetable prices have all risen!" the woman quickly replied, as she shook a small piece of shoe polish in her hand,

"One piece of shoe polish used to cost only a few yuan but now it has risen to more than ten yuan. If the price was still one yuan, we would not be profitable. The money we would make shining a pair of shoes wouldn't buy us a handful of the cheapest vegetables."

Mr. Dong Fang Dao was lost in thought hearing of her answer: The currency inflation is converting into the rise of commodity prices, and spreading to daily necessities. In the last quarter of 2008, in order to rescue the so-called GDP, the Chinese central bank continuously cut down the interest rate and deposit reserve ratio, and waived 5% interest tax, the so-called three-rate drop. The market began to be flooded with liquidity. However it was unexpected that the currency inflation was leapt and uncontrollable. M2 surged from CNY 45 trillion in October 2008 to about CNY 76 trillion at the end of April 2011. An increase of full CNY 30 trillion made the Chinese monetary stock the highest in the world. In fact the currency inflation had already been transmitted to rising commodity prices in 2009. Contrary the relevant statistical data resulted in a negative CPI due to the unreasonable classification of statistical objects, various unrealistic proportions, and an unscientific on-site enquiry for all kinds of commodities. That is, the commodity price soared broadly in reality however the data of the National Bureau of Statistics indicated the general decline. It is such a puzzling consequence.

"Hey, your shoes are finished!" The shoe-shining woman yelled, waking Mr. Dong Fang Dao out of contemplation. Mr. Dong Fang Dao handed over two yuan while asking curiously,

"Since the commodity price has added so much, why don't you shoe-shining women join hands, and raise the price to three yuan? Can't you make more money?"

The shoe-shining woman listened to Mr. Dong Fang Dao's question and laughed, "You are really interesting, people think two yuan expensive, and how can we add the price to three yuan? Last year a young man's shoes were polished, and I asked him two yuan, he not only refused to pay, instead wanted to beat me, saying that we were profiteering, and then he swaggered off. So the price should not be too expensive!" Her answer **touched** deeply Mr. Dong Fang Dao.

Let us now investigate the economic significance of shoe shine, namely how prices are structured. First of all the price of shoe shine service has risen from one to two yuan since 2009, which is a question of how will the price develop, or the price will run according to objective laws. Why does the price of shoe shine double? The law is as follows, the producer cost rose. Why did the production cost of shoe-shining women rise? As prices of her rent, rice, oil and vegetables, including shoe polish all rose. This matter is very complicated, and will be detailed later. This is the first question of shine business, i.e., the so-called scientific attribute that the price will rise to two yuan.

The shoe-shining transaction actually involves another question, namely, how should the shoe-shining price develop. When Mr. Dong Fang Dao asked why the shoe-shining women did not jointly monopolize the price to three yuan, actually the shoe-shining women gave an excellent answer: Ethics don't allow! Therefore **in the formation of every price, the relationship between supply and demand is one of determinants but morality is also one of the important factors that determine the specific price.**

Today Mr. Dong Fang Dao presents a **brand new** economic concept for the first time worldwide: **The relationship between supply and demand determines the gross price of commodity, and the moral factor of buyers and sellers determines the specific price of commodity. It is authentically incontestable for the whole theory of price formation.** For all commodities clearly marked price, the real price is more likely to be determined by the relationship between supply and demand.

For all commodities are not clearly marked price, the specific price is more likely to be determined by moral factors. Just that goods and services are not marked price, the price is hidden in the seller mind, and can only depend on the seller's conscience on the premise of the buyer without experiences.

The shoe-shining woman is unwilling to increase the price to three yuan as she cares about the buyer's evaluation on her except for craving money under her conscience constraint. In effect, suppose they monopolize together a certain area, the price can be raised sufficiently to three yuan. Although after rising to three yuan, some buyers will abandon the shoe shine in this market or turn to other low-price areas, for those eager to the shoe shine, it is also worth three yuan. Shoe-shining women are reluctant to ask for three yuan because on the one hand there is competition from the supply side, and on the other hand her ethics do not allow price discrimination. It is evident that the formation of prices, including some commodities clearly marked price, is determined on the one hand by the relationship between supply and demand, and on the other hand by the moral cultivation. For example, the Chinese people often honor integrity management, no imposition on child and the elderly, and a century-old shop, which practically sellers' quality and prices are restricted by the moral philosophy. **This theory of Mr. Dong Fang Dao shocked the world combines exactly and perfectly with the market principle in the *Wealth of Nations*, and the moral principle in the *Theory of Moral Sentiments* of Adam Smith to hence open up a brand new field of economics.**

We have now discovered the momentous theory of price formation: The relationship between supply and demand determines the gross price, and moral factors determine the specific price in respect of goods and services. Once this great law of price formation is appreciated, various strange price phenomena can easily be comprehended, and grasped.

IV. Analyzing House Price Tend by Supply-Demand Relationship

We once more return to the price of Chinese commercial houses. Mr. Ren discussed that the price of commercial houses will not fall. His evaluation is from the perspective of so-called economic development trend, which is the question of how will house prices be while Mr. Guozhong Xie evaluation starts from that rising or flat house prices are not conducive to the Chinese economic development, which is the question of how should house prices be. Mr. Ren expounds the relationship between supply-demand and price while Mr. Xie illuminates the relationship between moral and price. At the moment it is much easier for us to analyze their right and wrong under the guidance of new price formation theory.

Above all, apart from the impact of ethics on house prices, we analyze the trend of Chinese housing prices merely from the relationship between supply and demand in the future. It is not easy to analyze the trend of one economic price.

In the first place prices of goods and services are measured by money. More specifically tens of thousands of commodities in supermarkets are marked a specific amount with price tag. Only on the premise of the steady monetary aggregate in one economic entity can we more accurately analyze, and calculate the impact of supply and demand two sides on the price of goods and services. It is inconceivable to analyze the influence of supply-demand relation on prices without this essential premise;

In the second place on the premise of the steady monetary aggregate in one economic entity, changes in supply or

demand have nine different consequential effects on the price, and quantity of goods and services. It is often said that supply exceeds demand, including two formalizations: 1. Supply increases and demand remains unchanged; and 2. Supply increases and demand decreases. The effect of oversupply makes prices decline. What it is often said that supply is less than demand (that is, demand exceeds supply), the price increases, also including two formalizations: 1. Supply reduces and demand remains unchanged; and 2. Supply reduces and demand increases. Namely supply is less than demand that determines the price increase;

In the third place we need further analyze the specific reason that affects the change in supply volume and demand volume. The reason that affects the increase or decrease in **supply volume** generally includes: 1. Price; 2. Cost, i.e., the input price in supply side; 3. Technological progress; 4. Increase and decrease in the number of sellers; and 5. Expectation, i.e., the psychological evaluation for future prices. The reason that affects the increase or decrease in **demand volume** generally includes: 1. Price; 2. Buyer's income; 3. Prices of relevant items; 4. Hobby, viz., preference; 5. Increase or decrease in the number of buyers; and 6. Expectation, i.e., the psychological evaluation of the buyer for future prices. To analyze the future trend of house prices, we must first determine the specific factor that affects the change in supply volume or demand volume so that we can calculate a more accurate consequence of rise or fall in house prices.

A person who analyzes the trend of prices cannot break away from the analysis of these variables that affect supply or demand. In particular it should be noted that **the effect of price on demand volume or supply volume** has a certain premise, that is to say, i.e., other conditions remain unchanged such as other five factors that affect demand volume remain unchanged, and other four factors that affect supply volume remain unchanged. Only on such premise do prices and quantities change along the demand curve or supply curve. The impact of factors other than price on demand or supply will lead to the shift of supply and demand curves. It is a very significant expertise. Steven N.S. Cheung also mentioned this in his blog posts. Almost all the experts in China currently do not distinguish the character of variables to make irresponsible remarks in analysis prices anyway. Especially some stock analysts take nearly nonsense. Therefore the former Prime Minister Zhu after retirement said that some news every day is nonsense. It makes sense.

Now we have the elementary knowledge of how supply and demand determine prices, and what factors affect the supply volume and demand volume, we feel so mysterious about the ever-changing price phenomena no longer, and need not obey blindly the so-called expert price analysis. The reason why millions of net friends follow blindly the nonsense of those experts is that they lack economic common sense. You will not be deceived, and will even be able to debunk those lies in a timely manner without losing everything provided learn some common sense. It is now active. We use these tools to analyze the trend of house prices this year and next year.

First and foremost we analyze the recent change in supply volumes of commercial houses. Among five factors that affect the change in supply volume: 1. Price; 2. Cost, i.e., the input price in supply side; 3. Technological progress; 4. Increase and decrease in the number of sellers; and 5. Expectation, i.e., the psychological evaluation for future prices. We just now need to find out the factor that affects the change in supply volumes. The third and fourth factors: Technological progress and the number of sellers can be excluded on the grounds that there is no major change in the production technology of houses and the number of property developers, which is similar to that over the years. Midst other three factors, price is the most influential factor on the supply volume of commercial houses, such as the price of commercial houses soared in 2010 that led to the increase in supply volumes.

Let us first review the increase in supply volume of commercial houses due to price rise across the country in 2010. According to the data of the *National Real Estate Market Operation in 2010* by the National Bureau of Statistics, in 2010 the housing construction area of national real estate development enterprises, new housing construction area, as-built area of houses and as-built area of residences were 4.055 billion m^2, 1.638 billion m^2, 760 million m^2, and 612 million m^2 at year-on-year growth rates of 26.6%, 40.7%, 4.5% and 2.7% respectively. **What does this data indicate?** This shows that the supply volume would boom inevitably, and the year-on-year growth rate was 26.6% in the process of rising house prices. The quasi-total supply reached 4.06 billion m^2 minus 760 million m^2 of as-built area at the end of 2010, and there will be a supply of 3.3 billion m^2 to the market in the second half of 2011 according to the main work construction cycle of one and a half years. This excludes the newly increased construction area in 2011 now that the supply volume in 2012 can only be affected according to the infrastructure cycle in case of neither illegal sales nor presale, apart from that.

Then we estimate preliminary the supply volume of commercial houses before the end of December 2011. The first algorithm is that the 4.06 billion m^2 under construction in 2010 will be all completed or available for sale before the end of December 2011. The new increase in supply volume will be 4.06 billion m^2 by the end of December 2011. It has certain basis in that 1.04 billion m^2 were sold in 2010, and can be regarded as the stock houses in 2008 and 2009. The second algorithm is that the 760 million m² all completed in 2010 was sold, and the supply volume in 2011 also is 3.3 billion m². This is a relatively conservative figure in respect of newly added supply volume, and is the visible supply volume of property developers. Even if it is calculated according to the largest sales area in 2010, the annual sales volume should be the order of 1 billion m², and it will take 3.3 years to sell out the supply volume formed by the construction in 2010. Suppose the supply volume was 4.06 billion m², it will take 4.1 years to sell out these area increments in consideration of that sales in 2010 hold the line in 2011, and the construction area increments in 2011 will not be presold. This huge increase in supply volume is mainly spurred by price rise, and the expectation of property developers that Chinese housing price can only increase. Sudden huge profits are generated compared to own funds. Property developers will not consider too much about the project at the cost of about CNY 1,000 per square meter with regard to the low-income housing construction. In a word there are two reasons for the huge increase in the supply volume of commercial houses: One is the price increase, and the supply volume increases significantly along the supply curve; the other is the expectation of property developer, which causes the supply curve to shift to the right. This is a specific analysis about supply volume.

In hot pursuit we analyze the demand volume for commercial houses in 2011. As mentioned earlier, the influential reason on the increase or decrease in demand volume includes generally: 1. Price; 2. Buyer's income; 3. Prices of relevant items; 4. Hobby, viz., preference; 5. Increase or decrease in the number of buyers; and 6. Expectation, i.e., the psychological evaluation of the buyer for future prices. Among five factors that affect the demand volume, the buyer's income (2), and prices of relevant items such as rental (3) currently have little effect on the demand volume, which is similar to that last year apart from that. Primary influential factors on demand include: 1. Price; 4. Hobby; 5. Number of buyers; and 6. Expectation, i.e., the psychological evaluation of the buyer for future prices.

At present we analyze the demand volume for commercial houses in 2011 since the regulation and control of the new *Eight National Clauses*. According to the data in the *Operation of the National Real Estate Market from January to April* from the National Bureau of Statistics, the sales area of commercial houses was 234 million m² nationwide from January to April. At this rate, approximately 700 million m² can be sold in 2011.

The data from 2010 to 2011 is synthesized from the National Bureau of Statistics. It can be found that in 2010 the construction of 3.3 billion m² of commercial houses was postponed to 2011 while the data in April showed that the construction area was 2.646 billion m², the construction area in April minus the new construction area of 457 million m² is the old construction area of about 2.2 billion m². **By the end of April the as-built actual area was 1.1 billion m².** Before the end of 2011 the construction area of 3.3 billion m² last year can be thoroughly completed, and enter the market at this progress rate.

So, how long can the supply volume of 3.3 billion m² in 2011 be sold out? It is calculated according to the **700 million m² sold in 2011, and it will take nearly five years to sell out.** In addition the new *Eight National Clauses* for this year stipulates that 10 million suites of indemnificatory apartments shall be completed in various regions. There are construction areas of 900 million m² by 90 m² per suite.

We this moment calculate how much it would cost suppose all 3.3 billion m² were sold out. According to the data in January-April 2011, the sales area of commercial houses nationwide was

CNY 234 million m², and the sales value was CNY 1.24 trillion. The average price is about CNY 5,300 per square meter by computation. It needs taking CNY 17.5 trillion (3.3 billion m² x about CNY 5,300 per square meter) to sell out. The trouble is where does the money come from? This **supply and demand relationship of commercial houses is that: The annual supply volume is 3.3 billion m², and the annual demand volume is 700 million m².**

However only "on the premise of the steady monetary aggregate in an economy" are these analyses meaningful, that is, only when the growth rate of money supply is less than 3% is it valuable. For the growth rate of the money supply is more than 15%, this analysis of supply and demand is of little value. Because on the premise of a large amount of money injected into the economy, all prices are chaotic, and the analysis of supply and demand does not matter.

Chapter 5

How the Government Maintains
High Prices by Monopoly

Prices of all commercial houses in China contain unreasonable element. It is unreasonable for the poor without indemnificatory apartments, the middle class buying high price houses, and the rich buying high-end houses. All prices contain unreasonable element, and any house price or price per square meter is unreasonable. All their secrets are contained in **monopoly**. Only by destroying the monopoly market and in a freely competitive market can there be reasonable prices for the people. In case someone wants to make a fortune immediately, he will have nothing but two tricks: The first is to rob, and the second is to create monopoly.

There is no other than two ruses to monopolize a market: One is to monopolize resources; the other is governmental regulation. Resource monopoly reflected in real estate is the land monopoly of local governments. This is an extremely ugly phenomenon due to reverse brazenly the historical trend considering that the goals of the *Fourteenth National Congress of the Communist Party of China* was to establish the socialist market economic system, train numerous producers, suppliers and buyers of the market to allocate rationally resources through price signals. Resources are allocated by the market rather than the mayor. On all accounts Two Laws and One Document are used to force all land to be sold merely to local governments, and everyone can only purchase land from local governments in China. Such local governmental behavior forcefully buys, and alone sells, that is, the phenomenon that there is mere one seller in the land market is called monopoly.

(Note: The author first appealed against the local government monopoly on land transaction. Decade later, the Chinese government finally agreed in February 2019 that the rural operational construction land can freely enter the land market, which broke initially the situation of governmental monopoly on land.)

Someone makes an excuse for monopoly: The local government taxation is taken away by the central government, and local finances lack revenue so they have to buy land. However this excuse not only is a ridiculous, but also violates the *Constitution*. If you can find an excuse to violate undisguisedly the *Constitution* for some reason, then this society will have too many absurd excuses. **Corporatization operation of local governments**, and land transaction for profit is a forever strange tale all over the world. Even the Yamen of feudal society would not forcefully buy, and monopolistically sell the farmer land. **After the land monopoly, a city has nothing but one price, that is, each mayor sets the price.** Three plots are supplied at three different unit land prices, two plots are supplied at two different unit land prices, and one plot is supplied at one unit land price which varies monthly. The result of controlling land prices is achieved by controlling land supply, this is monopoly. Monopolist also rater can price land. Hence all suppliers are just price acceptors in a competitive market. This is the root cause of high land prices in China.

Another reason for monopoly is a governmental regulation. It is not enough to merely monopolize the land because the land belongs to various economic entities, citizens, and farmers, who have own land before the monopoly, as long as they wanted, houses could be built on their own land at any time so that the purpose of monopolistic land and making a million immediately will not be achieved. Correspondingly government control countermeasures are introduced to create the monopoly on the supply of commercial houses. These countermeasures stipulated that enterprise shall not build secretly houses to distribute to its own employees, and raise funds or cooperate to build houses. If not, the local government will not approve the Land Use Certificate or the Property Ownership Certificate. Previously every enterprise may build houses, and can obtain Property Ownership Certificates. After the monopoly, houses can merely be supplied by the property developer. Without doubt local government agencies can raise funds to build houses without self-monopoly. Like this the supply of all houses in a city is monopolized by a few property developers.

Property developers are also monopolized. It is impossible that everyone wants to be a property developer. Property developers become a scarce profession under the government regulation. First of all many people do not have a registered capital about CNY 8 million; secondly, even if such a development company is registered, you cannot become a property developer just that you can't buy the land for building houses at all. You may find a lot of information on land sales but the purchaser of those lands has been already decided at the higher level but not officially announced; in the end, even if a plot of land is obtained, you can never start work or build houses without the permission of relevant departments. Some people grumble over that you needs to obtain 115 stamps for approval before and after the land may only be used to build houses. Observably, all sorts of such regulations lead the supply of commercial houses into the monopoly.

Also property developers monopolize the quantity of commercial housing supply, just like squeezing toothpaste over and over again, supply volume always is kept less than demand volume to maximize prices. The monopoly of property developer stems from regulations to them so they hide the supply volume to prevent buyers from the discovery of veritable quantity. Providing you go to the wet market one day to buy vegetables, and there are only three cabbages in the whole market (the rest are hidden), you must buy three cabbages in a hurry in spite of triple price. The behavior of creating supply panic by hiding effective supply volume is a monopoly supply, from the measure of which, every property developer commits a crime. Raising prices and depriving the huge wealth of the poor, the middle-class, and the rich result in unaffordable medical expenditure, and tuition fee of many families, worrying about mortgages all day long. It is an enormous sin. This is not as a consequence of any market but the secondary monopoly of property developers under the governmental monopoly.

However this indirect monopoly is still the most chilling. Since the housing system was reformed in 1994, a series of State Council documents have all required the construction of indemnificatory apartments, videlicet, affordable houses and low-rent houses, in order to meet the people's reasonable dwelling demand. These documents also stipulated that in case the house price is too high, the employer should give housing subsidies. However the local government does not fulfill the agreement, provide or rarely provide indemnificatory apartments and the employer does not subsidize the staff to buy houses. For this reason the more the young people is increasing later, the less they have houses, the more they can not afford houses. Thus property developers monopolize indirectly all markets.

Residence is for dwelling, not for speculation. The government should provide unconditionally adequate indemnificatory apartments, and fulfill the agreement in the document.

(Notes: This article had a huge impact after the author published in http://blog.sina.com.cn/jylw in China 2011. Residence is for dwelling, not for speculation, which now becomes the most common and authoritative governance slogan of the Chinese government. They also absorbed the purchase restriction proposal provided by Mr. Dong Fang Dao, and initially controlled the scale of the real estate market, thereby house prices are stabilized, and the real estate bubble does not burst. In this regard China is more successful than all Western countries seeing that the Chinese government has been good at listening to the people's opinions in recent years, and immediately implements in the form of policy. Similarly in the response to the COVID-19 epidemic situation in 2020, as soon as finds something is wrong the Chinese government will replace immediately main local leaders. They formulate the correct countermeasure after listen to the people's opinions. This may be the reason why China has become powerful in recent years. With regard to the opposition like Fang Fang, the government will be tolerant under the special context because the government wants to give disobedient bureaucrats a lesson by virtue of her opposition. The Author added supplementary notes in May 2020.)

Chapter 6

Warning of Modern War on Real Estate Bubble

Humankind cannot avoid life from being invaded by natural disasters but can avoid congener inroads. Therefore humankind invented a civilization method that stipulates that everyone's life enjoys certain rights, and no matter who you are, you shall not infringe these rights to protect the congener life and dignity. Regarding Libya in the midst of civil war, Muammar Muhammad Abu Minyar al-Qadhafi authorities on one side, revolutionary masses on the other side, multinational allied forces on the third party, which "interfere in the internal affairs", as a matter of fact, who is right on behalf of justice, the Chinese are arguing inextricably. It is by no means what the matter is with the world that can't tell right from wrong, only starting from the fact, and using conscience as a guarantee can right and wrong be differentiated.

I. United Nations Information on the Libyan War

Supposing, it does not seem to distinguish difficultly justice and evil on the Libyan battlefield from respecting human life and conscience. We don't need much information and evidence. The information posted on the United Nations website should be credible in that China is also its important member. Concerning the Libyan War the United Nations website says,

1. The Cause of the War Was That the Qadhafi Authority Suppressed the Mass' Peaceful Demonstrations by Force to Commit Crimes against Humanity.

Original text in the website: Since February 15, 2011, the armed conflict in Libya, a North African country, has continued to escalate, and then United Nations interventions have also increased. On February 26, the United Nations Security Council unanimously passed a resolution expressing severe concern about the current situation in Libya, and decided to impose tough sanctions on Libya. Meanwhile in accordance with the authorization of the United Nations Security Council, the Chief Prosecutor of the International Criminal Court, Ocampo announced at the Hague headquarters in the Netherlands on March 3 that the crime against humanity that may be committed by the Gaddafi authority to suppress the mass' peaceful demonstrations by force will be officially filed, and investigated thoroughly from today. The United Nations General Assembly convened a plenary meeting on March 1, and adopted a draft resolution to cancel temporarily the Libyan membership in the Human Rights Council.

As the Libyan Gaddafi regime failed to comply with the sanction resolution passed by the United Nations Security Council last month, it continued to suppress civilian protests by force, and gradually gained the upper hand in the process of confronting anti-government forces. The United Nations Security Council passed again a resolution on March 17, imposing a flight ban on Libya driven by countries such as Arab countries, the United States, the United Kingdom, and France.

Secretary-General Ban Ki-moon urged the Libyan government to stop immediately the violence, and guarantee the people's basic human rights. He indicated that actions of the Libyan regime violated severely the *International Human Rights Law* and *Humanitarian Law* were unacceptable. Concurrently he also pointed out that revolution must be initiated within Libya. On March 6 Ban Ki-moon appointed the former Jordanian Foreign Minister Khatib as a special envoy to mediate the Libyan crisis.

2. Multinational Coalition Forces Air Strikes against the Qadhafi Authoritative Army Authorized by the No. 1973 Resolution by the United Nations Security Council

Original text in the website: On March 12 the League of Arab States passed a resolution calling on the United Nations Security Council to ban immediately the Libyan military aircraft, and establish a safe zone in the bombed area. On March 17 the United Nations Security Council adopted the No. 1973 Resolution, decided to impose the flight ban on Libya, demanded that the Gaddafi regime to cease fire immediately, and authorized all necessary measures to protect civilians and their dwelling districts from the threat of armed attacks.

On March 17 the United States, France, the United Kingdom, Denmark, Italy, Canada, Belgium, Spain, Qatar, Norway, the United Arab Emirates, and other countries notified the Secretary-General that military measures would be taken to enforce the No. 1973 Resolution to protect civilians, and their dwelling districts under potential attacks in Libya.

On March 19 the United States, France and the United Kingdom annunciated that they had started to take measures for the authorization of No. 1973 Resolution constituted on that day: aircraft was utilized to prohibit all flights in the Libyan airspace; when necessary, preventing armed forces that may attack civilians, including armored vehicles.

On March 23 <u>France</u> and <u>the United Kingdom</u> notified respectively that further actions carried out under the authorization of No. 1973 Resolution by the United Nations Security Council since March 19.

II. From the Information Disclosure of the United Nations, We Can Conclude on the Libyan War

1. The imposition of Severe Sanctions on Libya is the Resolution adopted unanimously by the United Nations Security Council, including Severe Sanctions against Libya passed unanimously on February 26, and the Resolution passed again to enforce the flight ban on Libya on March 17. China as a permanent member of the United Nations Security Council, now that China has participated in sanction resolutions by the United Nations Security Council against Libya, China should obey the collective decision of the United Nations Security Council to establish the Chinese prestige in the United Nations as a major power. This reason is easy to understand. For instance, 9 leaders in one economic entity vote on something, and pass finally a resolution by the ratio of 5 to 4. After the resolution comes into effect, 4 opponents should support the implementation of resolution because all resolutions cannot be agreed by everyone, and vote can only be in line with a principle of the minority subordinate to the majority. The resolution was passed in accordance with the principle, and the minority should also maintain the legitimacy of resolution. Only like this can human civilization and rationality be reflected.

Suppose after the resolution is passed, the minority criticizes irresponsibly, and obstructs vigorously the resolution, the cultivation of minority will be doubted. On the grounds that the minority has violated its own established rules, contradicts oneself, and will not be trusted by others. In this point anyone who has participated in the resolution of meeting should be easy to appreciate. The same is true of the United Nations Security Council, where several people have a meeting for resolution nothing but those people on behalf of different countries. In this case I think that our country representatives participated in this resolution of the United Nations Security Council, our people should recognize the legitimacy of this resolution, and respect those who implement the resolution in order to reflect the national honest cultivation of great power among the people around the world.

2. The reason why the United Nations Security Council passed the sanction resolution is that the Qadhafi authority cracked down on the mass' peaceful demonstrations because Qadhafi authorities did not obey the advice of the United Nations Security Council, and continued to suppress masses. The United Nations General Assembly convened a plenary meeting on March 1, and adopted the Draft Resolution to cancel temporarily the Libyan membership in the Human Rights Council. Secretary-General Ban Ki-moon urged the Libyan government to stop immediately the violence, and guarantee the people's basic human rights. He indicated that the action of Libyan regime violated severely the *International Human Rights Law*, and *Humanitarian Law* was unacceptable. From the plenary session of the United Nations General Assembly convened to the Secretary-General Ban Ki-moon's condemnation against the Libyan authority, it can be clearly shown that the Qadhafi authority is the unjust side, and the opposition against the Qadhafi authority is the righteous side.

3. Multinational coalition forces carried out further air strikes against the Qadhafi authoritative army, and weapons authorized by the No. 1973 Resolution of the United Nations

Security Council. Supposing no one performed after the Security Council passed the Resolution, where is the prestige of the Security Council? In the future the Security Council will not have to pass any resolution, and even will not be necessary. Moreover China joining the Security Council has little practical effect. Who would be interested in an organization that passed but did not fulfill the resolution? Is the time wasted? China may not participate in the action of multinational coalition forces but some radical Chinese people say that the multinational coalition forces air strikes on the Qadhafi's army are conspiracy to oil or robber incursion. It is not accurate. That being said, others will pay no attention to. If the action of the multinational coalition forces is not authorized by the United Nations Security Council, they should be regarded as aggression. They have been authorized by the Security Council, and are still regarded as aggression. China has participated in the resolution of Security Council that is China actually has also passed the multinational coalition forces authorized by the Security Council. At the moment the subject of the aggression is not the multinational coalition force but the United Nations Security Council. The key is only whether the United Nations Security Council is illegal or is the headquarters of robbers.

III. Consequent Prediction of Qadhafi Regime

Qadhafi led the revolutionary army more than 40 years ago to defeat the Libyan emperor, and also has been in power alone for 40 years. According to some reports from www.ifeng.com, as long as some people in Libya make a fortune or make their enterprise larger, the Qadhafi family members will nationalize them in the name of "public or national interest." After being nationalized, they often fall into the possession of the Qadhafi family at all risks. According to other information, the opposition called Qadhafi as a lunatic and an abnormal person, and complained about Qadhafi who did not allow anyone in Libya to be better than him as if Libya had only himself.

After air strikes on Libya authorized by the U.N. Security Council, the nature of the war has fundamentally changed. Up till now, the opposition occupies 16 cities in Libya while the Qadhafi authority only occupies 11 cities. The opposition is attacking the cities occupied by the authority along the southern coast of the Mediterranean from the east while the southern cities of Qadhafi authorities have long been occupied by the opposition. The war situation is very unfavorable to the Qadhafi. To the west is the new Tunisian regime, to the south is the opposition blockade, to the east is the front attack of the opposition, and to the north is the warcraft of the multinational coalition forces over the Mediterranean. At present the multinational coalition forces and the opposition have formed a firm encirclement against the Qadhafi power. The author predicts that **the war in Libya will end with the victory of the opposition within a few months. Just now** military vehicles and fighter jets of the Qadhafi Army have been destroyed by missiles. What else can they use for fight? The outcome is likely for the Qadhafi's family members and cronies on the road to exile, and Qadhafi to die in battle.

IV. Warning of the Libyan War on Chinese Real Estate

This new-style war in Libya has a profound warning significance for the Chinese urbanization, especially for the real estate industry. This multinational coalition battle is qualitatively different from history. The strategy adopted by the multinational coalition forces is to attack only the key targets of the other's pivotal cities without mobilizing ground troops. This is a very clever tactic. In remote places, missiles and fighters are used to attack specifically the other's battle weapons so that the combat power of the other party is quickly disintegrated. Since modern warfare is mostly a war of high-tech weapons as long as the other party's weapons are destroyed, his combat power loses basically.

The lesson of this war is that pivotal cities in Libya become the key target of the attack, including Tripoli, the capital of Libya, Benghazi and some important oil cities. Therefore, the modern warfare tells us that urbanization is not a good thing. Especially the Chinese urbanization, it is very inappropriate to concentrate countrywide all of significant resources on Beijing, Shanghai and Guangzhou. In the event of a war, as long as a few missiles were fired, several cities collapsed, leading to the economic collapse across the country at a heavy cost.

In order to maximize profits, ignoring the scientific limitation of floor area ratio, high-rise buildings in Chinese cities are blindly seeking greatness, resulting in a high concentration of personnel or excellent talents. Once they are hit by a missile, the rate of casualties will be extremely high at an excessively disastrous cost. In consideration of tactics, resources and talents should be dispersed from large cities in the future. For this purpose, we must alternatively rely on some small and medium-sized cities, and engage in emerging industries. So many high-rise towers are built in large and medium-sized cities, once a bomb hits they will become immediately ruins. Whereas we reserve other assets, and can evacuate unhurriedly in advance, and the damage is much less. Evidently the real estate bubble can't be too large again that will definitely benefit to China in the future.

Chapter 7

Who Finally Benefits from High Housing Prices

Mr. Dong Fang Dao is turning on his computer, and writing an article with regard to real estate. He just writes an 8-character title, and hears someone screaming. Mr. Dong Fang is frightened, and then stands up, and sees the person next to him pointing at something behind an object, and screams, "Mouse, mouse!"

Mr. Dong Fang signals her not to panic, immediately, snatches up a broom, closes the door and windows, moves the object away, he finally sees a mouse that is neither big nor little, and is crawling stealthily like a thief. He is just ready to beat. The mouse suddenly drills into the pile of objects on the left. He uses the broom to poke the left pile of objects, and the cunning mouse also drills into the pile of objects on the right, and disappears. He uses once again the broom to pat objects on the right, thinking that this time, as long as the mouse appears, Mr. Dong Fang kills it with the broom. It is a long time for patting, and at all events the mouse neither comes out this time, nor makes any noise. As soon as Mr. Dong Fang moves the object, the cunning mouse also crawls under the pile of objects on the right instantaneously. After a few rounds, closing the door for beating can not touch the mouse. Mr. Dong Fang is already out of breath.

In this round Mr. Dong Fang has to use a tactic. He blocks the right channel with something, and asks other people to pat objects on the left. He is standing in the unique channel behind of the mouse on the rear left, preparing to hit hard as soon as the mouse appears. Along with the other people's actions, the mouse finally crawls out from the left. Mr. Dong Fang quickly hits with the broom, and at last presses the mouse. The other people reminds, "The mouse does not die, and it pretends to be dead!"

Then the other person passes a cold iron tong. Mr. Dong Fang presses the mouse with the broom in his left hand, and lifts the iron tong in his right hand. He slow dare not beat anyway, "Because the Buddha taught humans not to kill life, Jesus asked humans not to be violent,"

Mr. Dong Fang's mind fills with this peaceful thought. How dare he commit the violence to the mouse in front of him? An idea flashes in his mind at this time he wants to open the window, throw and free the mouse through the window. At this moment the other people (Mr. Dong Fang's assistant) bursts out, "Beat corrupt official, beat briber!"

On hearing of this voice, Mr. Dong Fang promptly presses hard the mouse with his left hand, and beats the mouse with his right hand, shouting by beating, "Beat briber, beat corrupt official!"

After a period of craze, the other people shouts, "Sir, Sir, the mouse is all smashed."

Mr. Dong Fang stops to notice that the mouse's head is smashed and bloodied. It is cruel but Mr. Dong Fang completes a job in the end.

After beating the mouse, Mr. Dong Fang sighs, "It is so difficult to beat a mouse, I am afraid it is not easy to fight a corrupt official!"

Three lessons learned are as follows:

1. Beating mice (corrupt officials) must close doors and windows, and can not let them run outside. Once arrive outside, it is difficult to beat;

2. Mice are so tricky that they can hardly be beaten even though the door is closed. In case of their hiding behind the protective body, corrupt officials are trickier. Beating corrupt officials must use tactics as beating a mouse, first isolate his protective body, then let him appear by a frightening way, and then beat him with a special attacker. The tactic only works;

3. Even if a mouse (corrupt official) is caught, the attacker will be lenient due to his instinctive sympathy. Mice are heterogeneous, and cannot manage to give gifts to people while corrupt officials can employ a lot of relationships to affect the attacker. Hereby there must be a great number of corrupt officials caught, and secretly released. Obviously the cost of cracking down on corrupt officials is costly. It is best to use the mutual restriction system among powers to prevent the emergence of corrupt officials. Everything is open to the public to make the mouse, and the corrupt official have no chance to make trouble.

After beating the mouse, Mr. Dong Fang returns to front of his computer, and is really both happy and confused somewhat.

"Whatever happens a life was killed, how to explain to Buddha? The article cannot be written continuously." Suddenly the movie of *Let the Bullets Fly* springs to my mind, which now has been intensely discussed. I try to watch free it online several times but it has been screened. Tonight, I must watch the movie *Let the Bullets Fly* to relax a little so I command my assistant, "No matter how difficult the problem is, you need get a free broadcast website for me."

The assistant makes a phone call to be highly successful eventually after a burst of clicks. The high-definition broadcast for 3 seconds just attracts Mr. Dong Fang to watch it through in one time. It turns out that the popular *Let the Bullets Fly* actually told a story of the struggle among corrupt official, gangster and local bully. The plot is ups and downs, the story is soul-stirring, and the subject is full of revolutionary passion, punishing evil and promoting goodness, and affording general satisfaction and is entirely in line with the main theme of socialism.

Wen Jiang, this man, is really clever. The reason why the *Let the Bullets Fly* is so popular is that it tells some truths about the officialdom of Chinese successive dynasties:

1. People who buy official position spend money act as a high and mighty official, definitely not for the purpose of serving the people but making more money by the official post.
2. In order to earn more money than the cost of buying an official position, the buyer will use various trickeries to concoct pretexts, and maximize his income.
3. Concocting various pretexts, the key is the word "concocting". In order to make money, the official position buyer must collude with local bullies to form a gang of interests, and even threaten and lure other rich people, and ordinary people "voluntarily" to pay by means of "gangster" tricks, letting those payers have a sense of identity "for public advantages".
4. Middle- and lower-class people who are squeezed are ultimately unbearable, and rise in revolt to unleash

them and use violence to overthrow the vicious power that manipulates the local regime.

In the movie, from the fight of justice incarnation, gangster Damazi Wang punishing corrupt official Bangde Ma, and corrupt official and local bully Silang Huang (who bought the position of county magistrate in 8 counties), it completely accords with the three principles of Mr. Dong Fang's beating mice:

1. Close the door to beat, Silang Huang surrounded himself with a high wall. Damazi Wang mobilized masses, and arrested rapidly local bully with the help of principles of closing the door to beat.
2. Use stratagem to beat. A mouse is so tricky, and Silang Huang is trickier. Fortunately Damazi Wang responded quickly, and effectively according to the current situation, as long as encountered a trick, Damazi Wang saw through it. It is best to counterplot. Silang Huang substitute as a weak spot was used to capture himself.
3. Even if caught the corrupt official and local bully Silang Huang, Damazi Wang inevitably sympathized with him, was unwilling to kill him personally, and let him commit suicide. Luckily, gangster Damazi Wang was not for money and beauty this time, otherwise Silang Huang's stakeholders would present money, and beauties to make Silang Huang also get away with murder.

The theme of *Let the Bullets Fly* is to promote the revolution, that is, advocate the violent overthrow of the corrupt regime. At all events Mr. Dong Fang Dao regards such a theme still quite timeworn nothing but very vigorous revolution formally, lacking of more rational revolution. In that such a violent revolution faces the biggest problem: What to do after the revolution? Will do the people live a peaceful and happy life? In case we continue the plot, Damazi Wang becomes the county magistrate, and starts to be very poor and productive but after a while, Damazi Wang grasps an absolute power so he must corrupt, and will become another corrupt official.

If I were Wen Jiang, I would modify the conclusion of the plot. That is, after Damazi Wang mobilized masses to drive Silang Huang out of power, an inauguration ceremony of new county magistrate was held. It is stipulated that anyone can run for the county magistrate but the people of the whole county vote. Damazi Wang's armed forces, as the county governmental neutral organization, are not controlled by any candidate. A completely independent county court is established to adjudicate on the election campaign, and ensure fair and equitable elections. Only in this way can competition be openly conducted under the sun, the outstanding county magistrate be elected so that local interest gangs from various parties will not use wicked methods to make profits. Since then the society is peaceful, the economy is developed, and the problem of buying and selling official positions is solved permanently.

Some people will raise the problem of vote buying. As long as one vote is given to everyone that authentically put it into practice, any candidate can't afford to bribe so many people as the cost is huge. However there are too small candidates such as two people designated, and the cost of vote buying is not large because the election is only between two people. On the contrary there are many candidates at the beginning, and no one knows whether who will be elected in numerous rounds of future selection, and the cost of vote buying will be increased greatly. Therefore it is only the real election, and the splendid county magistrate of both political integrity and talent can only be elected that gives the people the freedom to be candidates. Distinctly this is only called a real innovation.

Problem of house prices makes huge trouble like mice. It's hard! Why don't house prices just fall after so many policies are introduced? Because, in these policies, including land, fiscal taxation, currency, supply and demand, laws, regulations, documents, and so forth, for example, it counts up to 1,000 clauses, of which 990 clauses are for housing price decline but 10 clauses are for housing price rise. Whether housing prices will fall in reality? Not necessarily! Considering that the power of 10 clauses for housing price rise is strong enough to make another 990 clauses for housing price decline lose effect. Therefore, in the event that the government really wants to lower housing prices, they must find out, and revise 10 fundamental clauses for housing price rise in order to achieve the goal actually.

Next who is maintaining those critical provisions for housing price rise? It is necessary to analyze who profits most from high housing prices. House slaves use two or three decades of debts plus a lifetime of savings to buy a house, obviously not profitable. More specifically, a house of CNY 1 million buys only CNY 500,000. The homebuyer can use another CNY 500,000 to establish factories and enterprises to provide products and services. His money also has the possibility of appreciation, and solves the unemployment problem. Home-buyers who lose money are multitudinous, and who invest in computer stores, and shops in garment market, and lose everything is innumerable. Hence home-buyers benefit from high housing prices that cannot lump together.

Local governments, real estate developers and banks really benefit from high housing prices. In fact, it is not accurate.

Local governments benefit from it that may be unconvincing. For instance, a local government received CNY 10 billion from land sales, and borrowed another CNY 10 billion from banks to all invest in infrastructure, and the local government also lost CNY 10 billion. The local government doesn't benefit from it! Real estate developers earn a pure profit into their own account. Banks, like local governments, get some interest, but take two or three decades to recover the cost. So who benefits from it? Well, we can think of the plot of *Let the Bullets Fly*. The answer can be readily obtained.

In the *Let the Bullets Fly*, the county magistrate and the local bully used their old unfair tricks to accumulate wealth. Though they also concocted pretexts, it was unfavorable for the rich, and the poor people in local from payment because banditry, underworld, and other tricks were used. While today "concocting pretexts" are much smarter, allowing the local to thank payee after payment such as buying house to get rich, buying house for patriotism, and real estate as the national economic mainstay which are of an identical nature theoretically. It is the individual who really benefits from high housing prices not the government, and banks. They are those governmental officials who are secretly engaged in real estate business, bank leaders, and real estate developers. Some real estate developers like local bullies, regardless of whether governmental officials or bank presidents are changed at his will, they can share benefits. In general, just like the *Let the Bullets Fly*, the people are unbearable one day, and rise in revolt to eliminate local bullies and the vicious power, and high housing prices can only be reduced.

Chapter 8

How to Solve Issues of High Housing Prices

Today ten clauses left and tomorrow five clauses right, Chinese government introduces many real estate policies to regulate and control high house prices every year, in any case high house prices cannot be suppressed. High house prices make current central government, and the people feel uneasy even when eating and sleeping with worry! At this very moment, suppose someone provides a "panacea", it can solve the problem of high housing prices in China at once, I wonder if the central government will adopt? This "panacea" is: The central government should decree tomorrow to cancel all relevant control measures, and restore the free production and supply for the Chinese real estate market. The problems of high prices and short supply will be resolved on the day the decree is issued. The measures for supervision that should be removed include:

I. Canceling the No. 18 Document in 2003. Real estate has been clearly identified as the mainstay of the national economy in the document. In this document the real estate is described exaggeratedly colorful, and is endowed with a great many of goals of public interests such as being satisfied with the need of the people's lives, accelerating economic development, and expanding social employment. In short the real estate is particularly important, and can boost a great many of goals of public interests. However the governmental "Invisible Hand" theory tells us that the more the goal of public interests the government promotes, the more private interests increase conversely.

Most prominently it orders that: **No economic entity shall disguise the house allotment in kind or the real estate development and management in the name of fund raising, and cooperative building houses**. Like this the local governmental affordable houses disappear, and no entity dares fund-raising, and cooperative construction. Various other channels of housing supply are blocked by the government. All residents can only buy high-priced commercial houses from property developers due to the sharp decline in various houses freely supplied.

II. Canceling two legal provisions that contradict the *Constitution*. More severely, revised simultaneously the *Urban Real Estate Administrative Law of the People's Republic of China*, **Clause 9 stipulated that** after collectively-owned land in urban planning areas is converted into state-owned land via the requisition according to law, the right to use this plot of state-owned land can only be sold; and the *Land Administration Law of the People's Republic of China*, **Clause 43 stipulated that** each enterprise or individual who needs to use land for construction must apply for the use of state-owned land according to law.

Through the two legal provisions, the local governmental controller has monopolized firmly the land supply right. The *China Constitution*, **Clause 2** stipulated that **all power of the People's Republic of China belongs to the people; Clause 5** stipulated that the People's Republic of China shall govern the country according to law, and build a socialist country under the rule of law. All laws, administrative regulations, and local regulations shall not conflict with the *Constitution*. All governmental departments and state armed forces, political parties and social organizations, and enterprises and institutions must abide by the *Constitution* and *Laws*. **All behaviors in violation of the *Constitution* and *Laws* must be investigated.**

Most importantly the *Constitution*, Clause 6 stipulated that the foundation of the socialist economic system of the People's Republic of China is the socialist public ownership of means of production, that is, **ownership by the whole people, and collective ownership by the working masses. The socialist public ownership eliminates the human exploitation system of man by man,** and implements the principle of letting everyone do his best, and distribution according to workload.

The *Urban Real Estate Administrative Law of the People's Republic of China* and the *Land Administration Law of the People's Republic of China* stipulated that each enterprise or individual who is engaged in the real estate construction must apply for the use of state-owned land. Namely, **any enterprise or individual cannot use directly enterprise and peasant collective own land to build houses, and must purchase it from the local government until the land is monopolized by the local government with requisition before construction.** These two legal provisions on land monopolies violate Clauses 2, 5 and 6 of the *Constitution*, and must be eliminated. Neither does China have state ownership, nor local government ownership symbolize state-owned. **The local governmental acquisition, monopoly, and operation on land violate obviously the *Constitution*. According to the *Constitution*, Clause 5, all behaviors in violation of the *Constitution*, and *Laws* must be investigated.**

These two legal provisions on land monopolies, namely the governmental monopoly and intervention in the land, and real estate markets are the root cause of Chinese high house prices.

As long as these two unconstitutional clauses, and the provisions of the 2003 No. 18 Document prohibiting fund raising and cooperative housing construction are canceled, the problems of high house prices, and short supply that the Chinese people has been upset over the years can be resolved within **one day**, when the official document of cancel governmental control and regulation is issued.

Chapter 9

Why High Housing Prices Prevent Economic Transformation

When turn to annual government work reports from 2013 onwards, to 2004, from 2003 to 1998, from 1997 to 1994 you will find an interesting phenomenon, that is the authority necessarily mentioned two key points every year: One is to change the economic development mode, and adjust the economic structure; the other is to develop agriculture, and change the rural appearance. However, until today these two problems have not been resolved, and are getting more and more severe.

A country like a family, suppose a family chief goal is to earn CNY 100,000 yearly, is stressed year by year but can't be reached, additionally some false compositions are increased in calculation to deceive himself as well as others so that this goal loses its significance. Evidently this family also has **the goal of changing the income creation mode**: For example, never will the **male labor force** pull a handcart, and the female labor force go to the street as shoe-shining woman, instead husband and wife will run a shop together. The same is true of that the mode of family creation income will be more relaxed: That is to say from heavier manual labor to lighter physical labor so as to realize **the transformation of this family development mode**. The mode of a family creating income involves not only the problem of gross income, but also how to create this income. From pulling handcart and shoe shines to opening a shop, it has a large influence on this family, and a slight impact on society. However **the economic transformation of some families has a huge influence on society.**

Also another family called an Old Wang Family. In 1978, 3 mu of cropland, 0.3 mu of vegetable field, and 10 mu of mountain forest were obtained from the village distribution. Before 2003 the family earned annual income by three methods: Farming to produce rice and vegetables, and planting economic forests to sell fruits. The annual income was equivalent to CNY 15,000, of which CNY 10,000 was consumed by the family, and another CNY 5,000 was deposited. Although not much, the income can be obtained every year until generations. No doubt all of you will not deny that this is a sustainable way of creation income.

However **since 2003 the people suddenly started speculation in real estate nearby cities**, and can coin money from buying and selling houses. At the foot of the mountain of Old Wang Family, a coal mine was just discovered. Then the family immediately changed the mode of generation income into coal selling. They cut down a part of trees in the mountain forest for the construction of coal transportation road, organized manpower, put into machinery, and dug coal day and night. Why do they dig all day and night? The reason is that they can make a lot of money. To be specific the Old Wang Family can earn CNY 1.5 million by coal sales per year, which is 100 times of the original income.

Why can coal sales get such a high income? Because of the development of real estate in the city, the house price has increased from 700 CNY/m² to CNY 5,000 CNY/m². People in the city are speculating on houses, and house demand volumes are more and more. Property developers in combination with the government in the city have immoderately requisitioned arable land and mountain land, and demolished old towns, and built a large number of new houses. Building so multitudinous houses, roads and squares require a lot of steel, cement and lime. How are these main building materials such as steel, cement and lime produced? Steel is sintered by iron ore, and coal, and cement and lime are sintered from limestone and coal. It is obviously that these steel mills, cement plants and lime factories all require large amounts of coal, and the coal price rises. Therefore the Old Wang Family dug coal day and night to sell to these manufacturing enterprises driven by colossal profits.

Digging coal can earn 1.5 million per year, and the Old Wang Family was not satisfied. Seeing that the next door neighbor Wang Er, who was put in prison thrice due to burglary, was released from the prison after two years of reeducation through labor, and came to know the Director Hu in the city. Under the collaboration of Director Hu, Wang Er made a net profit of CNY 3 million by the real estate speculation in the city. The Old Wang Family was jealous, and determined to exceed the Wang Er's annual income. Hence the Old Wang Family shoveled off the cropland and vegetable field, dug underground constantly, exploded with explosives, and mined limestone. Because cement plants and lime factories require large amounts of limestone, the cropland and vegetable field of the Old Wang Family turned into a huge sink hole less than one year later. As a result of stone and coal sales, the annual income of Old Wang Family exceeded CNY 3 million. By reason of making a fortune, the Old Wang was "elected" by the county leaders as a deputy to the National People's Congress, and became an "government official" again. Since 2003 the way of Old Wang Family's income creation had been fundamentally changed, and the transformation was very successful. As long as house prices in the city do not drop, and a large number of houses are built, the Old Wang Family's coal mine will not stop coal digging, and the stone factory will not stop stone exploding.

This is the reason why the Chinese economic development mode has not been transformed. As long as high house prices remain steadily, someone will rack their brains to conduct railway, road and other infrastructure projects, and build houses. As long as houses in the city are built unceasingly, cement plants, steel mills, lime factories, and other building material manufacturers will produce in large-scale. The coal at the foot of the mountain, and under the ground in the countryside will be dug without a break. Countless mountain forests and arable lands will be destroyed, and limestone will be exploded continuously. Until one day underground natural resources will be hollowed out, and exhausted completely, and even the whole mountain will be all collapsed at a proper time. In addition, because quarrying and coal mining require chemical products such as explosives and petroleum, the water in the river and croplands are polluted. Along with the rice, vegetables and drinking water, the pollution source sneaks into the bodies of people in cities and villages to accumulate toxins. For instance, in 2008 the Old Wang went to a large hospital for health examination, and findings were shown that he had cancer. The Old Wang recalled that more than ten persons in the village had died of cancer. They had no money to cure the disease, and had to wait for death while the Old Wang had money though the Oncology Hospital in the city was charged CNY 10,000 every day. In less than three years, the Old Wang Family became a pauper again.

But the story is not over. The sharp decrease in the cultivated land, and the large amount of pollution in the township lead to three consequences:

1. Output of grain crops will be reduced inevitably;
2. Grain and foods with grain as raw materials are contaminated, and the number of patients increases. This can be proved by the endless flow of patients in various hospitals;
3. The effective rural labor force is decreased due to the decrease in the area for growing grain, and the increase in the number of the old, weak, sick and disabled in villages. This can be proved from the fact that farmers in their 70s in villages cannot retire, and must do farm work.

The three consequences will inevitably lead to a disastrous effect, to wit, the commodity price in the city must rise. No one can control it. Farmers' products will not be sold to the city at a loss, or else, they will abandon production, supply will decrease, and prices of agricultural products will rise even by a large margin so that some people cannot stay in the city, they have no alternative but return to the countryside. However they find that neither a drop of water in the countryside is clean, nor a mu of field is unpolluted; and every inch of cropland contains heavy metals on their arrival home. At this time so numerous houses in the city can only be permanently vacant as a witness to the abnormal development of China's economy.

Writing hereto, it occurs to the author that the period of the Great Leap Forward, and the Great Steelmaking began in 1958. Many people do not understand the essence of the Great Leap Forward, and the Great Steelmaking. What is the essence? Much to your surprise, the truth was to create GDP, also catch up with the United Kingdom, and surpass the United States of America! Today isn't it just for GDP when we get the real estate industry into full swing? We have long caught up the Britain, and are surpassing America! Current peasants recall the Great Leap Forward, and the Great Steelmaking, all of them regard it as a wanton mischief. Collecting farmers' pans and shovels, deforestation without restraint and building small blast furnaces were used to make scrap iron. Isn't it nonsense? Otherwise what is it? This moment I read Dehuai Peng's "Letter of Ten Thousand Words", how fabulous it is! Commander in Chief Peng is a talent who really understands economics. In another one or two decade, it will be distressing to look back at the overdevelopment, and destruction of real estate and natural resources today. The Great Leap Forward only destroyed the land surface while now the so-called development has destroyed deeply the soil, surface water, groundwater, air and so on. In the near future these reckless developments will bring grave disaster to the Chinese people.

A large number of people are now directly and indirectly defending high house prices. They cannot see beyond the length of their noses, survey the problem, can only see today, and no longer would like to consider tomorrow. Provided this continues ridiculously, what is the difference of building excessive houses, making overmuch steels and digging exhausted completely coal, overly digging the earth, and pollution without restraint from the Great Leap Forward and the Great Steelmaking in the past? Why do the Chinese create income by virtue of selling natural resources, destroying the environment, and polluting humankind? Why can't we increase properly some income on the premise of environmental-protection, ecological and green mountains and rivers? Getting healthy body, and earning those papers with red and green backs, which is more important?

For the sake of sustainable development, we must resolutely eliminate high house prices. In order to transform truly the economy, it is necessary to clarify the measures and indicators of transformation in the *Government Work Report* but the GDP indicators. Sustainable development refers to the investment in rural areas, and farmers to restore environmental-protection, ecological and green mountains and rivers, and fertile farmland without pollution. Allowing that a large number of modern, comfortable and livable houses are built in the countryside, why so many houses are built to waste resources in the city? Learning from the Western countries, the rich live in the countryside and outskirts. Urbanization, please stop your peremptory, rough and hypocritical steps! Rural modernization is only the tomorrow of China!

Chapter 10

Why House Property Tax
Cannot Reduce House Prices

House property tax is a big event. The pilot significance is very important, and is a landmark event of whether the tax is promoted nationwide. Since, allowing that the people dispute and argue, and the truth will become clearer before a major decision is launched.

I. Divide the House Property into Ten Classes, and Levy Different Classes at Different Tax Rates

It is said that these ten classes are formulated based on a differential land rent economically. This statement is very professional. What is the differential land rent? Bluntly it refers to **different prices for lots**. For example, a City A can be divided into first-class land, second-class land, third-class land, and others. Generally the first prosperous lot near downtown is called the first-class land, and the second prosperous lot is called the second-class land, and so on. The first-class land in the City A can be sold for CNY 30 million per mu, the second-class land can be sold for CNY 10 million per mu, the third-class land can be sold for CNY 5 million per mu, the fourth-class land can only be sold for CNY 1 million per mu, and the fifth-class land can only be sold for CNY 200,000 per mu, and so forth, and the tenth-class land can only be sold for CNY 10,000 or even several thousand yuan per mu. **The difference in market prices of land per mu in such different lots is the land differential.**

This price difference is a huge profit margin. Who owns it? It was beyond doubt obtained by those who bought the land when the land price was low in earlier years. They are local governments and property developers who buy, and sell land. One category of developer who only buys and sells land, and is also called a first-level developer. The other category of developer who buys land and then sells houses, further they divide the land into densely small plots to sell to home-buyers together with commercial houses. In a sight of northern cities, property developers only issue the House Property Ownership Certificate, and do not issue the Land Use Certificate. In the south all commercial houses are also issued the Land Use Certificate, showing that a house is bought, and meanwhile the government proves how many square meters of land use right the homebuyer bought.

Now the City A divides the local real estate into ten classes, and then levies different tax rates according to different classes. It seems to be several inadequacies:

1. **The advantage of differential land rent is that the land was purchased in advance by the property developer who sells high-priced houses while home-buyers have paid extra money, and some of them have also owed two or three decades in debt due to the high-price house.** According to relevant opinions, the more expensive the land is sold, the higher the tax rate is levied. Actually who leads to the

expensive land? Who gains the highest benefit from the differential land rent for land sales? Obviously they are local governments, and property developers. Therefore this basis for setting the tax rate seems to have a sense of peeling: First the homebuyer is peeled first by the high land price, and now is also peeled second by the high tax rate as though the homebuyer is pressed on the ground to peel every year. Is it reasonable?

2. **It is very difficult to divide the house property into ten classes.** By way of illustration two owners who have the Land Use Certificate, Person A lives on the east side of the road, and is levied at the tax rate of 3% in the first-class land, and Person B lives on the west side of the road, and is levied at the tax rate of 2% in the second-class land. The two homes are just ten meters apart, and the tax amount paid is largely different. How many social contradictions will this trigger? How to classify the land price class will result in a lot of power rent-seeking events. Can't it be worrying!

3. **Upper limit of 3% tax rate must be alerted.** According to the original expert prediction, the house property tax rate will be generally below 1%, and the opinion of 3% tax rate further confirms the foresight of anti-levy faction, viz., as long as this precedent starts, the tax rate will be increased greatly. **In order for increase revenue, local governments try to firstly expand the first-class land, and secondly raise tax rate as much as possible.** As long as the house property tax starts to be levied, these two tricks will be used absolutely by local governments as scheduled. Tax rate has been

increased to 3% without the pilot now. It is entirely possible that the tax rate is increased to 5-9% again with the advent of mayors Ma, Niu, and et al.

II. No One Speculates on Houses at the House Property Tax beyond 3% According to a Economic Law

I wonder which inferior enough expert "contributed" this economic law? Current economic textbooks, including ones in the latest edition, as well as some books dedicated to taxation research, do not expound this "great" law. According to conjecture it must be "a theory presented" by a third-class expert.

Regarding the impact of fiscal taxation on prices, almost all economic theories form a consensus, that is whether a tax is levied on seller or buyer will merely push up the commodity price, and in the mean time the market size will be reduced, and the tax burden will be borne by both buyers and sellers. Almost all economists theoretically oppose to taxation in that it will reduce consumer welfare. Likewise, today famous Mr. Xianping Lang and Mr. Zhiwu Chen held foreign doctorates firmly oppose to the house property tax though their reason is not thorough, and the point of view is supportable. In case their views were untenable, all economic theories about taxation would have to be rewritten.

Nowadays we analyze whether no one speculates on houses when 3% of the house property tax is levied. For instance, on January 26, 2014 the mayor announced that 3% house property tax will be levied for all houses on the first-class land. What will this result in? Considering that the object of house property tax is the potential house seller, videlicet, **the**

seller of house is levied. The tax rate is 3% provisionally, and the price of commercial houses on the market will increase by 2%. One house of CNY 1 million will rise to CNY 1.02 million after taxation. The seller can only get CNY 990,000. The buyer has to pay CNY 1.02 million. **The both parties buyer and seller have to undertake CNY 30,000 tax.** Manifestly this is just a metaphor. The theory is as follows, **the taxation will make the price the seller gets lower than the original price while the buyer pays higher than the original price.** This theory formed seems to make sense. Therefore those debates that the introduction of house property tax will reduce house prices should have no sufficient basis.

Furthermore the internal relation between house property tax, and house speculation should be seriously comprehended. What is the house speculation? It is a phenomenon with the intention of holding houses for making profit in a short time. It means the speculator who buys a house and sells to other immediately. Some people buy houses, and sell on the first day, or sell a few months later. Such speculations in very short ownership duration are called the short-term speculation. **Usually such house speculators do not apply for the House Property Ownership Certificate, and only sign the Sales Contract with property developers. For this reason the cost of house speculation can be greatly cut down.** The Chinese real estate market is chaotic mainly due to the house speculation without restraint, and in any case it is much better now. **Who are house speculators in the market?** In the event that property developers tell the truth, they include just a few types:

1. **Each government department**, in which authoritative officials are responsible for examining and approving permits, planning certificates, fire

protection, and others of land, roads, and buildings. In the early stage of opening sales they will instruct property developers to reserve some houses, or buy them in a token payment, and then sell them until the house price rises. It is so-called **a speculation house ticket**;

2. **Professional house speculators** that is citizens who speculate on contracts in the Building Sales Department or speculate on houses with spare money. Most of these house speculators do not apply for the House Property Ownership Certificate. Therefore the house speculation can be eliminated at the house property tax of 3% that is just the opposite theoretically. **Such taxation on house property owners for a long time will instead stimulate the desire of short-term speculators.** Visibly the cost of short-term speculation is not increased, and conversely their profits are increased due to the house price rise.

In summary the house property tax neither has any impact on short-term speculation, nor promotes long-term holders to sell at a low price. **The advantage of taxation merely makes local governments increase revenue. Taxation burden is apportioned between buyers and sellers. For the house renter, tax amount is transferred the tenant.**

What is the reason for house speculation? Because the purpose of power interfering in the market is to make a profit, and fake contracts are rampant and administrative strength is ineffective. Another overall reason is that the money supply of central bank is excessive and relevant regulation and control of authorities is weakly. The supply of more than CNY 100 trillion becomes already a "fierce tiger in cage" unable to exert the formidable force. In 2009 and 2010 bank loan officers lent out the money crazily. Is the money really so worthless? Currently, as long as the central bank deflates slightly, and the bank grumbles about tight liquidity. Actually the central bank carries out sharply the interest rate hike to make depositors increase. Will the bank have money to lend?

Chapter 11

House Property Tax Makes the Middle Class Poor Probably

Establishment and abolition of some major decisions in China are often intriguing and thought-provoking. For instance, before the introduction of land bid invitation, auction and listing system in China, experts at that time were full of enthusiasm and generosity to strive to implement the fair and impartial land bid invitation, auction and listing system due to the opposition to the rent-seeking, and corruption of local government officials in land transfer. Later the experts and the public opinion all won. So far the land bid invitation, auction and listing system has developed. During the *Eleventh Five-Year Planning* (2006-2010), local governments made full use of the auction, this modern weapon, and finally got more than CNY 7 trillion land sales revenue. To this day the central government and the people just feel the huge harm of land bid invitation, auction and listing system: the implementation of this system may push China to the edge of the cliff! **Nowadays the land bid invitation, auction and listing system has to be changed again, and cannot conduct the game of highest-price-bidder as winner.** But, what about the experts and leaders in decision-making department after supported vigorously the bid invitation, auction and listing system? Were they still responsible for the damage caused by this system to China? Obviously they were not. They were busy with other things afterwards, and didn't care about this system.

Like the land bid invitation, auction and listing system, plenty of major decisions have been enacted at will since the China reform and opening up, and cannot stand the time test. For example, in the enclosure for the construction of the development zone, this development policy promoted vigorously all the fashion from place to place; local governments made great efforts to establish their own bank- governmental foundation policy, policy of money supply at a putting rate of 25% into circulation per year, and the like. These decisions were rough, not scientific in introduction so that painful lessons were exchanged by huge investment.

Anyway China overall still made progress compared to that three decades ago (1978). Why say so? Just that a personal worship in vogue **three decades ago,** even though the Highest Leader was wrong, the mistake could only be conducted in the end, keeping straight on one way. At that time the People's Commune, the Great Leap Forward, and the Great Steelmaking, including the Cultural Revolution later, someone proposed one after another objections such as the Vice Premier of the State Council, the Defense Minister, and the State President, anyhow all were rejected, and cannot persuade the Highest Leader. These mistakes could only were executed all the time. What a huge mistake it would be! Even if tens of thousands of people died of it, the wrong decision would still be carried through to the end. **Three decades after the reform and opening up, the Chinese government also made mistakes, at any rate there was a great progress, that is once mistake was found, and it was corrected. Besides, the authority also advocated a scientific development concept, i.e., scientific decision.** This is a good proposal but the scientific decision-making overall level of government officials in China is still in an urgent need for improvement. Supposing decisions go always wrong, it will be utilized by some people. There is now a group of leftists who dream of returning to the era of the Cultural Revolution, which is out of the question. Think about it. **Who can accept a society without personal freedom, and property freedom, in which everyone is commanded daily?** Isn't it too out to **solve modern real-world problems by using old-fashioned political movements?** Thus human history can only progress, not turn back.

So does the house property tax that some experts now advocate. We can only progress, not turn back. What does it mean? It stands for making scientific decisions. Whether the decision is scientific or not, I think there must be a measurement standard, that is, the common people opinion, which is not march, fight, shouting or curse against each other during the Cultural Revolution but means that different interest groups sit down, speak facts and reasons, and debate on the principle of rationality, and then make decisions based on the approach of the minority subordinate to the majority. With regard to the levy of house property tax, this scientific methodology should also be adopted so as not to regret. As the expert from the Chinese Academy of Fiscal Sciences Ministry of Finance said, **the levy of house property tax involves in various interests. Due to the hindrance of stakeholders with vested interests, the reform problem is difficult to resolve in the debate. The best way is to put the debate aside for a while, and try to pilot the levy of the house property tax as quickly as possible.** This opinion is probably wrong, and is not the way to make scientific decisions. Based on the assumption that he puts aside the debate in the great event of house property tax that concerns the whole people's interests, in other words he rejects different opinions like this, and blunders definitely. **As an official of the Ministry of Finance, what he considers the most is how to collect money for the government rather than reduce house prices or adjust income distribution. These two goals can be neither achieved in the cities where the house property tax is piloted.** Because from measures, and remarks of current pilot cities, they do not have any sincerity in using the house property tax to suppress house prices, and adjust income distribution.

Presuming that they really care about the common people, they should have three sincerity points below:

1. They shall bulletin the housing situation owned by local civil servants and relevant government officials to the public in detail;
2. They shall bulletin the taxable housing object in detail;
3. They shall promise to disclose the specific list of taxation expenditures at any time.

Before discussion on the three issues, let's first analyze a fundamental question, what is the reason for the levy of house property tax? From the current situation it is nothing more than the following:

1. Increasing the revenue of local governments;
2. Adjusting the income distribution, that is, collecting some money from the Rich A gives the Poor B;
3. Suppressing house prices, that is, the taxation on homeowners with multiple suites every year until

their unbearable, throwing excess houses to the market to promote the house price slash.

The three purposes are applied to measure whether the house property tax is good. It should be fair and equitable. Supposing the house property tax begins to be levied now, whether the three goals can be achieved?

Goal 1, the increase in local government revenue, will certainly be achieved. Because as soon as the government gives a command, all the local taxmen start off, police office, procuratorate and court all pitch into the work, no tax amount is not received. The money will definitely be received in the local governmental vault as scheduled, and the amount is huge. Distinctly the goal 1 is no problem.

Goal 2, the effect of regulating income distribution, it is difficult to ensure that satisfactory results can be achieved. Considering that the government departments did not give public opinions on how to distribute, disburse, and monitor every expenditure in respect of the taxation from the house property tax received, and even without mention. Hypothetically speaking the goal of income redistribution is really to be achieved, the government should request the National People's Congress (NPC) to make a local legislation on the openness and rationality of taxation expenditures, and it merely ensures that the tax amount received is indeed used for people's livelihood. The current news reports only broadcast that the government collects the tax amount, and does not mention that finances are opened simultaneously. Distinctly it is difficult to guarantee the effect of income redistribution.

Goal 3 is to suppress house prices. Will the introduction of house property tax really suppress house prices? This question is so important that we have to analyze it in depth. As a matter of fact the goal 3 involves the benefit of three parties:

The first party is the local government;

The second party is the homeowner of multiple suites;

The third party is the person who has no house and wants to buy.

Up to now two of the three parties are most active in the collection of house property tax. Local governments would like to increase their income, and the persons who have no house, and would like to buy. The current situation is that local governments are taking advantage of the voice of the group without houses, "conforming to the public opinion" to levy the house property tax. In any case after the house property tax is levied, whether the person who has two or three suites will authentically throw one or two suites to the market? In reality it is hard to say. There may be several situations:

1. Homeowners who have a stable income source annually will not care about 1% of the tax amount, and will pay on time;

2. Homeowners who are sensitive to the house property tax maybe throw the second or third suite into the market;

3. Bribing the officials of the housing authority, and the taxation bureau keeps multiple suites in a disappearance state.

Evidently after the house property tax is levied, two types of homeowners who have more than two suites cannot be collected the taxable amount:

Firstly the homeowners with more than two suites have a governmental official background;

Secondly the homeowners have made a false transfer.

According to the news from relevant local governments that levied the house property tax, the municipal government did not require to disclose the property list or real estate list of government officials when the levy of house property taxes was announced. Apparently the fairness of taxation, viz., whether all homeowners with more than two suites are taxed equally has not made a corresponding explanation. The property list of government officials is not bulletined. In the current context of China the common people will question this taxation as a fake, and fight against. It is conceivable how much trouble this will bring to China.

Therefore when the local government begins to levy the house property tax, ignoring the three sincerity points that they should have, this taxation will become an **irrational tax** in reality, which will be scolded, and spat on by the people, and then ended in a hurry. **Mr. Dong Fang Dao reminds hereon that the house property tax may become a sword to pierce hearts of all urban middle-class families.** Until now there is the order of 200 million citizen households, and the vast majority of them already have a total of two suites, one suite of welfare home from original employer, and another suite of improvement dwelling. In addition the purchase of second suite of improvement dwelling by urban residents is justified perfectly, and encouraged by the government. They have already paid expensive land rent, why should they pay the house property tax? On the premise that the taxation expenditure and the governmental official property list are not disclosed, why does the local government levy the house property tax?

In practice, will the house property tax become a favorable weapon for local governments to exploit the people wealth **like the land bid invitation, auction and listing system?** Judging from all the current signs, it is very likely! The land auction system itself is excellent but is utilized by the local government for the profit that will definitely results in the local government maximizing the revenue from land sales, and competing with the people for profit.

Whether the house property tax is good or not in the end? It depends on who is levying and consuming taxes. The taxes received can be guaranteed to actually return to the local people, and the people can agree to pay a little. In case neither the taxation fairness nor the transparency of tax expenditure is guaranteed, **should the people's money be handed over to others for expense?** Practically as soon as the local government ensures fairness and justice, this strategy is enough alone if single-hearted: **That is, it is to disclose the governmental official property list, and then recover their surplus houses as the governmental indemnificatory apartments, which are provided to local non-house households. This is the most popular method.** Instead it is certainly unpopular to target the middle class in cities with taxation. Because the middle class has become the majority of the city, it seems illogical that the government does not give the middle class ballot ticket but asks them to pay this tax.

The introduction of the house property tax in a place is a major decision that affects both the broad general public in contemporary era and future generations. The mayor cannot make successfully it alone, it is better to adopt a scientific decision-making. For the scientific decision **the government** must **ask the people about administrative opinions,** and strive to establish, and perfect **a decision-making mechanism that reflects the people-oriented, and administration for the people requirements.** When making decisions, and formulating policies, the government must fully consider interests, and respect the masses' wishes to plan and coordinate the interest relationship of all parties, and must **persist in asking about the people's administrative opinions, demand opinions and advices, and persist scientific, democratic and legal decision-making**. The author personally believes that the scientific decision is on the premise of democracy. There are three asking, i.e., three strategies in democratic decision, namely **asking about the people administrative opinions, demand opinions, and advices.** The essence of democratic decision is to let the people make their own decisions. After the people form a resolution in accordance with the rule of the minority subordinate to the majority, the mayor executes the resolution, which only reflects the original intention of the people mastering their own affairs. Otherwise the people cannot apprehend the taxation connotation, and the government will force the collection tax amount, which will cause social unrest. Given that the people controversy is strong, this decision should be put aside, and it is better not to force to launch.

Part Four

Arcana of National Wealth System

Introduction

Only by identifying the nominal income

    Can you pursue the real income

    So far governments all over the world have a set of methods to calculate their own wealth, by which they squeeze their people, which has been used, and promoted by the United States since the 1930s, never has been questioned, and can be overthrown in theory by no one. Because this set of scheme is offered to the people around the world as the textbook of modern economics. As usual, the people merely learn, and obey habitually it rather than scrutinization. It turns out that the old set is in trouble, and the people can only try to discover the new one.

    This Part takes China as an example at first. From the contradiction amid GDP, CPI, and M2 data bulletined, it fundamentally points out Chinese mistakes in calculating national wealth (GDP). The author applies a strict logic, and scientific methodologies to calculate the nominal growth rate, real growth rate, real GDP, nominal inflation rate, and actual inflation rate of China in recent years, revealing the truth of wealth growth.

The author also discusses deeply the relation between nominal national wealth and actual national wealth, and the relation between actual national wealth and consumer product prices for the first time with innovative thought and systematic theory, and besides several new models for GDP calculation are constructed and invented. Perhaps a series of brand new theories are beneficial to national governments in crisis. Furthermore the author's viewpoints will provide a strong theoretical support for the international liberal economy.

Chapter 1

How Should Governments Operate Economics

What is and what should be the relationship between government and economics in the final analysis? They are two completely different issues.

In order to clarify these two issues, let us most of all turn our eyes to the human ancient primitive society. At that time there were a dense forest and luxuriant vegetation, and humankind thrived in the embrace of nature, and lived exactly like current monkeys in remote primitive mountains and forests. Once a person was born into this world, he acquired naturally rights: One right was to naturally satisfy the life growth, and the other right was to pursue a better life quality. When he or his family pursued these two goals, there was no an institution named as government to interfere or prevent.

By way of illustration, 6,000 years ago, a Huang's Family in China had a total of 9 members including grandpa, grandma, father, mother, and 5 children. They lived in a remote mountain of the Yangtze River Valley. As long as they were willing, they could make a living by picking wild fruits, growing rice or hunting in mountains. Furthermore they could also cut down trees from mountains by virtue of their ingenuity, and physical strength to build firm and safe houses with stones, and wood. Their activities such as picking wild fruits, planting rice, and hunting belonged to family production activities, which could also be called economic activities. Their activity of building a new house was also an economic activity. Notably the former economic activity was for survival, and the latter economic activity was for better survival anyway. When this family with 9 members struggled towards these two goals day after day, and year after year, there was no an institution named as government to interfere. As long as they were willing, they could migrate freely from the Yangtze River Basin to the Yellow River Basin, and further Russia or Turkey, somewhere in Europe, India, Africa, and so on, wherever they could arrive. In that there were no country at all, and naturally there were no border in ancient times. For instance, from China to Russia, at that time there was neither the country concept of China, nor that of Russia. As long as the Huang's Family had been going west according to the sun direction, they could reach a place of Russia to live and they could also make a living by picking wild fruits and hunting. Similarly a Russian family could always go east, and reach wherever in China to live, and they could make a living by hunting or growing rice.

As long as this Chinese family wanted, they could sell rice, and porcelain to Russia or anywhere across the world just that there was no country, border defense, and government. Correspondingly their long-distance sales profits did not need to pay any tax, and there was no any taxation. A world is equal to a large place. Only in this primordial situation without any country, border defense or government is there 100% pure liberal economy, and free trade in this place.

In ancient times because there was no country, government, border, and frontier defense, resources around the world could be shared freely. At that time although science and technology was not developed, a family might merely produce, and live within a 20 km area but all members of this family had been enjoyed free production, life, and trade rights wherever on the earth since they were born in this world. Although this kind of right might not be understood at that time, it actually existed in the human society, and animal society. This is the origin of "natural rights" in the *American Constitution*. Many people in modern times can't apprehend why the founder of the United States wrote the "natural rights" into the *Constitution*, and further criticize that the "natural rights" can't stand scrutiny. In fact they may forgot that as long as a person was born into this world, he would have freely and equally production, life, and trade rights as the same as others of this world in the human society of ancient times. As soon as a life was born, such rights were naturally granted invisibly. Although it was not written on paper, and there were no ceremonies to announce, it actually existed in reality at the time. Considering that there was no country, no government or no restriction, all people were completely free from their birth at the time. This freedom can be summarized into two rights: One is the life right to live freely and the other is the right to pursue freely a happy life. This is the "natural rights".

However after the establishment of countries all over the world, the earth was artificially divided into pieces, and they were determined by borders, and troops. Humans in this piece of place cannot reach that piece of place freely, vice versa. In every place a country was established, and where a government was established, In which this group of leaders managed their own people internally, and did not allow their own people or people of other countries to freely enter, and leave this country externally, where was called the state-owned land. Under this kind of control the inherent "natural rights" that human beings had inherited from ancient times were crushed by an institution called the country, and the government. After the establishment of country and government, humankind has lost the right of free production, action, and pursuit of happiness.

Today the Adam Smith's market economy theory, viz., the liberal economy theory, is highly praised all over the world. However has everyone thought about it? The world should not have so-called liberal economy, and illiberal economy. If borders of all countries throughout the world are eliminated, and the people of every country can move freely, isn't it the best liberal economy? Even if the country, and the government exist, as long as the country border defense is canceled, the people of every country will be granted a part of "natural rights", i.e., the right to reach freely a place for free production, life, and certainly for trade. Thus the people have the right to choose country, and government. Like this the human society strides towards freedom. On the grounds that once the border defense is canceled, the people can freely choose country, and different countries and governments have to compete to attract the people. It is precisely on the score of state-to-state competition that rulers of all countries must treat their people in the country kindly, and make every effort to govern successfully own country. Once the dominator does not treat own people friendly, the people will immigrate to other countries, and the dominator will become a loner. From the status quo of very few authoritarian countries in the modern era, dictators are most afraid of people escaping their own countries so they try every means to strengthen their border defenses. They are very clear in case they are not watertight guard, and do not defend desperately, all the people of their country will immigrate overseas, and they will collapse thoroughly because lose the regnant object. Distinctly from the essence of state and governmental establishment, it is not conducive to the human liberal economy. That is to say the establishment of state and government is a restriction on the liberal economy, or all countries or governments are abolished, the people's economy worldwide will right away return to the status of liberal economy just that there is no illiberal economy by the moment, and whatever the people do not care the concept of liberal economy. From this perspective the reason why the Adam Smith's liberal economic theory has such a strong vitality is that he represents the human conscience, and voices a real cry for human freedom rights that have been suppressed by all national governments for thousands of years!

Since the establishment of state and government, humankind has been arguing around a question for thousands of years: What should the relationship between the government, and the people be? Indeed including what about the relationship between the government, and the people's economy? The government is represented by the ruler. Concretely speaking, in reality what should the relationship between the ruler and the people be. Thinking about this question, China, Europe, India, and other countries have born many great ideologists since ancient times. At all events what did they all think about: What the relationship between the ruler and the people was? As for another more essential question: What the relationship between the government (represented by the ruler) and the people should be? It actually has been ignored for thousands of years. This question is only fundamental, and involves:

1. How did government come about?
2. Whether government should exist?
3. Advantages, and disadvantages of whether government exists or not;
4. Can the people live better without government?
5. Will there be government in truly free society?

These questions connect directly the essential key of human society, and while promote the progress of human society. At the moment the author puts forward these questions, and looks forward to next generation of people who have the courage to think can explore and figure out!

Regarding the question of what should the relationship between the ruler, and the people be, the author thinks that taking China as an example is very representative on the grounds that China is a great country, and rules and ruled histories have been for above 5000 years. What should the relationship between the ruler and the people be that was debated most intensely during the Spring and Autumn and Warring States in China. It was the most fruitful so as to form several schools such as Confucianism, Taoism and Legalism. Because at that time, kingdoms were established in great numbers, and competed with each other to drive various idealistic competition. It authentically reached a situation where hundreds of ideological schools contended just like all flowers blooming together. Among them main ideas included Confucianism, Taoism and Legalism. In any wise the three schools mainly discussed in terms of the ruler managing the relationship with the people properly. The essence is to offer the ruler with governance approaches.

First of all we study the Confucianism that has been ruled in the longest term, and widely used by rulers of all generations in China. In fact when you earnestly study so-called Confucian classics the *Analects of Confucius* (Dialog Quotations between Confucius and Disciples) created by Confucius, founder of Confucianism, Zeng Zi (Confucius' disciple), and Kong Ji (also known as Zi Si, Confucius' grandson, and Zeng Zi's disciple), the *Great Learning* (written by Zeng Zi, explaining Confucius important views), and the *Doctrine of the Mean* (written by Kong Ji, explaining Confucius methodologies), you will find that the

246

so-called theories of Confucius, and his disciples are multifarious, and there is no systematic views and rigorous argument at all. Although we cannot evaluate the ancient with the contemporary requirement, when we review the Confucian classics in a rational and objective attitude, we will find that their value is indeed not great, and their views and assertions can not withstand scrutiny. In regard to the emperor admiration for Confucianism in all dynasties, that is another matter. As a researcher his scientific approach should discard the environmental influence, and evaluate the true feature of things.

The *Analects of Confucius* recorded the conversation among Confucius, numerous disciples, and contemporaries. Each article was titled with the first two or three words of the content. There is no logical relationship among articles. When the title is deleted, the article is a long Confucius Dialog Quotations to record the viewpoint expressed by Confucius on the society at that time. That's all! Today we record the daily conversation between a teacher, and his students at a university, and perhaps it will be wonderful, and attractive. At all events this teacher's every sentence is regarded as classics, and the people of the whole country are required according to what the teacher said, isn't this an insult to the people? In reality Confucius was in the Spring and Autumn, and Warring States period, hundreds of ideological schools contended just like all flowers blooming together. His views represent just one school, and are completely unable regarded as classics to popularize highly. The reason why these views and assertions of Confucius have a huge influence is that his disciples recorded, and promoted them. On the contrary in case someone recorded, and promoted specially a farmer's daily conversation randomly at that time, it would maybe become classics. For thousands of years the Chinese people's superstition and confinement to the Confucian views have been very foolish. This will confine the people's thought to make the entire Chinese nation backward, and beat. Think about it. Behaviors and thoughts of thousands of the people in one nationality are required with the daily expression, and casual speech of one person who has died for more than two thousand years. Isn't it ridiculous and stupid? What hope and future are there for such a nationality? Just now we enter the sacred mansion of Confucianism to see what treasures there are inside, and whether they are real treasures.

After visited the three sacred mansions of the *Analects of Confucius*, *Great Learning*, and *Doctrine of the Mean*, we find that Confucius ideology and assertions were concealed in the *Great Learning*. From a general survey of these three masterpieces, we will find that Confucius actually has no too much thought. He primarily put forward some requirements for the king and the people at that time, that is, some behavioral rules such as the king must obey the rule of being a king, the courtier must obey the rule of being a courtier, and the people must obey the rule of being a people. These rules were indiscriminately imitated from the rules and regulations established by the King of Western Zhou Dynasty as source, and were played a role. Let's start from how the ruler managed the relationship with the people to research what views Confucius put forward.

The *Great Learning* is the maximum guideline of Confucianism. From how emperors should deal with the relationship with the people, the book put forward some requirements on rulers so scholars of all ages called it the "Science of Emperor". For instance, the three basic principles of "developing and expanding illustrious virtue", "rejecting the old for the new, repenting and being good to correct own conduct", and "arriving at absolute perfection and supreme goodness". Eight steps in life that should be taken to achieve these three goals such as "investigation and research of things", "awareness and knowledge", "sincerity", "integrity", "self-cultivation", "family alignment", "governance country for peace and stability", and "peaceful world", which are well-known for our Chinese people. These contents extracted by Zeng Zi highly summarized Confucius' thoughts, and increased a certain systematization and logicality.

The foremost ideology of Confucius is as follows: Awareness, and knowledge is acquired by investigation, and research of things, after which ideology becomes sincerity, after which all kinds of restless emotions are eliminated, you do not be covered by material desire to keep the psychical quiet, i.e., integrity, after which own moral character is constantly improved, i.e., self-cultivation, after which, family is kept harmony, i.e., family alignment, after which country is administered by means of virtue, and governed into a state of peace, and stability, after which benevolent governance is extended all countries to make the world peace. From the emperor to the civilians, everyone all takes the cultivation of own moral character as the foundation. The main idea of this passage is: Only after understand the truth of things can awareness be clear, only after which can ideology be sincere, only after which can thought be correct, only after which can own moral character be cultivated surpassingly, only after which can the family be reorganized, only after which can the state be governed successfully, and only after which can the world be peaceful. Therefore it is essential for everyone to cultivate own moral character from the emperor to the common people.

His causal inference seems to be very reasonable, and actually ignores the largest premise, that is where does the emperor power come from? As Confucius said, numerous civilians achieved absolutely a perfect moral realm by self-cultivation, who should become in the emperor? According to the Confucius' logic, only after a personal own moral character is cultivated perfectly can his family and clan be reorganized in good order, only after which can the country be governed successfully, only after which can the world be peaceful. Confucius found the foundation of country governance. The state and society consist of clans, which consist of families, and which consist of individuals. Accordingly he emphasized the importance of individuals, and families to the country, and further his argument was to emphasize the importance of personal cultivation. Thus starting from the goal of personal cultivation, he put forward the cultivation standards of the monarch and the people, which will be discussed later. We analyze whether the logic of this so-called Confucius' "Chinese Scripture" can withstand scrutiny at first.

As a matter of fact it involves the relationship in the midst of individual, family, clan, and country. This is an ancient, complex and distant relationship, and is not as simple as what Confucius and Confucianism had said. Back to the beginning of this article, we return to the human society more than 6000 years ago. At that time there were only families or clans, and were no country or government. Anyone born to this world was granted the rights to survival by God, and to continuous pursuit of the individual and family happiness. At that time there was no institution that stipulated individual self-cultivation standards for each family or individual, nor was there any institution to levy taxes on individuals or families, and to intervene in individual or family thought, production, life, trade, and so on. In this context all individuals and families are completely equal. This is only an interpersonal and inter-family inherent relationship in human beings.

However when discussing the relationship among individuals, families, and country, Confucius emphasized that the successful governance of individuals, and families laid a good foundation for the country governance. In the family he advocated filial piety, that is, children respected their parents, and younger siblings respected their older ones. Family sequence was determined based on filial piety. Confucius further evolved the filial piety of the family into the loyalty of the courtier to the king, and then into the filial piety of the king's family. Taking the filial piety of the king's family as the example, a social order was established. To all appearances, Confucius completely confused individual, family, and state governance. He didn't understand the inherent relationship amid individual, family, and country at bottom. This was the largest mistake Confucius made. We know that any individual or family has the right to freely engage in family affairs, and personal affairs at any given time. A family member must manage the family appropriately, and arrange production orderly, in other words, when they should do some things, their work schedule must be arranged, there will earn income, simultaneously life must be arranged suitably. It is necessary to arrange the life of both own family members, and parents, and show own filial piety to parents, and more. How is this family managed well? It is not that only by the Confucian filial piety can this family be managed appropriately. Children show filial piety to their parents both materially, and spiritually. It is impossible to have a filial spirit and attitude alone, and parents' actual problem cannot be solved. Thus it is necessary to have a material piety. Children must produce and trade to obtain income. Only if the income obtained is enough to support own family, extra money can be used for the material piety to the parents. When a child's family is poor, and his family members are hungry, and can't eat their fill, and his family food is taken away to filial parents without worrying about food or clothing, isn't it a false filial piety? Parents accept the filial piety, and instead feel uneasy. It is thus evident that the filial piety does not have much to do with the excellent family governance. To manage family appropriately, the key is to improve production, life, and trade, and increase income. Only when the family income increases can the filial piety for own elders have foundation, videlicet, "Only granaries are so sufficient that they could take into account etiquette". Therefore the filial piety is only one part of family governance. In family affairs, the uppermost is production, life, and trade, that is survival, and development affairs; the second is children cultivation; the third is only filial parents. Confucius only emphasized the family filial piety while ignored other family affairs, and simply summarized the family governance as filial piety, which was merely his personally biased standpoint.

With regard to the relationship between family, and country, Confucius more randomly connected. The family is governed in the spirit of filial piety. What is the relationship with the country governance? Theoretically the filial piety of family members to parents, and elders is purely a family private affair. How much filial piety, and how about filial attitude are completely a kind of tacit, and harmonious personal relationship formed by parents, and children of this family in the long-term practice. It is not much related with other families, and the country. However Confucius stiff insisted that this was wrongly related to the national governance. Actually he couldn't distinguish state affairs from family affairs! Since ancient times, state affairs have been dominated by public affairs, and country has established the rule and the ruled relationships with ordinary families through governments at various levels. Country is governed successfully, firstly main affairs are also development production, life, and trade to increase own national and governmental income so that the country can only be powerful. Secondly it is necessary to adjust various domestic contradictions to avoid wars. Thirdly it is necessary to manage properly the relation with foreign countries. All of them are only main affairs of national governance! Filial piety of emperor family was their private affair. It cannot be said that this emperor was filial, and can govern the people while that emperor was not filial, and cannot govern the people. Like this it is totally not objective that an emperor is one-sidedly evaluated, and judged by "filial piety"!

Therefore the relation among self-cultivation, family governance, and national governance cannot be simplified into what Confucius said. After a person finishes faultlessly the self-cultivation with filial piety, honesty, and loyalty as contents, he can not necessarily govern ideally own family. Family is particular about filial piety. A clan pays great attention to filial duty. All of them have little to do with the country governance. Since Confucius loved sacrifices since childhood, enjoyed studying the etiquette, and established practices of the Zhou Dynasty, and his hobbies were strongly recommended to the Chinese ruler through students, and instilled to the Chinese people through the ruler. How sad it is! The above statement completely refutes Confucius with his logical loopholes. Next we will analyze various rules Confucius set for the emperor, and the people.

Four main requirements of Confucianism for rulers include:

1. Lead by example, and strive for putting oneself in the other position. Manage interpersonal relationships at all classes in careful, and skillful;
2. Exercise government by means of ethics to gain popular support. Only when liking and hating the things were the same as the people can the emperor be supported by the people;
3. Recommend and appoint sage, value the sage, and abandon the villain;

4. Pay attention to the way of making money, and using money, and oppose to venality, and regard righteousness as profit.

In the view of Confucianism, the emperor who can meet the four requirements above was an excellent emperor, and the country can be governed successfully. The four requirements actually demand the ruler to respect the people, and regard the people interests as own interest so as to be an excellent emperor, and govern the country well. Nonetheless in reality, even if there is such a wise emperor, he certainly can not govern his country properly in that the courtier is loyal to the supreme splendid emperor, and the common people are obedient to the local magistrate in the rigidly hierarchical society advocated by Confucius. No matter how wise, able, and sagacious the ruler is, he cannot govern his country resoundingly.

Firstly no matter how diligent, and judicious the emperor is, he cannot know what the public mind is. Because the people are composed of millions, tens of millions and even hundreds of millions of individuals, only the people themselves can know own will, interest appeals, and minds. How can one emperor understand the people's public minds in the rigidly hierarchy advocated by Confucius? It is impossible in terms of space, and even more impossible in terms of time seeing that the public mind is changing again. Although the ruler can obtain a very small amount of the people feedback from some channels (courtier reports, incognito emperor private visits in plain clothes, and official documents), such public sentiment is all amended, and is not true. Distinctly "Those who win the people's public mind win the country" that was touted by the Confucian actually does not exist.

Secondly it is a very vague standard for emperors to cherish the sage, and abandon the villain, and cannot be achieved in reality. What is the sage? What is the villain? Will the sage write a "virtuous" word on his face? Will the villain write a "vile" word on his face? Confucianism simply divides persons into the sage, and the villain, which is extremely crude. The problem is not viewed from development or objectivity. A person is very wise and able at first but may become corrupt, vile, and harmful to the people once acting as a governmental official for a long time. How does the emperor know if the person he employs is a veritable sage or a false sage? Even if he employs a veritable sage, how can the emperor ensure that the sage will not go badly in the future? Distinctly this employment criterion was also fabled by Confucianism, and the emperor could not achieve at all.

Thirdly the emperor should regard righteousness as profit to seek the public benefit of the whole people. This is actually the most hypocritical proposition of Confucianism! It required that the emperor should not scramble for profits from the people, should save costs, and should not be extravagant, and wasteful, which distinctly is conducive to the establishment of the emperor image. The emperor is not greedy for money, and the people burden will naturally be alleviated but the people may not be prosperous. Considering that the people have ample foods and clothes that rely on mainly the improvement of production technology, productivity, and output. No matter how frugal the emperor is, the output does not increase, and the people do not live happily. Although the emperor's expenses were cut down, the amount was also huge. Because according to Confucius' hierarchical specifications, imperial family standards in all aspects were the highest, and it need cost a lot of money to maintain the specification. It was possible for the frugal during the emperor enthronement of the New Dynasty because he just came to power but he must be luxurious, and cost the people's blood and sweat money too much with time. With regard to the emperor to seek the public benefit of the whole people, it was even Confucian deceit. On account of the greatest benefit of all citizens, the decision-making power of public affairs has been monopolized by the emperor alone. How there can be the public benefit of the people? For example, a robber appears in your home, and says, "You must be obedient to my orders from now on, and I can protect the benefit of your whole family!" Will you believe this robber? Because your most important decision-making power is taken away, have you other benefits? Therefore what people say, "Little thieves are hanged, great ones become dukes" are very reasonable.

Fourthly all of these regal standards are based on a cloud-castle. For instance, the emperor led by example, and self-cultivation in the first standard. It is the most unreliable. In accordance with the hierarchical system advocated by Confucianism, splendid emperors are supreme, the courtier is loyal to the emperor, subordinate governmental officials obey their superiors, and the whole people are obedient to local magistrate. Under this system no one dare restrict the emperor at the top of the power in that the power is too high, and survival rights of all courtiers, and the people are controlled by the power will. Therefore the emperor is like a tiger in cage for courtiers, and the people, and is possible to eat people at any time. However this invisible cage is "the emperor led by example, and self-cultivation" as Confucianism preached. When the emperor is rational, and would like to accept opinions, he may not slaughter people. In any case the emperor is also a person, and also has seven emotions, six desires, pleasure, anger, sorrow, and joy. His mood is changeable. Once he is angry or doubts about someone, he may slaughter indiscriminately the innocent, and even start a war. The so-called companioning emperor is tantamount to living with a tiger!

Therefore Confucianism advocated that a preeminent emperor governed the people, and strove for it ceaselessly. This is just an illusory ideal or goal that will never be achieved. Next what kinds of behavior standards were Confucian proposed to the courtier, and the people? They are mainly as follows:

1. Courtier treats the monarch with great respect;
2. Children treat their parents with all kindness;
3. When touch elbows with others, we treat our friends with great loyalty.

The main ethics Confucius put forward to the people are family-based filial piety, and love, and respect for own elder brother, and further this family relationship was extended to the political domain such as loyalty, faith, and respect. This is the origin of his view of exercising government, and administrating country by means of ethics. The rulers should lead by example to abide by their own moral codes, and also required his courtiers and people to abide by the moral codes. At all events Confucianism never touched the problem essence, that is to say higher level problem: Should his courtiers and people be unconditionally loyal after the emperor himself was obedient to the so-called moral standards? Suppose the emperor was morally corrupt, can his courtiers and people overthrow him? Where did the emperor power come from? Confucius only said that his courtiers and people should be loyal to the emperor, and did not involve a series of such major issues. Therefore the emperor would lay down a large number of laws in the light of the spirit of Confucianism in all dynastic rule history. His courtiers and people were required to be loyal to the emperor while the emperor was only self-restraint. Since the idea of loyal to monarch was so ingrained in China that the emperor became insatiably greedy, and extorted excessive taxes and levies, courtiers and people did not dare to resist. Clearly the ideological practice of Confucianism actually becomes the laws formulated by the ruler that are used to rule the people by violence while the people must honestly abide by. Practices over thousands of years have proved that Confucianism is a psychedelic created by Confucius to maintain the autarchy of a handful of rulers who use violence to take the political power. Confucianism will only imprison the people's thought, and put the entire nationality in a backward and beaten state.

Chapter 2

How the Government Operates Economics with Economic Indicators

We above all analyze the authenticity of GDP growth data from 2001 to 2012. From the URL of the National Bureau of Statistics, we can find nominal GDP, and GDP index, and then calculate the real GDP, and GDP growth rate. All of these are calculated with the commodity price in 1978 as the benchmark (100, control standard), and have a certain degree of credibility.

Table 5: China nominal GDP (CNY 100 million), nominal growth rate (%), real GDP (CNY 100 million), real growth rate (%), and GDP index (the GDP of CNY 364.52 billion in 1978 as the benchmark 100) from 2001 to 2012

	Nominal GDP	Nominal growth rate	GDP index	Real GDP	Real growth rate
2001	109655.2	10.5	823.0	30000.0	8.3
2002	120332.7	9.7	897.8	32726.6	9.1
2003	135822.8	12.9	987.8	36010.9	10.0
2004	159878.3	17.7	1087.4	39637.9	10.1

	Nominal GDP	Nominal growth rate	GDP index	Real GDP	Real growth rate
2005	184937.4	15.7	1210.4	44121.5	11.3
2006	216314.4	17.0	1363.8	49713.2	12.7
2007	265810.3	22.9	1557.0	56755.8	14.2
2008	314045.4	18.2	1707.0	62223.6	9.6
2009	340506.9	8.4	1862.5	67891.9	9.1
2010	401202.0	17.8	2074.8	75630.6	11.4
2011	471564.0	17.5	2265.7	82588.6	9.2
2012	519322.0	10.1	2442.4	89030.5	7.8

The data in the above table is very important for judging the authenticity of China GDP. The nominal GDP is vital data disclosed in the bulletin of the National Bureau of Statistics while the nominal growth rate of GDP, real index of GDP, and real GDP are the data that the National Bureau of Statistics has never been willing to release in the *Press Communique*. Concerning the real growth rate of GDP is calculated at constant price (comparable price), although it is announced quarterly and monthly, the real GDP calculated at constant price is never announced. Instead, after the nominal GDP is announced, the growth rate of GDP suddenly appears at "comparable price". This behavior is irresponsible to the country, and the people. When the statistical department bulletins GDP, and other data, in order to gain the people's trust, they must release regularly nominal data, real data of GDP, nominal growth rate, and real growth rate of GDP.

In fact the National Bureau of Statistics has always calculated the real GDP data of subsequent years with the commodity price of 1978 used as constant price, and never released to the society. This is a dishonest behavior to the people. Certainly the National Bureau of Statistics released quietly the real GDP index on the website, equivalently indirectly released the real GDP. To be specific, the nominal GDP in 2009 was CNY 34 trillion, and real GDP index was 1862.5 (the GDP of CNY 364.52 billion in 1978 as the benchmark), then the real GDP in 2009 would be CNY 6,789.19 billion by calculation. Why we use the commodity price of 1978 to measure the output of 2009? Since the output calculated at a constant commodity price excludes the factor effect of rising commodity price, it can reflect the real growth in output over time. For one country or the people, the increase in real output is only the real growth, which only manifests that wealth has genuinely increased. Assuming that we only focus on the growth of nominal GDP, it is simple, as long as the central bank commands to change CNY 1 into CNY 100, the nominal GDP in 2009 will become immediately CNY 3,400 trillion. However the GDP in 2009 was also CNY 6,789.19 billion with the price in 1978 for calculation.

Now suppose a Country A produces only one commodity, rice. The output in 1978 was 1 billion catties, and the price was CNY 1 per catty. GDP in 1978 was CNY 1 billion. By 2013, the president of Country A wanted to increase the nominal output value, and enlarged its money supply by 10 times. The rice output in 2013 was assumed to be 2 billion catties, the current price of rice became CNY 10 per catty, nominal output value was CNY 20 billion. For this purpose the president of Country A was very bragging that the output value increased by 20 times compared with 1978. Some people who did not know the truth also lavished the president achievements of Country A, and the people of Country A never felt the material benefit of income was a factor of 20 higher anyway. How to uncover the president lie of Country A? We use the rice price of CNY 1 per catty in

1978 to calculate the rice output of 2 billion catties in 2013, the output value in 2013 was only CNY 2 billion, just double in 1978.

Markedly it is very important to choose the constant price of benchmark year recognized by the people of one country to measure the output value in subsequent years, which can limit the impulse of various government authorities to money over-issuance. When constant prices are used to measure the output value, the authorities want to exaggerate the output value or boast about their achievements, there is just one countermeasure to make up output, that is, the quantity of goods and services but it is easily penetrated by peers. For example, there is a Garment Factory (b) in City B. The Factory (b) production of 100,000 garments in the 2003 was completed in the statement when it was counted by the government of City B while another Factory (c) of same size in City C produced only 50,000 garments during the same period. Factory (c) may judge that Factory (b) exaggerated more 50,000 garments in the statement. However in order to see through the trick of exaggerating production in City B, product types, and quantities of City B must be disclosed. As soon as it is disclosed, the fake data of City B government will be penetrated immediately by the people.

Let's go back to China GDP in 2009. The nominal output value was CNY 34,050.69 billion, and the real output value was CNY 6789.19 billion. The real output value is divided by the nominal output value, and the GDP deflator is 5.02. This indicates that the output measured by the commodity price in 2009 is higher than that by the commodity price in 1978, and the commodity price is increased by 4.02 times or 402%. Distinctly this is merely calculated on the basis of the data provided by the National Bureau of Statistics.

We want to estimate how many times the commodity price in 2011 has actually risen compared to the commodity price in 1978, we can also use some simple and convenient methods to reckon. It may not be accurate but may be closer to the people's feelings. We most of all choose four common consumer products of the people:

Rice per catty,

Fish per catty,

Meat per catty,

Egg per catty

CPI of Chinese rice, fish, meat, and eggs in 2011 with the commodity price of 1978 as the benchmark

Then we find the commodity price in 1978: (The unit price of this year was provided by net friends, and was verified by the elderly over seventies.)

CNY 0.18/Rice per catty

CNY 0.4/Fish per catty

CNY 0.7/Meat per catty

CNY 0.8/Egg per catty

Gross price of these four commodities is CNY 2.08.

Then we find the prices of four commodities in 2011: (The unit price of this year is from conventional varieties such as eggs are native eggs, only which are comparable. Fish are grass carp, the common people ate chub, and grass carp in 1978 so grass carp are comparable.)

CNY 2/Rice per catty

CNY 5/Fish per catty

CNY 16/Meat per catty

CNY 11/Egg per catty

In 2011, the gross current price of four commodities was CNY 34, which divided by CNY 2.08 in 1978, is 16.35, i.e., CPI in 2011. CPI in 1978 is taken as 1. It means that the commodity price in 2011 increased by 15.35 times or 1535% of that in 1978!

For any sake it is far from the CPI bulletined by the National Bureau of Statistics. CPI announced by the website of the National Bureau of Statistics was 519 in 2009, and announced no longer later. In some financial and economic websites, such as some key data after 2009 are blank in Sina.com, and ifeng. com. However according to the year-on-year growth rate of CPI of 3.3% in 2010 and of 5.4% in 2011, we can calculate the CPI in 2010 as 536.1, and the CPI in 2011 as 565.0. Certainly these data are calculated on the strength of the CPI in 2009 provided by the National Statistics Bureau. It regards the gross price in 1978 as 100, namely the gross price in 1978 is 1, and the CPI in 2011 is 5.65 while the CPI calculated above is 16.35 in accordance with the price of several commodities in the people's real life. Evidently the CPI of the National Statistics Bureau is very different from the CPI experienced by the people. Let us now verify the rise in real commodity price since 1978.

Table 6: Currency inflation rates calculated based on GDP deflator and CPI

	Nominal GDP	Real GDP	GDP deflator	Inflation rate	CPI	CPI rise rate
2001	109655.2	30000.0	365.5	2.03	437.0	0.7
2002	120332.7	32726.6	367.7	0.6	433.5	-0.8
2003	135822.8	36010.9	377.2	2.5	438.7	1.2
2004	159878.3	39637.9	403.3	6.9	455.8	3.9
2005	184937.4	44121.5	419.2	3.9	464.0	1.8
2006	216314.4	49713.2	435.1	3.8	471.0	1.5

	Nominal GDP	Real GDP	GDP deflator	Inflation rate	CPI	CPI rise rate
2007	265810.3	56755.8	468.3	7.6	493.6	4.8
2008	314045.4	62223.6	504.7	7.8	522.7	5.9
2009	340506.9	67891.9	501.5	-0.6	519.0	-0.7
2010	401202.0	75630.6	530.5	5.9	536.1	3.3
2011	471564.0	82588.6	571.0	7.6	565.0	5.4

Generally the currency inflation rate (i.e. CPI rise rate) is calculated by two methods internationally: One is based on the CPI, and the other is based on the GDP deflator. The inflation rate calculated by two methods should be close. On all accounts we find in line with the above table that the inflation rate calculated based on the GDP deflator is very different from that based on the CPI every year. The annual CPI increase rate bulletined is all 1.5-3% less than that calculated based on the GDP deflator, of which 3%, and 2.6% are unexpectedly less in 2004, and 2010.

In China the inflation rate calculated based on nominal GDP, and real GDP data should be more credible. Because nominal GDP data, and real GDP data are statistics on all types of goods, and services domestically produced within a year, and CPI data only counts the price of eight categories of consumer goods such as rent, food, clothing, transportation, education, and entertainment. Generally speaking the increase range in the GDP deflator in the same period should be smaller than that in the CPI. It can also be said that the increase range in the CPI should be larger than that in the GDP deflator during the same period. The increase range in CPI over the same period should be higher than that in the commodity price calculated by the GDP deflator. Naturally this conclusion may have exceptions under special circumstances.

Table 7: Comparison between Chinese nominal growth rate (%), real growth rate (%), and inflation rate released by the National Bureau of Statistics, and inflation rate calculated based on GDP deflator from 2001 to 2011.

	Nominal GDP (1)	Nominal growth rate (2)	Real growth rate (3)	Inflation rate (A)	Inflation rate (B)	Inflation rate (C)
2001	109655.2	10.5	8.3	2.2	0.7	2.03
2002	120332.7	9.7	9.1	0.6	-0.8	0.6
2003	135822.8	12.9	10.0	2.9	1.2	2.5
2004	159878.3	17.7	10.1	7.6	3.9	6.9
2005	184937.4	15.7	11.3	4.4	1.8	3.9
2006	216314.4	17.0	12.7	4.3	1.5	3.8
2007	265810.3	22.9	14.2	8.7	4.8	7.6
2008	314045.4	18.2	9.6	8.6	5.9	7.8
2009	340506.9	8.4	9.1	-0.7	-0.7	-0.6
2010	401202.0	17.8	11.4	6.4	3.3	5.9
2011	471564.0	17.5	9.2	8.3	5.4	7.6

In Table 7, there is a big secret under cover: After calculation, the actual growth rate of GDP released by the National Bureau of Statistics is consistent with the real GDP annually. That is to say the actual growth rate of GDP of the National Bureau of Statistics is calculated on account of the actual data of GDP in their statistics each year, and there is no contradiction with the actual growth rate released. However they never bulletin the nominal growth rate of GDP, why? Because there is an important formula worldwide, i.e., nominal growth rate of GDP-real growth rate of GDP = currency inflation rate.

The nominal growth rate of GDP is given, and the real inflation rate can be easily calculated. The value of inflation rate

(A) (second item-fourth item) in Table 7 is probably the real inflation rate in China. By comparing the column of inflation rate (A) in Table 7 with the column of inflation rate (B) bulletined by the National Bureau of Statistics, it is found that the figures in other years are quite different except the figures in 2009 are completely consistent. In Table 7, the data of inflation rate (A) column is very close to that of the inflation rate (C) column calculated on the strength of the GDP deflator. Table 7 can prove that the popular calculation method of nominal growth rate of GDP -real growth rate of GDP = inflation rate is relatively reliable all over the world. It can be said that nominal growth rate of GDP -inflation rate = real growth rate of GDP. It can also be said that nominal growth rate of GDP = real growth rate of GDP + inflation rate. However the sum of the real growth rate of GDP and inflation rate bulletined by China is much smaller than the nominal growth rate. More specifically the real growth rate of GDP was 9.2, the inflation rate was 5.4, and their sum was only 14.6 while the nominal growth rate of GDP in 2011 was 17.5 in 2011. Whatever happens, the nominal growth rate of GDP can be easily calculated by anyone now that the GDP bulletined yearly and quarterly is nominal, and is easy to calculate, and just it is ignored by a large number of people.

We further verify the authenticity of Chinese nominal data of GDP, and real data of GDP. Why verify the authenticity of nominal GDP, and real GDP? This actually involves the total amount of real wealth created by a country or a government, and people within one period but does not involve how real wealth is distributed fairly among the people. The authenticity of nominal GDP and real GDP can also reflect the real commodity price increase. Taking the data in the year of 2010 in Table 5 as an example, the CPI is 5.361, and the GDP deflator is 5.305 (with total price of 1978 as 1). According to the passage above, the

CPI in 2010 is the order of 16 by computation. This shows that in the light of the statistics of the National Bureau of Statistics, the CPI in 2010 rose only 5.36 times, and the price of all goods, and services in 2010 rose only 5.3 times compared with 1978. Whereas in the light of the price in the people's several representative consumer goods, the CPI in 2010 rose by 15 times compared with 1978.

Why there is a huge gap between the data officially published, and the data verified from the common people? This must investigate the relationships between nominal GDP and real GDP, nominal GDP and CPI, and real GDP and CPI. Three major relationships are the basic framework of current macroeconomics in the world, and the basis of every country government administration in the world since the 20th century. There are huge crises in the economic field of various countries, which is accurately caused by the inherent error in their dominant economic theories across the world today. Hereby the author will expose these errors for the first time throughout the history of humankind to correct the progress direction of global economics.

Chapter 3

Revealing Laws between Nominal GDP and Actual GDP

This is a very complicated issue that has not as yet been finalized in the international economics circles. The author believes that there can merely be three relationships between nominal GDP, and real GDP:

1. When nominal GDP increases, real GDP may increase, remain unchanged, or decrease;
2. When nominal GDP remains unchanged, real GDP may increase, remain unchanged or decrease;
3. When nominal GDP decreases, real GDP may increase, remain unchanged or decrease.

In order to facilitate the explanation of these relationships, we assume that Country A produced only one commodity in 2011, rice. Further assume that 100 million catties of rice were produced in 2011, and average unit price of rice was 1 yuan. The nominal GDP of Country A in 2011 was 100 million yuan.

I. The government of Country A decided to double domestic money supply at the beginning of 2012. Supposing that after three months, the rice unit price in Country A rises to 2 yuan, the increase in rice retail, and wholesale prices stimulates wholesalers for a period to enhance the unit price of purchase rice, correspondingly promotes rice producers to expand their planting area, and improve planting varieties, as a result production is increased to 110 million catties. As far as rice, the nominal GDP of Country A in 2012 is 220 million yuan, and the real GDP is 110 million yuan. In 2012, the nominal GDP of Country A increases by 120 million yuan while the real GDP increases by only 10 million yuan. The increase of real GDP of rice reflects that of real production.

However after the expansion of money supply in Country A in 2012, meanwhile stimulating the growth of rice production, the real GDP of Country A does not necessarily increase. The first reason, in reality the people of Country A not only produces rice, but also tens of thousands types of other commodities are produced such as vegetables, and clothes. The second reason, the material capital, human capital, natural resources, and technological level of Country A are basically or largely unchanged in a short period. Under the stimulus of excessive money supply, the people of Country A increase the rice production, and in the meantime may reduce the production of other commodities so that the GDP of Country A remains unchanged or decreases. Needless to say the excessive money supply stimulates the increase in rice production, and meanwhile may not affect the increase in production of other commodities but one of following conditions must be met at least:

a. Human capital attracted by Country A increases within one year;
b. Technical level of one or more productions in Country A is significantly improved;
c. The people of Country A are more diligent, and prolong working hours.

In case Country A does not meet one of three conditions above by the end of 2012, the monetary stimulus increases the rice production, and simultaneously the real GDP of Country A in 2012 cannot increase, and even may decrease. Obviously the view of money to stimulate economic growth implies numerous uncertain risks. Only when certain conditions are met can the real GDP increase. However, the monetary stimulus will definitely lead to the rise in domestic commodity prices, which will sequentially increase in the nominal GDP.

II. When the nominal GDP remains unchanged, the real GDP may increase, remain unchanged or decrease. Suppose the government of Country A decided to keep its domestic money supply unchanged in 2012. The CPI of Country A in 2012 will remain the same as that in 2011. Although prices of some commodities may rise in 2012, prices of other commodities will fall. After the weighted average the CPI will maintain unchanged. On the premise of constant money supply the GDP growth of Country A can only depend on the real growth of GDP, viz., the growth of real production. On the premise of constant money supply in 2012, in case the real production increases, the commodity price may drop, and its monetary purchasing capacity will increase in Country A.

Providing Country A produces only one commodity (rice) in 2012, rice price may be lower than the average unit price of 1 yuan in 2012. For example, in 2012 the people of Country A increases rice production to 110 million catties through one of improving varieties, strengthening management, expanding planting area, enhancing technology, and lengthening working hours. The nominal GDP of Country A in 2012 is less than 110 million yuan, and the real GDP is 110 million yuan. For instance, the actual GDP of Country A increases significantly in 2012. On the grounds that monetary aggregates remain unchanged, the commodity price of Country A may fall significantly in 2012. Although the GDP of Country A increases, the nominal GDP may be equal to or less than the real GDP on the score of the fall in commodity prices. Definitely on the premise of the constant money supply of Country A in 2012, the rice production of country A is reduced due to the number of laborer, work efficiency, natural conditions, and the rest, resulting in the reduction in the real GDP.

III. When nominal GDP decreases, real GDP may increase, remain unchanged or decrease. The nominal GDP of Country A in 2012 is less than that of 2011, there are only two possibilities: Firstly the government of Country A decided to deflate the money supply in 2012, compared to 2011, thereby the commodity price in 2012 is reduced. Secondly the annual production of Country A declines in 2012. At present economic circles and governments around the world have merely considered the first situation where the nominal GDP and real GDP increase, and never considered the situation where the nominal GDP remains constant or decreases. All of them require merely the economic growth, and do not allow the economy to stagnate and reduce naturally, which will lead to the world economy toward an edge of cliff of limitless growth. World economy should have included growth, stagnation, and decline. It is impossible to grow forever. It is abnormal and unsustainable no other than growth.

Suppose the government of Country A decided in early 2012 to deflate the domestic money supply to a half of 2011, and the commodity price in 2012 falls to a half of 2011, videlicet the average price is 0.5 yuan, and Country A only produces rice in 2012, rice production may be 90 million catties, 100 million catties or 110 million catties, then the nominal GDP in 2012 is:

1. 90 million catties * 0.5 yuan = 45 million yuan;
2. 100 million catties * 0.5 yuan = 50 million yuan;
3. 110 million catties * 0.5 yuan = 55 million yuan;

In above three situations, in other words the actual production of rice in 2012 may decrease, remain unchanged, and increase, the nominal GDP of Country A is significantly smaller than the actual GDP. Due to the price drop, even though the production increases to 110 million catties in 2012, the nominal GDP is only 55 million yuan, far less than the actual GDP of 110 million yuan. This reveals a major shortcoming of countries around the world nowadays to count the GDP in monetary unit: Under the condition of sharp deflation in the money supply, even though the real output increases, the nominal GDP in statistics will also drop significantly. No matter what the nominal GDP decreases, it does not affect the increase in the real GDP. When we count the GDP based on rice production alone, i.e., 100 million catties in 2011, and 110 million catties in 2012, this output value is calculated merely by weight but by money. When we only focus on comparing the quantity of goods and services, it is also feasible to count the quantity of various types of goods, and services alone. In any sort tens of thousands of kinds of commodities can only be compared against the quantity without price such as how many catties of rice, how many pieces of clothes, and how many customers had their hair cut, which will be very troublesome. When the current price per unit is used to calculate respectively how much monetary amount, and then to get a sum or the total GDP, it is obviously easy to compare.

On every account when calculating the GDP in monetary amount, governments from various countries do not expect the nominal GDP at year-on-year decrease, even if the real

GDP increases, it has no effect on the economy, and does not mean a so-called recession, they are dedicated to stimulating the "recessionary" economy various state. Therefore when the nominal GDP decreases, we must distinguish that the reason is whether the decline in real output or in price. With regard to the truth of the U.S. economic recession in 1929-1933, we have to review whether the reason for the price decline or the output decline? We can not only accept the Milton Friedman's analysis, and instead we further understand what are the change details of real GDP (more information on the quantity of various types of goods, and services from 1929 to 1933) in order to explain authentically the substantial problem.

One view that is widely popular in the international and domestic economics circles is that one country money supply must grow moderately at a rate of about 3% in order to benefit the country economic growth. Almost all mainstream economists claim that the money supply can only increase, and can not decrease. When the money supply is deflated, the economic growth rate will definitely decline. Naturally this will reduce the nominal GDP but not necessarily the real GDP.

Currently let's take a Farmer Family F in the south of the Yangtze River China in 2011 as an example. The Family F has 5 members, and 3 mu of farmland. The farmland produced a total of 3,000 catties of rice in 2011. The monetary income of Family F was CNY 1,500. The cost of seeds, pesticides, chemical fertilizers, etc. for 3 mu of farmland was exactly CNY 1,500. After CNY 1,500 monetary income of the Family F fully invested in 3 mu of farmland, 3,000 catties of rice were harvested in 2011. Granting that in 2012, the monetary income of Family F only is CNY 750 due to various reasons, will the rice output of 3 mu of Family F exceed 3,000 catties in 2012? This depends on the following factors of the Family F:

1. Family F determined that the rice output exceeds 3,000 catties;
2. Whether the Family F can have CNY 750 credit loans;
3. If no loans, whether the Family F has the ability to borrow relevant items of CNY 750;

When the Family F determined to exceed the output of 3,000 catties, the Family F can always borrow relevant items of CNY 750 to invest in the farmland, and strengthen the management. It is entirely possible to reach 1,100 catties per mu, and the total output of 3,300 catties in 3mu. In 2012 on the premise of reducing a half the money supply, the Family F can still increase 10% of the rice production, whether the resources related to rice cultivation such as seeds, fertilizers, pesticides, machinery, water, and labor can be allocated, the key is not that the Family F has enough money investment but whether these inputs are sufficient in society? When these inputs are sufficient, the Family F can easily complete the transaction by credit without money. Money is merely the exchange medium so does credit like barter. Therefore it has no basis for the reduction in the money supply that will trigger surely the decline in real output. As the money supply decreases, people can use credit or barter to achieve exchanges, and thereby inputs are allocated, and output is increased.

Chapter 4

GDP Calculation Models Originated by
Dong Fang Dao

The relationship between nominal GDP and CPI is also complicated by so-called mainstream economists in modern times. They do not explore the relationship between the two issues in essence but do empirically verify the relationship between the both on the basis of some data in the past. Milton Friedman is such a typical representative. He just found the law from the empirical data of money supply, commodity price, GDP, and others. It is obviously from the phenomenon but does not explain the problem from the essence.

Today the author tries to analyze the relationship between nominal GDP and CPI from essence. As we all know the nominal GDP refers to the gross value of all final goods, and services produced in a country within a certain period. This gross value refers to the sum of output (quantity), and market price (current price) per unit of all kinds of goods and services. Intrinsically the nominal GDP is determined by the output amount, and what price per unit. The increase in nominal GDP is either an increase in real output or a result of rising prices. Also the CPI (Consumer Price Index) is also the sum of output, and prices per unit of all types of commensurate goods and services used for consumption. On all accounts the quantity of selected types of goods, and services is fixed. CPI compares the total price of equal quantity of goods and services in different periods, and is also determined by the output amount (relatively unchanged), and unit price.

The composition of nominal GDP and CPI shows that they are the sum of the same kind of goods and services with corresponding current price per unit. Nothing but that the nominal GDP is aggregated by all kinds of goods and services, and corresponding current price per unit while CPI is aggregated by a fixed quantity of consumer goods, and corresponding current price per unit. Nowadays we discuss several intrinsic relationships between the both.

We introduce the so-called identical equation on the GDP composition in economic textbooks throughout the world:

$$Y = C + I + G + NX \qquad \text{(Formula 1)}$$

Y represents GDP, C represents consumption, I represents investment, G represents government expenditure, and NX represents net exports (exports-imports). The premise of this equation satisfied is that GDP must refer to the market value of all final goods and services produced for one country within a given period, namely indicating that all the goods and services are produced, and exchanged in the market. With respect to all goods and services, as long as the transaction is concluded, the seller's income must be equal to the buyer's expenditure. Accordingly the sum of all the buyer expenditures must equal that of all the seller incomes. To be specific there are 200 vendors (sellers) in a vegetable market, and various vegetable sales incomes from 200 sellers amount to 100,000 yuan on someday. Without doubt expenditures from multitudinous vegetable buyers are also 100,000 yuan. Income per yuan corresponds to expenditure per yuan, and thus this equation is satisfied.

All expenditures in one country can be divided into four categories such as consumption, investment, government expenditure, and net import. However what nature of expenditure is ranged consumption, and is ranged investment, and so forth, it is sometimes difficult to divide. What is the nature difference between consumption expenditure, and investment expenditure? Whether such a division is valuable? They are worthwhile to research. This identical equation based on the relation between purchase and sell can only use the current price to measure the value of all commodities and services entering the market, and the one outside the market can not be measured. In respect of some regions and countries, this method is unscientific, and is difficult to really and comprehensively measure all GDP of a country or region. A brand new GDP calculation mode invented by Dong Fang Dao is as follows:

$$Y= A+ B+ NX-D \qquad \text{(Formula 2)}$$

Y represents GDP, A represents tangible commodities, B represents intangible services, and NX represents net imports. Only in this way can we measure accurately the GDP of a country or region in a given period. As long as tangible commodities are produced, it can calculate definitely by quantity. As long as there is market, it can measure definitely by market prices. As long as intangible services are generated, it can also measure by quantity or price. As well as net exports, certainly, the total value of a certain amount of goods and services sold to foreigners by own country, minus the total value of a certain amount of goods and services purchased, and imported by own country from foreign countries. It can calculate definitely by quantity, and price.

However all tangible and intangible goods and services produced constitute the total wealth for a certain period in one country. This is a biased concept. Because the production of all tangible goods and intangible services is at the cost of consuming the earth resources or human energy, and physical strength, the total wealth is only the total gross income of one country or region in a given period, which must subtract the total cost D of creating this total wealth. The total cost D is the expenditure of this country or region caused by the environmental pollution, occupational disease treatment, waste resources, and others in a given period. The GDP calculated like this is more valuable, and measures the total net income of one country or region, i.e., total income-total cost = total net income. This GDP integrates organically one country economic metrics into one company metrics. Every enterprise always promotes human progress in pursuit of maximum profits but maximum total income. When one country measures the GDP, the total cost must be also subtracted before it can reflect that this country is authentically pursuing the increase in pure wealth.

Classification of the GDP is also objective, and true in another form:

$$Y = E + F + NX - D \qquad \text{(Formula 3)}$$

Y represents GDP in a given period, E represents the market value of domestically produced and traded goods and services, F represents the market value of household production, self-use goods and services, and NX represents net exports. This is extremely accurate to measure one country GDP. Considering that it is to measure the total value of production, as long as goods and services produced domestically within a given period should be regarded as the statistical object. Whether and when newly-produced goods and services enter the market for exchange depends entirely on the owner production purpose, and demand extent for exchange. It cannot be said that goods and services are not used for exchange, and do not belong to the production value. This is completely wrong.

In addition the relationship between E and F is very important. For instance, a certain commodity, the more household self-produced, and self-sold quantities, the less transaction quantities to the market, and vice versa. More precisely, rice, wheat, and vegetables, 700 million farmers in China almost all produce, and most of them can meet their own needs. Their excess products are only exchanged in the market through various channels. Merely Chinese urban citizens exchange to the market because they do not produce rice, wheat, and vegetables. Chinese 700 million farmers are all the most veritable investors because in order to produce various products quarterly or every year, they must invest in pesticides, fertilizers, seeds, houses, and labor. The farmer investment is also the most meaningful seeing that their various agricultural products substantially increase the real domestic output. Undoubtedly household self-produced, and self-sold products are very closely related to the same products that are delivered to the market for transactions: The more families have the same item outside the market, the less the demand for the item in the market, and the price must fall; the less families have the same item outside the market, the more the demand for the item in the market, and the price must rise.

So-called commodities are products, and services used for exchange: When one product is placed in own home, it is just an article; when the owner transports it to the market for transaction, it is called a commodity. Therefore the principle that the commodity price is determined by market supply and demand reflects merely part of the authenticity of price formation. The complete situation is that the commodity price is determined not only by the market supply and demand, but also by the quantity of households have the product outside the market.

NX is also inextricably related to E and F. The more one country imports the same kind, category, and class of commodity, the lower the commodity price will be caused whether it is household self-use or is traded into the market. When the more the household imports for self-use, the less the imports for purchase in the market, this commodity price must fall in the market. When the more this commodity imports in the market, this commodity price will also cause to fall. Exports are opposite as follows: When exports of the domestic item are increased, the supply in the domestic market must be reduced, and the commodity price in the market must be increased. Concerning one country, the governmental responsibility is to allow its own country people to buy domestic products at the most preferential price so as to make own people rich, and powerful. When one country does not export own surplus products abroad but exports the product that own people need abroad, the intention of such exports is questionable! The export purpose is to import better, more, and newer commodities in order to finally meet domestic demand, and only make own people richer. At all events, with regard to imports, on the understanding that there must be more commodities exported. Therefore the key is to increase the productivity of various domestic products. Only if more products are produced domestically, which meet not only the demand of the domestic people, but also surplus for export, can imports be increased. When an item that one country households averagely want to have is less, and the country exports a lot of such items, even if the country GDP is large, it is disturbing just that this national people are not richer due to the GDP.

Evidently E, F, and NX are only the best means to measure one country GDP. It shows the values used for transaction, for household self-use, and for net exports.

There are also many GDP classifications such as primary, secondary, and tertiary industries.

Y = primary industry (agriculture, forestry, animal husbandry, and fishery) + secondary industry (mining, manufacture, and construction) + tertiary industry (services in circulation links such as wholesale, retail, and transportation)-D   (Formula 4)

It is classified according to the type of producers of goods, and services. As long as the added value of goods and services produced by all economic entities in these industries is calculated in a given period, the GDP can be obtained.

According to the final destination of all goods and services, the GDP can also be classified for measurement. There are only two possibilities for all products and services produced by all enterprises (state-owned enterprises, joint-stock enterprises, and individual enterprises), and households in one country within a given period: One is bought, and the other is not bought. All products and services without procurement have also another two possibilities: One is for the producer own use, and the other is for inventory, and will be bought later; All products and services bought have also another two possibilities: One is buyer direct use and consumption, and the other is that the buyer utilizes it to produce goods and services for profit after procurement. When the buyer directly uses, and consumes, they are called as consumer goods. When the buyer utilizes them to produce goods and services, they are called as investment goods. Many goods and services in the market can be either consumer goods or investment goods in accordance with different buyer use natures. When investment is apprehended restrictively into fixed capital such as houses, buildings, machinery, and equipment, it is very unscientific. Investment can also be classified more scientific. The more thorough the investigation is conducted, the greater the significance is.

According to different buyer (owner) natures of all final goods and services produced in one country during a certain period, the GDP can be also expressed as:

$$Y = C + G + NX - D \qquad \text{(Formula 5)}$$

Y stands for GDP, C stands for the private nature purchase of enterprises, households, and individuals, G stands for public purchase viz. governmental purchase, and NX stands for the value of one country domestic products and services sold to foreigners minus that of foreign products and services purchased domestically. Because all kinds of products and services are produced in one country that can only be bought by families, economic entities, and governments. Generally speaking the vast majority of products and services purchased by families are directly used as consumer products, that by economic entities (enterprises) are used as investment products for profit, that by the government are used as various public goods. Considering that consumer goods are closely related to the people's livelihood in one country, all countries have established CPI. How are various consumer goods available on the market produced? Obviously various economic entities (enterprises) organize production capacity, and produce on the basis of the consumer demand. Various economic entities (enterprises) must purchase and produce simultaneously, one is to buy various new workshops, machinery and equipment, raw materials, and the like directly used for production, and the other is to buy various consumer goods for workers, that is to say, when organizing production, various economic entities (enterprises) must consume. So it is not rigorous to regard the purchase of economic entities (enterprises) as an investment in modern economics. Government purchases are divided into the procurement of various public goods, the first is the procurement of public goods in various fixed assets, such as squares, highways, railways, parks, and schools, the second is the procurement of various consumer goods for government agencies, and personnel, the third is the procurement of various public services paid by the government. Therefore GDP can also be indicated in detail as:

$$Y = C1+C2+C3+G1+ G2+G3+NX-D \qquad \text{(Formula 6)}$$

C1 stands for all household expenditures for consumer goods, C2 stands for expenditures of consumer goods of various economic entities (enterprises), and C3 stands for governmental expenditures for consumer goods domestically. Like this the destination of all consumer goods is clarified in one country. G1 stands for the investment expenditure of various economic entities (enterprises), G2 stands for the governmental expenditure on various public goods, and G3 stands for the governmental expenditure on various public services. Likewise whereabouts all kinds of capital goods, and public goods are clarified in one country.

The relationship between investment and consumption is that investment is to save current consumption, and produce products and services in the future. At all events whether various public goods purchased by the government are investments should be clearly distinguished. Because investment is most importantly characterized by profits, and public goods purchased by the government such as parks, squares, railways, and highways should not be used for profits or else it cannot be called public goods, and can only be a commodity of ordinary connotation. Public goods for the non-profit purpose purchased by the government should be classified as consumer goods. Since handed over to the public by the government, these public goods (parks, highways, railways, etc.) have been consumed by the public, have non-profit purpose, and will not increase revenue. On the contrary the government must increase continuously expenditures to maintain these public goods. Regarding whether purchase, and expenditure of such public goods are as desired by the people, and whether they have other values, it is another matter. Public goods are the people's common consumer goods, not investment goods.

In conclusion it is defective that the GDP is indistinctly divided into consumption, investment, and net exports. Like the United States it is also unscientific to divide the GDP into consumption, investment, government procurement, and net exports. Considering that private investment contains consumption, and the nature of consumption and investment in government procurement is difficult to distinguish. Therefore it is necessary to distinguish in detail like the above formula (Formula 6), and is only meaningful.

This equation indicates that the relationship among investment, government procurement, and CPI: When investment is added, future production capacity will increase, at the same time it will drive up the increase in consumer demand to trigger rising commodity prices, and vice versa. When government procurement is added, it will also drive up the increase in consumer demand to trigger rising commodity prices. Monetary sources of government procurement are particularly worthy of attention, and include only four: Taxation, inflation, borrowing money, and capital income. Whether the government procurement is cost-effective should be analyzed, and evaluated from the monetary source. Undoubtedly the excessive government procurement is an inflationary source. Only by reasonably controlling various government expenditures can the wealth flow to the people, who become wealthy.

Chapter 5

Revealing Laws between Money Supply and GDP

In each country actual GDP and CPI may only have the following relationships:

I. Specify the Price of a Certain Year as Benchmark, and Money Stock of One Country Will Not Change in Subsequent Years.

Under such circumstances a country real GDP increases year by year (consumer goods, investment goods, and net exports increase at the same proportion). The country commodity price declines year after year, reflecting in the prices of commensurate consumer goods, the price must be a gradual decline, CPI decreases year by year, and currency inflation is negative.

For example, small Country A produces only one commodity, rice. In 2001, rice production was 100 million catties, unit price was 1 yuan, and the money supply was 100 million yuan. From 2001 to 2010, Country A maintained 100 million yuan money supply. By improving varieties and technology, Country A has increased rice output at 10% annual growth rate. The annual output of rice was 100 million catties in 2001, 110 million catties in 2002, 121 million catties in 2003, 133.1 million catties in 2004, 146.41 million catties in 2005, 161.051 million catties in 2006, 177.1561 million catties in 2007, and 194.87171 million catties in 2008.

It can be found that the rice production increased by one time or doubled at 10% growth rate in only seven years from the first year (viz., 2002) to 2008. When the money supply of Country A remained unchanged at 100 million yuan, 100 million yuan money corresponded to 200 million catties of rice, and the unit price of rice would drop by half, namely 0.5 yuan per catty, and 1 yuan can buy 2 catties of rice by 2008. Assuming that the rice CPI in 2001 was 1, and the CPI in 2008 was 0.5, the inflation rate in 2008 was -0.5 x 100% = -50%. It is so-called deflation. There are two situations in deflation: Firstly output increases, and monetary aggregates relatively shrink under the premise of stable money supply; secondly when output remains unchanged or increases, the absolute monetary aggregate amount shrinks.

How to evaluate deflation? In the former case, output increases on the premise of stable money supply, even as the rice case, from 1 yuan /catty in 2001 to 0.5 yuan /catty in 2008, there is no bad influence on everybody in the Country A who has money. 1 yuan can only buy 1 catty of rice in 2001, and can buy 2 catties of rice in 2008.

For the buyer he can buy more rice with the same money, because for everyone rice consumption is limited yearly, the excess money can be deposited. By way of illustration a Citizen D in the Country A can be only enough to eat when buys 300 catties of rice per year. He spent 300 yuan on rice in 2001, and only 150 yuan on rice in 2008. The Citizen D can deposit the surplus 150 yuan. The accumulation of 150 yuan is his benefit brought by the year-by-year increase of rice production in the Country A agriculture. Just because of the increase in rice production, the Citizen D had become richer than that in 2001.

For the seller 1 catty of rice was sold for 1 yuan in 2001, and was sold for 0.5 yuan, and 2 catties of rice only was sold for 1 yuan in 2008. Therefore only by being sold the double rice can the rice seller exchange the same money. Suppose a Farmer F in the Country A grows rice to make a living. The Farmer F eats 300 catties of rice every year, and the excess rice is sold. The Farmer F's rice output per mu was 600 catties in 2001, and was 1,200 catties in 2008. The Farmer F sold the excess 300 catties of rice for 300 yuan in 2001, sold 600 catties of rice for only 300 yuan in 2008, and sold the excess 900 catties of rice for only 450 yuan. For the Farmer F, the increase in rice production in 2008 brought him a benefit of 150 yuan, which was due to the yield improvement per mu on the premise of improved varieties, technological progress, and the same investment. As a result the increase in unit output, and the decrease in commodity price benefited both buyer and seller.

Anyway for the Farmer F, in the event that the rice gross output of Country A is increased rather than the increase in output per mu, the Farmer F cahnot benefit, and can only lose due to the increase in national output. For example, on the grounds that the Country A government increased the number of rice-growing households to double by adopting physiocratic measures by 2008, rice production in 2008 doubled than that in 2001, and rice prices in 2008 dropped to 0.5 yuan per catty. In 2008, the rice output of Farmer F was 600 catties. He ate 300 catties by myself, and sold surplus 300 catties for only 150 yuan. For the Farmer F, compared with 2001, the income was reduced 150 yuan in 2008. The Farmer F situation was not improved due to the increase in rice gross output across the Country A, and worsened due to his output increase. No doubt it is also very important how to increase the gross output of commodity. Just as the manufacture industry needs to enhance productivity in order to generate more wealth, agriculture must enhance the output per mu for agricultural products to make farmers become rich. If it is not the increase in output per mu, and the increases in the gross output or in the number of peasant households cultivating farmland throughout the country to make the agricultural gross output increase, such increases in output will instead cause the price of agricultural products to fall, resulting in the increase in grain output, and the decline in farmer income throughout the country. From the Qin and Han Dynasties to the Qing Dynasty in China, after the reunification of every dynasty, the construction of water conservancy, the expansion of agricultural acreage, and the increase in the number of farming households led to the increase in the national grain gross output, and the decline in prices. As a consequence "whole country has no idle fields, farmers still starve" every time. It is just because the increase in actual output is not based on the increase in output per mu.

Under the precondition of stable monetary aggregate, the increase in output is good for everyone. Although the price drops, the seller may enhance a part of the output to make up for the loss of price decline by boosting productivity, and surplus also adds the seller proceeds. No matter what the increase in gross output is caused by the increase in the number of suppliers, such an increase in gross output will promote the commodity price fall, instead the supplier income reduces, and they become poorer than before.

II. Specify the Price of a Certain Year as Benchmark, and Money Stock of One Country Will Increase with the Improvement of Output Growth Rate in Subsequent Years.

Under such circumstances, the real GDP of one country increases year by year (consumer goods, investment goods, and net exports increase at the same proportion). Commodity prices remain stable that are reflected in the prices of commensurate consumer goods, prices hold steady, the CPI is approximately equal to 1, and currency inflation is zero.

For instance, a small Country A, which produces only one commodity, rice. In 2001, rice production was 100 million catties, unit price was 1 yuan, and the money supply was 100 million yuan. From 2002 to 2010, money supply of the Country A had increased at 10% growth rate. By improving varieties and technology, the Country A has increased the rice output at 10% annual growth rate. The annual rice output was 100 million catties in 2001, 110 million catties in 2002, 121 million catties in 2003, 133.1 million catties in 2004, 146.41 million catties in 2005, 161.051 million catties in 2006, 177.1561 million catties in 2007, and 194.87171 million catties in 2008. It can be found that from the first year (viz., 2002) to 2008 at 10% growth rate, and rice production increased by one time or doubled in only seven years.

The money supply of Country A was 100 million yuan in 2001, 110 million yuan in 2002, 121 million yuan in 2003, 133.1 million yuan in 2004, 146.41 million yuan in 2005, 161.051 million yuan in 2006, 177.1561 million yuan in 2007, and 194.87171 million yuan in 2008. By 2008 the money supply of Country A was twice over that of 2001 in only seven years. How would the rice price change under the condition that the money supply increased with the output growth rate like the Country A? We have to specifically analyze how to increase 10% money supply. Provided that in January 2002, the central bank of Country A loaned 1 million yuan to a Commercial Bank of Country A, and the deposit reserve ratio was 10%. In terms of the deposit multiple effect, the deposit of Country A increased by 10 million yuan in the next period of 2002. That is the money supply increased by 10%, and the money stock of Country A at the end of 2002 was 1.1 trillion yuan. The Commercial Bank B borrowed 1 million yuan in cash from the central bank of the country in January 2002. In order to earn the interest margin as quickly as possible, the Commercial Bank B would lend the money to consider reliable customers as soon as possible. Suppose the Farmer F was trying to improve rice varieties, and engaged in plantation in a high technology at this time, and thus borrowed 1 million yuan from the Commercial Bank B. After receiving this money, the Farmer F immediately built water conservancy, improved soil, and introduced excellent varieties. By the end of 2002, the yield per mu increased from 600 catties in 2001 to 660 catties in 2002. Granting that the Farmer F earned 100,000 yuan on account of grain yield increase by 100,000 catties, after the Farmer F repaid 1 million yuan to the Commercial Bank B at the end of 2002, and he still profited 100,000 yuan for deposits. How was 100,000 yuan profit earned by the Farmer F created? Evidently he obtained it by selling rice of yield increase to the market. His 100,000 yuan came from customers who bought rice. Because the Farmer F first obtained loans, his yield increased first. When he first put the yield increase into the market, the buyer in the market did not immediately feel that the rice supply increased significantly. The Farmer F would try his best to sell the rice of yield increase at the price of 1 yuan per catty due to yield increase. Therefore the Farmer F first benefited from the loan.

We next analyze the law of currency circulation increase. When the Farmer F received the 1 million yuan loans in January 2002, he may deposit all 1 million yuan as current deposit, and then would pay for the input of commodities such as pesticides, fertilizers, and seeds, and pay various labor wages and expenses with the production progress. Suppose an Individual N had business relationship with the Farmer F. After the Individual N got his proceeds from the Farmer F, he deposited the money in the bank to earn interest. After the bank got the takings, it immediately loaned the money to an Individual M on account of requisite interest margin. At deposit reserve ratio of 10%, the deposits of the entire commercial bank expanded to 10 million yuan. In the process of the Farmer F's 1 million yuan deposits becoming 10 million yuan deposits of the entire banking system, somebody received pure deposits while other deposited, and burdened by loan debt. For instance, businessman who supplied seeds to the Farmer F, peasants who worked for the Farmer F, after earned proceeds from the Farmer F, their money obtained has a pure deposit connotation, and will not be used for loan repayment. Whereas the Farmer F is different as he borrowed 1 million yuan from the bank, he must earn 1 million yuan from others for repayment bank.

Next let's assume that the Farmer F took out 1 million yuan loans from the bank in January 2002, and paid the Individual N who had business relationship with him. The "new" word was written on all banknotes before making the payment. Continuously let's assume that 1 million banknotes with "new" word all were paid. The Individual N received "new" banknotes, and can turn all of them into bank deposits. The 1 million yuan may be withdrawn by the Individual N at any time to buy commodities in the market. After the commercial bank obtained the 1 million banknotes with "new" word, it can loan 900,000 yuan of them, such as lent to a Farmer G. After the Farmer G received the loan, he paid again, and another Individual M received 900,000 yuan proceeds from the Farmer G. The Individual M deposited the 900,000 yuan banknotes with "new" word in the bank, and received a 900,000 yuan of current deposit slip (debit card), and can buy commodities at any time, and so on. When the initial 1 million yuan "new" money generates 10 million yuan deposits, it also generates 9 million yuan loans. These borrowers must get 9 million yuan "old banknotes" from others in some form on the market for repayment bank. If the Country A has only one final product, rice. Let's also assume that all borrowers in the Country A are engaged in rice production. These borrowers increased the rice gross yield by 10% or 10 million catties in 2002. Before the increase production rice of 10 million catties was sold in the market, all borrowers had completed the relevant payments, and correlative personnel had increased 10 million yuan deposits. Holders of 10 million yuan deposits can buy rice with current deposits at any time. If they purchased 10 million catties of new increase rice production, the rice price would not rise due to the new increase deposit of 10 million yuan, corresponding to new increase rice production of 10 million catties. The original 100 million yuan "old money" of the Country A still corresponded to the rice of 100 million catties so the rice price would not rise. By 2002 the rice price was likely to be 1 yuan per catty.

At all events if the new increase deposit of 10 million yuan is formed prematurely, and rice production and sales are later, the situation of 110 million yuan deposit corresponding to below the rice of 100 million catties will be formed, which is likely to cause the rice price rise. Therefore after the issuance of new increase money, the time for new increase deposit, and the time for new increase production must match so that the commodity price will not rise. If the time for new increase production lags behind the time for new increase deposit, the commodity price will rise. Clearly the new increase money often brings a lot of uncertainties to the price. Because as for new increase loans, usually multiple deposits are formed first, and producers use loans to increase production second. In consequence the producer to receive firstly new loans increases production at first, his products foremost enter the market to obtain the largest benefit while the producer to receive finally new loans increases production at last, his products enter ultimately the market, and thus gain smaller profits or losses in stronger competition.

Next we will analyze the impact of new increase money supply on sellers and buyers more specifically.

In respect of buyers, on condition that the Country A did not increase the money supply in 2002, it is equally possible for farmers to increase the rice yield by 10% through variety improvement, and technological progress. The buyer of Country A may buy 1 catty of rice with only 0.9 yuan. Nevertheless after the money supply has now increased in accordance with the yield growth rate, buyers take a risk that the deposits of Country A will rapidly multiply, and the output will lag behind, that is, the rice price will rise at any time. In 2001 the buyer of Country A was able to buy rice at unit price of 1 yuan per catty. Anyhow, even if the rice price of 1 yuan per catty did not rise in 2002. However the rice buyer of Country A did not enjoy the benefit of agricultural technological advances of Country A for rice farming. In the light of the principle of specialized production, and market exchange, specialized production gains yield, supply increases and price falls so that buyers can get the benefit of yield gain. Only when the specialized production of each type of commodity all gains yield, and unit price falls can all sellers and buyers benefit from them, and make a fortune in that they are both sellers and buyers. If monetary aggregate does not increase, they can always buy more commodities with less money. No matter what central banks of various countries newly add loans, all buyers risk that monetary aggregate will multiply with loans, and whether yield will increase, and increase on time. Even if the time for the yield gain coincides with the time for the monetary aggregate growth, and the commodity price is steady, buyers do not benefit from the specialized production. Therefore **the Milton Friedman's famous monetary theory: The growth of money supply increases synchronously along with the yield growth rate, which is a distortion of the increase**

in buyer welfare by specialized production. Because under the guidance of his theory, even though prices remain stable, in other words, the currency inflation rate is zero, it is also unfavorable to consumers. Although the buyer can buy the same commodity with 1 yuan, the yield gain of this commodity due to specialized production does not benefit buyers.

In respect of sellers, this policy of increasing the monetary aggregate growth along with the yield growth rate is also complicated. As mentioned above the first person who gets new loans from bank invests in production, and pays for various costs before the input price rises so his cost is the lowest. Furthermore his input expands, and yield increases foremost. When he puts the yield gain into the market, he most likely obtains the maximum benefit given that he faces less supply competition, and can sell the product at the highest price. On all accounts all this is based on the premise that the first producer to receive new loans successfully boosts productivity. When producers in the second, third, fourth, and the others batches receive new loans also invest in production, the situation changes. First the price of input products rises at the beginning, and then is getting higher and higher, and input cost increases. Second the later borrowers complete the goal of yield gain with loans but when their products are sold in the market, pressure from their supply competition increases, and the price is likely to fall. The last producers who use new loans are likely to cope with losses due to product oversupply or even their incomes are insufficient to repay loans. Therefore in an environment where monetary aggregate increases with yield, the impact on different producers is different. Only a small number of new loan users can benefit, not only can they use their income to pay off bank loans, but they also reap profits. However the majority of new loan users is likely to face losses from the supply competition for new yield gain and price fall, and cannot even afford bank loans.

At any cost when new borrowers in the first, second, and even nth batches use loans, they have to complete various types of payments and allocation, and purchase of various resources in society during the payment. Then those payees of new money will pay the new money to the relevant people. In that way new loans become the people's deposits batch by batch. In this process, sometimes new loans can create or just transfer the employment opportunity, increase social gross product, and only transfer social production when purchasing various resources. It depends on whether new loan users purchase social idle resources to put them into production.

Above analysis shows that new loans are used in the production field, and may lead to various relationships between monetary growth, and yield gain. Nevertheless, when new loans are used in the transaction field, what impact will it have on commodity prices? Just like the initial 1 million yuan loan was borrowed by the Rice Merchant W of Country A in January 2002. After the Rice Merchant W borrowed this new money, there may be only a couple of purposes:

1. Buy rice to Place A with low price (such as 0.8 yuan per catty), and sell it to Place B with high price (such as 1 yuan per catty);
2. Hoard most of the rice in a certain place, and sell it bit by bit in a price increase mode;
3. Transport the domestic rice to the foreign place with high prices for sale, or import the foreign rice to China.

Like the first purpose, new loans are good for rice sellers but are not good for rice buyers in the Place A because the purchase of Rice Merchant W raises the rice price of Place A but it is beneficial to rice buyers in the Place B just that the Merchant W rice supply will make local supply increase, thus prices are forced down.

Save and except for rice transportation, the Rice Merchant W is actually engaged in monetary transportation. He first transported the new money to the Place A, and then transported the rice to the Place B. After selling out the rice in the Place B, he recovered the old money of rice buyers in the Place B, and deposited it in the bank. What impact does the circulation of such commodities and currencies have on the Places A and B? With respect to the Place A, the rice was transported to the Place B, and the rice was reduced, anyhow the new money brought by the Rice Merchant W was gotten by the rice seller. After the rice seller received the new money, it might be deposited in local banks immediately. If the rice seller in the Place A receives the new money, and purchases local rice, numerous rice producers will sell the rice, and get the new money. After receiving new money, numerous rice producers will buy locally various urgent need commodities so that the new money will be also paid to various local commodity suppliers. In this way, after the new money enters the Place A, it will raise the price of local commodities. New money flows counter-currently along commodity circulation channels, and where new money flows, commodity price rises. As far as this model is concerned, new money enters the Place A allowing people who get the new money to buy urgent need commodities, and it also pushes up local commodity prices.

Like the second purpose, the new money is used by the Rice Merchant W to hoard rice, and control the local rice supply. The Rice Merchant W must purchase most of the rice from local wholesalers, and sell out at a higher price. Like this the new money will soon flow to the wholesaler, then flow to the place where the rice price is the lowest, and then flow to the producer. The higher the price of Rice Merchant W purchases rice, the faster the new money flows. Since rice is necessity, the Rice Merchant W likely makes huge profits in where rice is hoarded, at any price, the Rice Merchant W runs a significant risk, when he raises the rice price very high, other rice suppliers will swarm, which thereby will make the supplier of final price reduction lose everything. The utilization of such "new" loans does not increase production, and instead make the local people poorer. When this large amount of "new" money flows to producers, it will also give producers a wrong message in mistake for the rice price rise, thereby expanding production. When producers produce more rice, they can only sell it at a lower price. Obviously, when "new" loans are utilized to hoard any commodity, it will beyond doubt distort the authentic supply-demand relationship in the market, undermine drastically production, and crack down on producer enthusiasm.

Like the third purpose, where "new" loans are used to import and export rice. It has different effects on domestic rice prices. More specifically after receiving the new money, the Rice Merchant W immediately purchases rice to the domestic market. As thus the demand for rice would increase by a "new" amount compared with previous years, causing the price rise of domestic rice market. The Rice Merchant W exported rice to foreign countries, and received foreign exchange. If the Rice Merchant W deposits the foreign exchange into his foreign account, this transaction will only do harm to the domestic people. The Rice Merchant W brings the foreign exchange back to China, and sells it to the People's Bank of China. The central bank will print and issue more corresponding banknotes to the Rice Merchant W. After using the money exchanged by the foreign exchange for domestic payments, the Rice Merchant W will push up the price of domestic commodities. The Rice Merchant W purchases commodities with the foreign exchange overseas to import into China, which can increase the domestic supply of such commodities, and benefit domestic consumers. Therefore it should be scrupulous to use domestic new increase loans for exports. Only by exporting surplus domestic commodities abroad, and then returning the commodities needed by the domestic people will it benefit own country people. While imports always tend to be beneficial to own country people but imports should be based on the export value of domestic surplus commodities.

We next analyze the impact of the central bank proportional increase in new loans on commercial banks. Assuming the Country A owns a Commercial Bank H. In January 2002, the Commercial Bank H borrowed 1 million yuan from the central bank, and the loan interest rate is 2% per annum. The Commercial Bank H then lends to someone of the Country A at annual interest rate of 5%. The Commercial Bank H can immediately increase income 30,000 yuan due to the new additional 1 million yuan loans. In the event that the Commercial Bank H correctly evaluates the mortgage assets for loans, in any case the Commercial Bank H will newly add 30,000 yuan income on account of the new addition of 1 million yuan loans. Moreover there are branches more enough in the Commercial Bank H to implement the principle of linking deposits and loans, the Commercial Bank H is likely to derive 10 million yuan deposits, and 9 million yuan loans (at 10% deposit reserve ratio) due to the new increase 1 million yuan loans, and the annual interest income of the Commercial Bank H will reach 270,000 yuan instead of 30,000 yuan. Noticeably the benefits of new increase loans to commercial banks are huge. Therefore only by lowering the interest rate, and interest margin of deposits and loans can it benefit the domestic people. Supposing by the end of the year, the central bank withdraws the 1 million yuan loans, and locks it into the vault, the Commercial Bank H can earn 270,000 yuan from the client. Money supply also decreases by 10 million yuan. Thereafter commodity prices will generally fall, and the Commercial Bank H profit of 270,000 yuan can be lent as loans. New increase loans can bring steady and high returns to commercial banks. Functions of commercial banks are mainly to direct depositor savings to producers with the highest production efficiency. After the producer obtains the loan, he allocates resources, and produces products. Only by selling the product to the market can the producer obtain income and profit. The profit margin of Chinese manufacture industry is generally only about 5-8% from 2008 to 2010. Comparatively speaking commercial banks only guide the flow direction of funds, get profits by borrowing others resources, namely borrow depositors or the central bank to operate, and rely on mortgage assets, and the profit rate may be as high as 20% or more. Rapid expansion profits of banks become capital, either forming the plunder to producer labor products in the market or lending as loans to expand the money supply exponentially so as to trigger currency inflation in the market.

We then analyze the impact of new increase loans on the central bank. As is known to all, the central bank is the bank of all commercial banks, and all commercial banks must deposit in the central bank (central banks of some countries give interest on these deposits such as China, and central banks of some countries do not give interest on these deposits such as the Federal Reserve). The deposits of these commercial banks in the central bank are called reserves. Each commercial bank must deposit the stipulated proportion of its deposits (i.e. the statutory deposit reserve ratio) in the central bank. It is thus evident that the central bank always has money. It can refund the reserves of commercial banks to various commercial banks. Supposing all the reserves are refunded, and the commercial banks still feel that the money is not enough, the central bank can also create money. There are diversified forms for the central bank to create money, one is to increase the number of sheets printed (new banknote quantity) according to the original denomination (such as CNY 100), and the other is to overprint banknotes with large numerical value by the method of frugal paper (such as changing the amount in figures of CNY 100 into 1,000 or 10,000.). After the central bank ordered the banknote printing, and minting factory to print the new money, it was put in the vault for preservation. For instance, a central bank newly printed CNY 1 million, the central bank can lend it to a commercial bank or the central government or be presented to a certain government department or a certain enterprise through commercial banks (such as bad loans written off). Regarding the owner of the newly-printed CNY 1 million, unless the central bank admits to give away, the central bank is still exercising its ownership whatever happens. The ownership of newly printed banknotes is listed as a liability in the central bank balance sheet. Who is the creditor? Obviously it is the debt to all money holders of the country that is the debt to the whole people. Considering that newly printed banknotes of the central bank are put into the market, which dilute the purchasing power of all money holders, and infringe the whole people's interest, the ownership of newly printed banknotes should belong to the whole people of the country. At any cost the newly printed banknote can also be merely used as a method to regulate the money supply in the market. In other words after the central bank lends the newly printed banknote to the commercial bank, it must be recovered on schedule, and put in the vault for seal. On the assumption that the central bank is worried that it cannot resist the temptation to destroy the recovered new money, the new money will disappear, and the ownership will also disappear. In some countries the government has unlimited powers. The central bank is only a branch of the Ministry of Finance. Provided the government would like, it can command the central bank to start the banknote printing machine at any time, and print new banknotes directly to the Ministry of Finance for expenditure. Like this the ownership of newly printed banknotes immediately belongs to the government department. This allows new banknotes to be paid through the Ministry of Finance, and thus currency inflation is unavoidable. From the measurement from all aspects, the new increase money strengthens the power of the central bank, and the governmental purchasing capacity.

III. Specify the Price of a Certain Year as Benchmark, and Money Stock of One Country Will Increase with beyond the Actual GDP Growth Rate in Subsequent Years.

In this case according to different actual situations (year-on-year increase is positive, and year-on-year decrease is negative) of one country actual GDP growth rate (consumer goods, investment goods and net exports), the commodity prices are maintained moderate, and rise or substantially rise to reflect in the prices of commensurate consumer goods, prices rise continuously, CPI is larger than 1 or N multiple of CPI in benchmark year, the year-on-year inflation rate is generally within 10%, some more than 10% or 20% or even 1000% in extreme case.

Since the 1930s, when an American economist Milton Friedman summarized the lessons of the Great Depression of the United States in the 1930s, a wave of bank bankruptcy was attributed to the Federal Reserve failure to supply money in a timely manner. More fundamentally at that time the central bank let a bankruptcy wave of commercial banks alone in order to fight for the power of local banks. In view of this Milton Friedman's insight, central banks of various countries have been brave to act as "lender of last resort", and print recklessly banknotes to supply commercial banks whenever commercial banks risk going into liquidation since then. Milton Friedman also proposed a famous theory that the growth rate of money stock, and the growth rate of actual yield increase simultaneously to keep stable commodity prices. In the subsequent practice some western countries have controlled sternly the monetary growth rate in the light of his theory, and can maintain domestic commodity price stability. Nonetheless almost all developing countries have put money at a value that greatly exceeds the actual GDP growth rate, leading to tempestuous waves of domestic inflation. **Now we focus on the analysis of how those currencies that exceed the actual GDP growth will trigger the commodity price rise**.

For instance, a small Country A, produces mainly one commodity, rice. In 2001, rice production was 100 million catties, unit price was 1 yuan, and the money supply was 100 million yuan. From 2002 to 2010, the rice supply of Country A had increased at a rate 10%, and money supply had increased at a rate 20%. The annual output of rice was 100 million catties in 2001, 110 million catties in 2002, 121 million catties in 2003, 133.1 million catties in 2004, 146.41 million catties in 2005, 161.051 million catties in 2006, 177.1561 million catties in 2007, and 194.87171 million catties in 2008. It can be found that the rice production increased by one time or doubled in only seven years at 10% growth rate from the first year (viz., 2002) to 2008.

The money supply of Country A was 100 million yuan in 2001, 120 million yuan in 2002, 144 million yuan in 2003, 172.8 million yuan in 2004, 207.36 million yuan in 2005, 248.832 million yuan in 2006, 298.5984 million yuan in 2007, and 358.31808 million yuan in 2008. By 2008, the money supply of Country A was 3.6 times that of 2001 in only seven years.

Supposing that the Country A need maintain the rice price of 1 yuan per catty, there was only excess money of 10 million yuan in 2002, of 23 million yuan in 2003, and so on. By 2008, Country A yield was the order of 200 million catties, and money supply was the order of 360 million yuan. Money supply is 1.8 times of the actual GDP. How will this excessive monetary aggregate 160 million yuan promote the commodity price rise of Country A? Provided that we analyze this excessive monetary aggregate 160 million yuan, and it is accumulatively increasing year by year, especially money supply in 2008 was increased by about 60 million yuan than that in 2007. Whether this excessive monetary aggregate 160 million yuan is increased year by year or suddenly, no matter what it is, we study largely how the excessive money promotes the price rise.

Assuming a Country A only owns a Commercial bank H. In early January 2008, the Commercial Bank H received 160 million yuan new money from the central bank regardless of whether borrowed from the central bank or returned the deposit reserve from the central bank, whatever the Commercial Bank H added new money, and the statutory reserve ratio was 10%. In January 2008 the Commercial Bank H may lend the 160 million yuan of new money to the following types of population: 1. engaged in production or transaction of consumer goods; 2. engaged in production of investment goods; 3. engaged in import and export trade.

Assuming the Country A produces only one consumer product, rice. Actual yield of rice in 2008 was 200 million catties. Compared with 2001, rice yield increased by 100 million catties but the money supply increased by 260 million yuan. On all accounts the excessive money supply 260 million yuan may be unable to enter the field of rice production. According to the analysis in the previous section, as long as the monetary aggregate of the Country A has increased at a rate of 10% since 2001, price stability can be ensured, that is to say, when yield increased at a rate of 10% from 2001, the excessive money corresponded to the surplus output. It guarantees that price will not drop when yield increases. In the light of this principle, the money supply in 2008 should be 200 million yuan rather than 360 million yuan. Whereabouts will the excessive 160 million yuan currencies go by 2008?

We must examine minutely how the money supply of CNY 160 million is generated. For example, at a deposit reserve ratio of 10%, the deposit of 160 million yuan generates among commercial banks provided that the central bank of the Country A lends 16 million yuan to a commercial bank. Now suppose there is a Citizen F of the Country A. In January 2008, he first of all borrowed the new loan of 16 million yuan from a Commercial Bank H, and the annual interest rate of the loan was 5%. The Citizen F then deposited this new loan in the Commercial Bank H as a current deposit (the deposit interest rate is almost zero). The problem now is that when the Citizen F borrows this new loan, he must use it, and otherwise he will lose 5% of the new loan at the end of 2008. Obviously before the Citizen F applies for this new loan, he must have a specific purpose. He will either put this new loan in production (investment) or in circulation (trade), such as import and export trade. The worst possibility is that he uses this new loan for his own consumption, that is, borrowing money is not to make money but he directly enjoys it regardless of consequences.

When he puts this new loan in production, it can be divided into several situations: The first is the production of consumer products such as rice, pork, clothes, and furniture, the second is the production of factories, warehouses, machines, equipment, and other fixed investment goods, the third is the production of public consumer products such as roads, railways, squares, parks, and public facilities. These public consumer products are now generally included in the scope of governmental investment, it is inappropriate to be also called investment. Because the investment is made for profit, and the purpose of these public consumer products should not be for profit but for satisfying the people consumption by the government.

Even if the Citizen F invests this new money in the production of consumer goods, the actual output of Country A merely increases by 10% year-on-year. When there is only one commodity rice, according to the previous assumption, the total output was only 200 million catties in 2008. Given that the increase in total output is subject to material capital, natural resources, labor force capital, and science and technology, it cannot be solved immediately by the excessive money supply. When the Citizen F all paid all 16 million yuan new money in 2008, the increase output by his investment in 2008 must also be included in the 10% increase output of the Country A in 2008, that is, included within 200 million catties of rice yield. However, after the Citizen F completed the payment, before the end of 2008, the 16 million yuan loans became cash, and deposits of an Individual N related to the Citizen F. When the money of the Individual N deposited in the bank, and it was loaned to an Individual M by the bank. Therefore the money supply may soon form 160 million yuan deposits among banks. Some of the 160 million yuan deposit holders may use the money for savings, and not for purchases, and other holders may use the money to increase purchases. Although they have different purposes for holding deposits, they have such a huge new increase purchasing power that they may enter the market at any time, and lead to a sharp commodity price rise. Distinctly even if the excessive money supply beyond the yield growth rate enters the field of production necessities, it will inevitably lead to serious currency inflation. When the Citizen F directly used this new loan for merchandise trade, the situation was basically the same as the analysis mentioned above. However when the Citizen F directly used this new loan to hoard a certain commodity, the new loan always flows among large or small and medium commodity purchasers or wholesalers, and producers so that the flow channels of new loans are relatively single in the purpose of buy low and sell high. This will quickly trigger speculative funds to control the supply and sales channels of commodities, and increase commodity prices. In this way, due to the Citizen F's initial investment of 16 million yuan, 160 million yuan deposits, and about 150 million yuan loans are quickly formed in the wholesale, and retail chains, resulting in a huge speculative fund scale, which is likely to make a commodity price soar.

What happens when the Citizen F put the new money in investment areas at the earliest, such as the factory building construction, machinery equipment purchase or construction of roads and railways! It is also necessary to research in detail how new loans flow. The new loans always flow in the time and order of payment, thereby forming a new expansion currency. Taking a road construction as an example, supposing from Jan. 1 to Dec. 31, 2008, the monetary aggregate of Country A was at 10% growth rate. At the end of 2008, the money supply of Country A was only 200 million yuan. Commodity prices will not rise. Now we change the situation at the beginning of 2008. To be specific there is a City B in the Country A. Because the City B plans to build a road, the City B applied for 16 million new increase loans from the Commercial Bank H at the beginning of the year. Then the Commercial Bank H borrowed this new money from the central bank, and loaned to the City B. The City B will pay the new money to the general contractor after the road bidding. The general contractor will pay part of the new money to sub-contractors of various types of work. The subcontractors then pay the new money to various suppliers, and workers. Like that the 16 million yuan of new money will flow to the relevant personnel along the road construction procedure, resulting in the money supply of 160 million yuan through bank deposits, and loans. On the premise of constant conditions, the first side the new loans first lead to the price rise of materials, and equipment, and personnel wages related to road construction. The second side the new loan allocates limited social resources to road construction. It will lead to the decline in the output of other sectors. For example, the peasant-worker comes to build road, they will not farm probably, resulting in the decline in rice yield. The third side after the wage hike of all the people with regard to the road construction, it will certainly increase the purchase of domestic consumer goods, and hence CPI rise is caused. When a country uses a large amount of new loans for the construction of roads, railways, public infrastructure, and residence, the new loans will allocate a large amount of resources of the country to real estate, which will affect the production of consumer goods to reduce its output. Furthermore the huge monetary aggregate is generated by the construction of these real estates to form a current purchasing power, which make the price of consumer goods rise.

Conversely when a private capital finances directly the road construction, it will generally not cause a country monetary growth. For instance, the Citizen F builds a road, and borrows someone else cash, which is transferred to the Citizen F purse without increasing the money supply. When the Citizen F borrows someone else deposit, their money is transferred to the Citizen F's account, which will not increase the money supply. Only when people deposit their cash in hand to the bank, and then the bank lends it to the Citizen F, the money supply will double. However as long as a country does not add new money, generally the whole people have the cash within certain limitations, such as 100 million yuan. Admitting that all cash is deposited in the bank, the reserve ratio is 10%, it will expand 1billion money supply at most. For instance, in a country original deposit is 1 billion yuan, and the maximum monetary aggregates are only 10 billion yuan. Anyway when the central bank of the country injects continuously new currencies, the money supply will expand without limit.

Annex

Discussion on the Relationship between Spirit and Economic Growth

Songs include revolutionary song, popular song, folk song, and so on, anyway, as long as it is a song, someone sings, we can still find a unique relationship between songs and GDP growth. Everybody knows that governments at all levels in the Chongqing City have been continuously singing revolutionary songs in recent years. According to the report of the municipal governmental leadership regarding the *National People's Congress (NPC)*, and the *Chinese People's Political Consultative Conference (CPPCC)*, the GDP growth rate of the Chongqing City ranked first throughout the country in 2011. The urban practice seems to indicate that singing revolutionary songs are helpful to increase production. From the large-scale singing activity in the Chongqing City, the author thinks of a new knowledge, singing economics! The fundamental theory is analyzed as follows. It is hoped that experts at home and abroad can use this as a starting point to carry forward this subject knowledge.

I. Singing Status in Macroeconomic

Songs, also known as singing industry, music industry or entertainment industry, is currently an important occupation in the global and the Chinese economics. The song position in the macroeconomic industry is indeed not specifically discussed. In accordance with the division of primary industry, secondary industry and tertiary industry, the things like singing or entertainment culture are classified as tertiary industry or services. That is to say, song is really a part of GDP. The more the people sing song, the rapider GDP grows. By way of illustration, an entertainment company rerecorded disc, and released 10 new songs in 2011, the local government where the company is located increased GDP by sales proceeds of 10 new songs. As for whether the company produces new folk song, popular song or revolutionary song in 2011, that is the company's own business. Anyway, as long as the company creates, and releases new songs, there will be sales proceeds. The proceeds will increase the GDP. Therefore songs contribute to the GDP growth.

However it is necessary to clarify that song is only a part of GDP, specifically refers to, the "singing" that specializes in, and is manufactured for exchange purpose, such as exchange other labor products in the form of live singing or records. The remaining "singing" for various purposes cannot be included in GDP. In this regard it is a rigorous "boundary" when all modern countries count GDP. For example, a person named Tom loves singing. He sings alone at home every day. Sometimes he sings for himself or his family members. Such singing definitely cannot be counted as GDP. On the grounds that he is not for the purpose of "exchange", how about the song he sings at home, what level, and whether he could exchange other person's labor products, only he himself could evaluate, others could not. In another example, Tom helps his wife to wash clothes or dishes, and cook the meal every day at home for the purpose of pleasing his wife. These labors cannot be counted in GDP. Additionally Tom singing is appreciated by an entertainment company, and he was hired to sing in a Singing Hall. The entertainment company gave Tom CNY 200 for each song. Such songs Tom sang should be included in GDP.

Therefore only with the purpose of "exchange" can the singing be regarded as a component of GDP. "Exchange" is the principle, and "watershed" for dividing whether singing belongs to the GDP queue.

II. Relationship between Government Organizational "Singing Songs" and Economic Growth

Over more than 30 years of reform and opening up, we have heard that the governmental investment is related to GDP, and few that the government organizational singing is also related to GDP. Government investment indicates that the government purchases various fixed assets such as new roads, squares, factories, machinery and equipment, and other products. The reason why they can promote economic growth is that genuine wealth is added. It is easy to appreciate. In any case, government organizational song first heard of also promotes economic growth. According to some net citizens in the Chongqing City, since the municipal government advocated large-scale singing revolutionary songs, broad leaders and masses have been clean and upright, and are full of tremendous enthusiasm, and thus production is developed and the people's livelihood is improved greatly. The reaction of these net citizens poses a large question for economists, what is the essential relationship between the government organizational singing, and economic growth? Because the reaction of these net citizens is just an individual perception without a rigorous logic and data support, it cannot convince others in essence. According to Mr. Dong Fang Dao's comprehensive and in-depth investigation regarding the both relationship, he finally obtained the significant theory with respect to the government organizational singing, and economic growth:

The government organizational singing first and foremost is manifested economically as a "governmental expenditure" to purchase that "the masses sing for themselves".

Net citizens in abundance and 99.9% of the 1.36 billion Chinese do not quite understand how the Chinese cultural sector specifically organizes, and implements those large-scale "masses singing activities". For instance, in 2011 the municipal government should organize 60 "revolutionary song concerts" freely watched by large-scale masses in 10 grand plazas across a City A under the superior arrangement. Specific implementation is the responsibility of the City A Cultural Bureau (hereinafter referred to as the Cultural Bureau A). After receiving this "political mission", the Director General of Cultural Bureau A is secretly pleased, and has to laugh on the other side of his face, "Lord Mayor, in order to ensure the completion of this sacred mission, at any cost I would rather finish desperately well. In spite of this, so many venues, facilities, professional bands, stereos, recording, and broadcasting, also 20 or 30 national topmost actresses and actors all are required. As regards 60 concerts, even if CNY 200,000 per concert at the minimum price, 12 million is needed at least! Lord Mayor, you see, in case the money is not in place, the work will not start!"

The Mayor frowned, "Don't complain of being hard up before me! 6 million is for you, and the rest you will find your own way."

Whereupon large-scale singing activities are carried out under the specific direction of director general of the Cultural Bureau A, after obtaining the CNY 6 million, the Director

General of the Cultural Bureau A leaves one half at first, i.e. CNY 3 million, and even three quarters, i.e. CNY 4.5 million, and then throws the remaining CNY 1.5 million to the Head of Division W, "You take this money to hold 60 concerts well, you must ensure the completion of 'political mission'. Is it not enough? You find your way to settle it!"

After receiving this "political mission", the Head of Division W will not be stupid enough to organize authentically "revolutionary song concerts" with the CNY 1.5 million so he launches a special "cultural investment promotion activity" citywide. A great many of advertisement companies, musical instrument companies, actor agencies and television stations come to negotiate business, and bargain with the Head of Division W one after another. Then the private enterprise that wants to beg for leftovers gets busy about while the Head of Division W is only responsible for supervision, and charging a certain "rebate". After received this command, the private enterprise tries to recover the cost, and profit from other economic entities under the banner of revolution to scare and deceive people. Eventually, in sometime 2011, 60 large-scale mass singing movements are launched in the whole city. A number of production enterprises are forced to fulfill "political tasks", despite understaffed, they have to suspend the work of numerous atmosphere persons, and train them at own expense before going to compete for places in citywide singing movements.

Above contents about the inside story of "government organizational singing" are provided by a net citizen called as "Zheng Yi Zhe" to Mr. Dong Fang Dao. Only by holding these contents can we veritably analyze the relationship between government organizational singing, and GDP growth from the economic perspective.

First of all the government should be pure expenditure. Government expenditure can purchase real fixed assets such as squares, factories and machines, or local people "singing for them". As mentioned above, the government of City A spends CNY 6 million to purchase local people "singing for them". Even all CNY 6 million is all spent on figurants for 60 concerts. It will not promote the investment growth considering that the personnel who got CNY 6 million were not for production but consumption. After receiving the CNY 6 million, numerous figurants will buy various goods and services to thereby push up local commodity prices. After all it also promotes CNY 6 million consumptions. Anyway like the City A above the CNY 6 million cannot all promote consumption because a large proportion of the money merely enters a few people's moneybags, figurants who practically participate cannot earn any income. Therefore such government expenditures can promote neither production nor consumption. This is nearly a wasteful expenditure.

In the next place the government organizational singing is too expensive in terms of opportunity cost. We know that opportunity cost is the main indicator to measure the resource allocation. Like Tom, his career is carpenter, and he can earn CNY 200 every working day. One day there is a pig killing job to cost CNY 50 in his family. Tom himself can also kill pig, and so does the butcher Harry. In case Tom kills pig, he will lose CNY 150. So Tom will definitely ask a favor of the professional butcher Harry to kill the pig. This is an example of opportunity cost allocating optimal resources. The government organizational singing is a professional behavior for the Head of Division W Cultural Bureau A hereinbefore but the opportunity cost is too high for thousands of companies, and public institutions in the City A.

More specifically an enterprise produces electronic products, in order for participation in this government activity, it is necessary to transfer the most beautiful girls and the most capable boys from staff to attend relevant training except for too fat and ugly employees so as not to affect the corporate image. The enterprise has to organize specially manpower, material resources and funds to undertake the entire activity. Thus production will definitely be affected to reduce output. Even if output does not decline, participants must hand their work to other colleagues, which is unfair. Beyond all doubt, government organizational singing activities substantially interfere with the professional production of all economic entities, and the whole society has to lose a huge opportunity cost. As always the GDP of City A must plummet.

In the third place it is impossible to meet the authentic interest of local people for such expenditures like the government organizational singing. As mentioned above, in the event that there are 10 million people in the City A, and local governmental officials truly respect the people's wishes, they must let the people choose which songs they love by themselves, and they must completely trust the people's judgment. In the 21st century, can the people be too stupid to know what songs they like to listen to? Unquestionably some elders love revolutionary songs, some youth love pop songs, and many people are very fond of foreign songs such as Mr. Dong Fang Dao is keen on Indian songs. Should the government go so far as to intervene in this hobby of listening to songs?

Suppose the revolutionary song producer does not use the public expenditure, competes fairly with other music producers, and gains the most income. It means that the revolutionary song has high market share, and contributes more to the GDP growth. However it is valueless for city A that spends a lot of the public expenditure at all costs to purchase "the masses sing for themselves". Also such expenditure of CNY 6 million in the City A will affect medical, educational, housing, and other expenditures, or else there are only three possibilities: Firstly the central government transfers payment that is the central government gives money; secondly the local government borrows money; and thirdly the local government increases tax revenues. Among them the central government giving money is unfair to other local governments, local government loans are unfair to the next government, and taxation increase is unfair to enterprises and employees. Will such expenditure meet the people's fundamental interests?

III. Relationship between Government Organizational Singing and Spirit

In order to understand thoroughly the relation between government organizational singing and labor production, we analyze further the essential relationship among singing, human spirit and human labor efficiency. For some Chinese people have been worshiped almost superstitious the spiritual power of singing able to promote the material power of labor production for nearly 60 years. It may be instructive to the Chinese development for the discussion from this relationship.

Singing also has certain benefits for improving labor productivity. Some songs can overcome fatigue in work, encourage energy, and maintain passion and strength for work, which is helpful to increase productivity. These songs at any rate must be related to the labor productive process such as, the Chinese working people enjoy all long singing *Operating Iron Rammer Song, Oil Squeezer Song, Chuanjiang Boatman Labor Song, Picking the Pomegranate, Picking Rape, Four Seasons Song in Northern Huaihe, Ramming Song, Threshing Flail Song, Smooth*

Water Work Song, Seeing Beach Song, Threshing Wheat Song, and the like. Such songs are related to the labor process, singing while working, may have a refreshing effect to overcome fatigue in a continuous production, which thus is conducive to the output growth. These songs are named as a labor chant or the yo-he-ho theory for the mutual encouragement between working people during collective labor, and there is no contradiction with labor, singing in labor or working in singing has a certain positive effect on the increase in output.

However there are generally two ways for the government appeal to singing, one is to gather the people to sing specially at the designated venue, and the other is to sing in the work unit. The former one is dedicated to singing, and participants obviously have a spiritual excitement during singing but it is useless for production after singing. The latter, when someone sings *Azalea, Red Star Shining, Folk Song to the Party, Our Workers Have Power, Liuyang River, Oriental Red, Reddest Sun, and Dearest Chairman MAO*, and others, which have nothing to do with the labor process, it is not only useless for the increase in output but harmful. Because when someone sings, other colleagues will be distracted to make output drop. As a matter of fact whether the working people sing or not, what song they should sing, and whether singing helps to refresh, should be chosen, and judged by the people in the work unit.

In case the working people sing some extolled songs all the time, they will gradually lose their ability to judge, spiritually generate a strong sense of dependence on the chanted object, and eventually lead to a personal worship. In this regard the People's Commune was given a lesson paid for with lives during the Cultural Revolution.

During the Cultural Revolution, students sang carols every day. When the working people had meetings, carols were often broadcast on the radio. On the spot, carols were often sung. It is obviously unfair for competitors to promote someone like this by virtue of public resources. During the Cultural Revolution, many old revolutionaries were overthrown, and intellectuals were criticized and denounced. It is a direct causality with some people who employed public resources to sing forcibly themselves. In order to win the people support, the governor and the opposition must abide by the principle that they cannot employ public resources without authorization, and must compete on an equal footing. As long as the ruler employs public resources to sing carols for himself directly or indirectly, competitors will be in a very disadvantageous situation. Once the ruler obtains the benefit of taking advantage of public resources to serve him, and he will expand continuously the utilization of such resources at all hazards, and even desperately maintain private interests to the end even at the expense of production.

In the People's Commune, working people also listened to revolutionary songs, and sang carols. All of these were organized and enforced, and the people had no a choice right under all circumstances. At that time only such songs could be sung, the people sang, and then scattered after completion. They still sang the labor chant at work. As a consequence such carols go bad, and become a tool for someone to protect own interests. There is no connection to the goal of increase production with such encouragement enthusiasm and vigorous work. At that time young Red Guards lost ego by singing carols, and carried out a lot of bloodstained activities such as beating, smashing, and robbing to destroy production and wealth.

During that period the government organizational singing was a regular activity. The people could sing only the song chosen by the governor, and could not sing own favorite during the Cultural Revolution. Will there be a situation where thepeople are not allowed to sing their favorite songs supposing it follows the same old disastrous road now, and the people are required to sing designated songs by employing public resources recklessly? At present the government organizes singing, and a lot of money is spent. This money comes from the people's hard-earned money. Why not use it to do a few practical things?

Epilogue

Loose Governmental Regulation

I. Realization of "Chinese Dream" Only Depends on Private Enterprises Closely

Whether the China's economy can grow in a "steady progress" expected by the central government in 2013 is a touchstone for testing the new governmental ability to govern. There are merely three strategies to increase healthy veritable GDP year-on-year in China:

Firstly products and services of private enterprises increase year-on-year;

Secondly the government makes investment increase through state-owned enterprises and platform companies;

Thirdly exports are increased.

Since 2008 the countermeasure of Chinese governmental response to the world economic crisis has been the governmental investment, and increase exports that have proved to be impractical. Governmental investment has resulted in the scale of Chinese government debt exceeding CNY 12 trillion. The original Ministry of Railways alone is up to CNY 3 trillion in debt, which is shocking! These huge debts seemingly need not be borne by the Chinese individual but sooner or later will have to be paid by every Chinese through commodity price and taxation increase, and chaotic debt accounting records. Given that these huge debts not recovered are more delayed one day, the inflation threat to China will more remain for one day. Due to the extension of these debts, the Chinese M2 reaches so huge 100 trillion that shock the world. Foreigners all want to see the outright catastrophe trick of inflation in China while the Chinese themselves are still unexpectedly calm proud of it, concealing own fault for fear of criticism. Regarding money supply, even enthroned aggressive Emperors Wu in Han Dynasty, Li Shimin in Tang Dynasty, and Qianlong in Qing Dynasty were all careful. They did not dare to overprint and over-issue indiscriminately so as to ensure prosperous country, wealthy people, and steady society. Nowadays provided that China cannot recover dozens of trillions of government debts on schedule, I really don't know how the huge debt will end in the future.

In the case of exports it has long been pointed out vividly that the Chinese used the money in hard cash at the expense of environment and health in exchange for USD 3 trillion. The USD 3 trillion only exists in the account of Bank of America, and even banknotes are not available. For instance, Chinese people spend USD 1 trillion to buy something in the international market. Do you think the American will agree? Therefore currently the China's economy growth is dependent on government investment and exports that is a road to lead to nowhere. It turns out that it will not work. The 2013 *Central Economic Working Conference* has also deeply recognized this point so it proposed to "boost the domestic demand and expand consumption". It refers to the increase in domestic investment, and consumption, we cannot rely on the government but only tens of millions of private enterprises.

II. Realization of "Chinese Dream" Need Depend on Numerous Private Enterprises

With regard to government investment, this concept needs to be corrected. In economics there has never been a concept of government investment abroad in the four parts of investment, consumption, net exports and government purchase to form the GDP. It is just blindly meddled, and entirely made up by Chinese cynic economists. Economically no government can engage in economic investment except for war materiel requirement. The character of governmental purchases cannot be anything but consumption, and is mainly used for governmental personnel expenditures. It is not a good thing for more government purchases, and it should be evaluated respectively in accordance with different purchase purposes. Consequently the "government investment" has been aimlessly operated in China for decades but must be written off from Chinese future documents, and reality. China is safe, the government is safe, and the people are safe, as well as it lays a foundation for the realization of "Chinese Dream" only in this way. Otherwise government investment indulges unceasingly, government debts will increase by 70 trillion in recent years, and M2 will explode exponentially. I am afraid that the Chinese people will have no chance to dream by then, let alone the Chinese dream.

All in all the Chinese economic growth can only rely on tens of millions of private companies. Without cautious and conscientious work of tens of millions of private entrepreneurs and employees, it is also impossible for the China's economy to remain unchanged year-on-year apart from year-on-year growth other than recession. In that way, how many private enterprises are there in China? According to relevant information estimation, and the data in 2011, there are roughly 11 million enterprises in the form of sole proprietorships, and 36 million enterprises are registered as the self-employed, amounting to nearly 50 million enterprises, which account for 98% above of the number of Chinese enterprises, contributing 85% to Chinese new jobs, occupying 75% of new products, 65% of invention patents, 60% of GDP, and 50% of taxation. Significantly whether it's employment or innovation, SMEs contribute to economic development vitally important.

50 million private enterprises are only one type of calculation. Mr. Dong Fang Dao believes that this data is inequitable because China still has 600 million farmers, about 200 million peasant households. Although they do not register at the industrial and commercial bureau, they are also authentic "enterprises" that invest, and produce agricultural and sideline products. Only 200 million peasant households are real leading enterprises of Chinese products and services, and tens of thousands of agricultural and sideline products they produce ensure that the Chinese CPI does not skyrocket. The reason why China can still be basically stable is that 200 million peasant household enterprises are neither forced by the government to register, nor regulated, and thus the Chinese people still have ample foods, clothes, and daily necessities.

III. Governmental Regulation Microeconomics Overshadows Economic Growth

At all events it is completely different for those 50 million SMEs. They all have a bitter history of "governmental regulation". The first is registration review. Ordinary natural persons cannot register companies in China. Basically the government departmental license system gets in the way during establishment applications for companies in any industry. For example, it was required by a printing business license for printing industry, license issued by the cultural department for publication and distribution industry, also special industry license for waste collection and purchase, and so on. Before setting up a new company, the industrial and commercial administration requires you to apply for them at first. The authority to examine and approve these licenses is firmly controlled by public officials with real power in government departments. Citizens have to get this paper at the expense of tens of thousands, hundreds of thousands, and even hundreds of thousands of CNY. For instance, there are 100 persons who want to start such an enterprise, and anyway the "license" can be daunting, and obtained by mere 3-5 persons in the end. Others can only give up entrepreneurship. In case the 100 persons want to invest CNY 200,000, and employ 20 persons for jobs, it will lose CNY 19 million of direct investment by citizens, and 1,900 persons or so of employment, which thereby will directly hit the Chinese economy. Behind such a huge loss there is the shameless corruption of a few who are in power for license. Certainly there are also those officers who "play fair".

Even the registration of general enterprises without "license" restrictions is extremely difficult in most cities in China. Industrial and commercial departments at all levels have enacted different entry standards to make the establishment of new companies under a difficult circumstance. By way of illustration it is required CNY 2 million of assets for the registration of provincial company, CNY 500,000 for that of municipal company, and CNY 50,000-100,000 for that of district level. There is not so much money, and you can ask the agency for help. After the advance fee charged by the agency due to the payment completion to relevant industrial and commercial department instead of you, and the capital verification fee charged by the accounting firm, the new company needs to spend several tens of thousands, or even hundreds of thousands to only open a temporary account in the bank.

Followed by the endless "investigation and examination" of four major departments of industrial and commercial administration, quality supervision, taxation and banking. It is required to prepare more than 30 pages of materials by industrial and commercial administration, fill out a lot of forms by quality supervision and numberless information as the sand by taxation, as well as the procedure by the bank. Four major departments have rigorously governed the establishment of every enterprise. Every department asks for money, and SMEs dare not reject them. Supposing that you don't spend money to find an agency, and "do things according to the rules", your new company won't be able to establish until one or two months.

Beyond doubt one side many people want to set up SMEs for investment and entrepreneurship in China but they have to give up due to masses of cumbersome procedures in the four major departments of industrial and commercial administration, quality supervision, taxation and banking. Other side our government wants to boost investment and domestic demand every day but it also sets up a lot of cumbersome procedures for the establishment of new companies to keep out the majority of SME investors. Suppose 100 companies are not successfully established, and each company only invests CNY 200,000, the Chinese domestic investment loses to CNY 200 billion per year. Even if each company employs only 20 persons, lost employment positions amount to 20 million. What our government is trying to achieve now is to introduce large amounts of investment, and despise the investment of SMEs. Actually they do not know that only by small-scale investments of SMEs can local employment issues be solved fundamentally, and economics be developed permanently.

According to the author's analysis of first-tier cities such as Beijing, Shanghai, Guangzhou, and Shenzhen, and second-tier cities such as Wuhan, Changsha, Nanchang, and Kunming as well as some small counties, first-tier cities have loosed control over the establishment of SMEs, the regulatory system is not very strict in departments of industrial and commercial administration, taxation and quality supervision so the economy is developed. Conversely second-tier cities are more rigorous in control over the establishment of new companies than first-tier cities so many people are deterred from investment and entrepreneurship, and the economy lags behind. Especially in some small counties the functionary from industrial and commercial administration, and taxation chases after SMEs every day, restraining private enterprises tight, which makes these investors daunt so the economy is very backward. Nowadays does GDP compete between provinces or cities? Hereby economists can tell provincial governors and mayors a secret, whoever allows industrial and commercial administration, taxation and quality supervision to ease the regulation and control for private enterprises, the GDP of province or city who leads can increase rapidly. Whoever immediately withdraws, and merges the industrial and commercial administration, and quality supervision bureau, the GDP of the place who leads will be far ahead.

This is "free ideology, and reform and opening up!" Removal of government control, and allowable the people to invest, produce, and operate freely are authentic and essential connotations of "free ideology, and reform and opening up". As a matter of fact it was also the pursuit of open-minded monarchs of all generations in China, and our governments throughout ages rarely regulated and controlled private investment and entrepreneurship. In the history of thousands of years in China, anyone with capital can start a business anywhere, and was not required to register to any governmental office. Furthermore there was no national boundary, and all foreigners were welcome to start up business in China, watching Chinese dramas during the Tang Dynasty so that officials judged mostly lawsuits, and regulated and controlled rarely the economy.

IV. "Automotive Annual Detection" Transformed into Compulsory Behavior of A Few Stakeholders in the Department

The "automobile annual detection" is apparently not as important as the governmental regulation mentioned above. Since the industrial and commercial administration, quality supervision and taxation departments regulate potential producers and potential outputs they have a direct and obvious impact on the economic growth of a place. The "automobile annual detection" is much more important for vehicle owners. For this reason it also has a certain effect on economic growth.

One is to increase the vehicle owner's direct cost. Compulsory insurance is one of compulsory payment costs. Also there are a detection fee, and various expenses to the detection site.

The second is opportunity cost. That is to say, for the sake of detection the vehicle owner's employer and related personnel must abandon production, and specially line up for detection, which will cause certain damage to the economic growth.

The third is to encourage corruption. In order to cope with the automobile detection, intermediary companies were set up. Provided that vehicle owners paid up, in reality, vehicles need not to be driven to scene at all. Intermediary companies support a corrupt chain to simply make the purpose of automobile detection useless.

Each private car owner knows that the car quality is nowadays significantly improved, and it does not need to be overhauled for seven or eight years. There is a regular maintenance every 5,000 kilometers. Thus the car annual detection is completely a superfluous formalization. It is recommended that the central government should cancel the mandatory "automobile detection" system for private cars from economic growth to allow the people more time to invest in entrepreneurship, or should decentralize the detection authority to all automotive maintenance, and repair shops because only the maintenance personnel can know whether the car is safe.

Review Requested:

We'd like to know if you enjoyed the book.
Please consider leaving a review on the platform
from which you purchased the book.